TITTERS 101

AN INTRODUCTION TO WOMEN'S LITERATURE

TITTERS 101

Compiled and Edited by

Anne P. Beatts, M.A., Oxford University
Ruth L. McCarthy Scholar
Chairperson, English Department
New York State University, Weemawee, New York

Dr. Judith Jacklin
Holder of the Eames Chair at Princeton University
Professor Emeritus of English
Prell University, Minocqua, Wisconsin

Deanne Stillman, Ph.D., Cambridge University
Carmelita Pope Fellow, Yale University
President and Owner, Helen Putnam University, Lake
Morongo, Louisiana

Guest Editor

Emily Prager
Visiting Professor of Women's Studies
With an Honorary Degree in Bachelors from
Harvard University, Cambridge, Massachusetts

A Perigee Book

THIS BOOK IS AN INSULT TO TREES!!

TITTERS 101
Designed by Judith Jacklin

Library of Congress Cataloging in Publication Data
Main entry under title:

Titters 101.

  "A Perigee book."
  1. Parodies.   2. Women authors—Anecdotes, facetiae, satire, etc.   I. Beatts, Anne P.   II. Jacklin, Judith. III. Stillman, Deanne.   IV. Prager, Emily.   V. Title: Titters one hundred one.   VI. Title: Titters one hundred and one.
PN6231.P3T57   1984   817'.54'080352042   84-5893
ISBN 0-399-51079-6

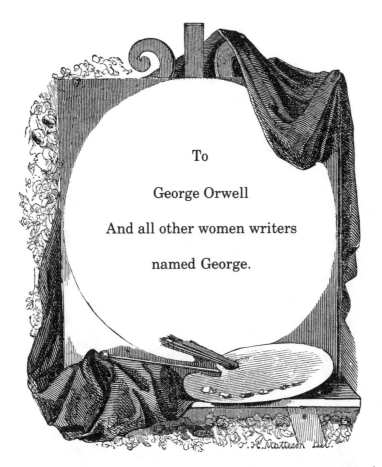

To

George Orwell

And all other women writers

named George.

George Eliot
George Sand
George GERSHWIN
GEORGE BRETT
Oh, BOY! GEORGE

Now, I don't claim

To be an "A" student

But I'm tryin' to be.

I think that maybe by bein'

An "A" student, baby, baby

I could win your love

For me.

—Sam Cooke
"Wonderful World"

CONTENTS

Eighteenth Century

The Age of Creative Ferment: The modern novel is born and survives to the present day despite attempts to kill it on the part of Truman Capote and Tom Wolfe.

A young girl puts on men's clothing; stows away on a seafaring vessel; ends up stranded on a desert island without any guys or moisturizer.

Nineteenth Century

The Age of Romance and Industry: A new element enters into literature; women writers are accepted on a par with men as long as men don't know they are women.

A complicated story that's too complicated to explain. Not only that, it was written by a guy who thought he was a gal! You figure it out.

Poems about death, depression, and deep-dish pies. Nothing about guys. Hey, that rhymes!

Cranky, folksy commentary on life on the Mississippi penned by a half-Jewish, half-Negro woman who combined the skills of cooking and satire, in a literary style as crusty as her chicken pot-pies.

From the far-off, way out, exotic world of Japan, where they don't even have an alphabet, we find that women, no matter which way their eyes slant, have the same problems: guys, clothes, and personal hygiene.

Twentieth Century

A Crazy Jigsaw Puzzle Patchwork Quilt of Time: Lots of action here, including the Roaring Twenties; the Brother, Can You Spare a Dime Thirties; the How Ya Gonna Keep 'Em Down on the Farm Now That They've Seen Paree Forties; the Hepcat, Rock Around the Clock, I Like Ike, Hey, daddio, let's smoke some reefer and dig that crazy Miles Fifties; the wow, man, far out, like, heavy, Paul is dead, and Johnny Winter's at the Electric Circus tonight and I've got some dynamite crystal meth and the Angels'll be there Sixties; the Dump Nixon, get clear, get est, and get into Studio 54 Seventies; the "It's a jungle out there, sometimes I can't help but wonder how I keep from going under," "Girls just wanna have fun" Eighties.

A wise-cracking coffee-shop waitress whose infamous witticisms made her the talk of the late-night counter crowd, and whose coffee intake ultimately sent her into a caffeine-related neurotic tailspin, or was it a nosedive? It's not clear.

The only member of the "Northern School" of writing, this Eskimo gal writer set her sights on Hollywood but left her heart in the igloo. *Canned Salmon* was her swan song, and, not incidentally, her diet, for the last years of her life.

Travel with Anaïs through the mysterious and perplexing Sargasso Sea of adolescent consciousness. This is one tense teen.

A chick is finally in the driver's seat in this beatnik odyssey which carries the reader along a metaphorical six-lane highway, where we encounter crash pads, the Holy Goofus, and guys.

THIS CAT IS RETIRED ON CATNIP

INTRODUCTION

HOW did *Titters 101* grow from a sheaf of blurry mimeographed papers clutched in the sweaty palms of students at an obscure hick university to the handsome, elegantly designed, lavishly illustrated tome it is today, with ten weeks on the *New York Times* best-seller list? How did it get to be Book of the Month Club Featured Alternate, a Quality Paperback Book Club Main Selection, winner of the National Book Award, and nominated along with V. S. Naipaul and Shelley Winters for the Pulitzer Prize? And what about those B. Dalton's windows? Don't they have anything else to put on display?

Funny you should ask. Well, it was like this. The contents of this book originally comprised the required reading list for Titters 101, a freshman English course first given in 1974 at Helen Putnam University, a tiny academic sanctuary nestled under the Spanish-moss-laden cypress trees in that sizable chunk of Louisiana bayou country which had once formed a part of the old Titters plantation.

Basically a Mickey Mouse survey course, Titters 101 focused on excerpts from women's literature through the ages, from Ancient Greece to the present day. It was popular with women students who wanted to take advantage of this important opportunity to explore their literary heritage, which had heretofore been suppressed by the male-dominated publishing industry. And frosh men signed up for it because they thought it was a good way to meet chicks. In fact, it was during a Titters 101 weekend seminar that Phil Donahue met Marlo Thomas.

The original Titters 101 course was taught by three young women with stars in their eyes and not much in their pocketbooks. At the time they were all engaged in graduate study at Helen Putnam University, or as they fondly called it, P.U., where they roomed together in a former slave cabin and spent their off-hours whooping it up, skinny-dipping and drinking Wild Turkey juleps with the officers stationed at the Naval Training Center on nearby Lake Morongo.

It was after one such late-night soirée that one of the editors had an out-of-body experience. She found herself hovering over Lake Morongo, while a voice tittered in her ear—doubtless one of the eerie tittering voices, famed in tales of the Old South, that had given the old Titters plantation its name. "Don't be a moron," it seemed to repeat. "Publish or perish." This confused the editor in question, who at first thought the voice was saying "Paris," a place she had always wanted to go.

However, this confusion was cleared up when her astral body returned to the cabin and discovered that the other editors had received a message from another weird apparition, an old lady in a rocking chair, who held a glowing phosphorescent book marked "Titters 101." She bade them, "Rest ye not until ye see this book on the cover of *Newsweek*." She then tittered mysteriously and vanished, leaving them with a strange appetite for hot chocolate and Sara Lee Pineapple Cheesecake, which they were enjoying when the third member of their party was reunited with her physical body, which, oddly enough, also had this same strange craving.

It was there in the kitchen of the slave cabin that the editors, over hot cups of Nestle's Quik, gave each other the pinky shake and pledged solemnly to heed these visions. The result of this endeavor has just been nominated, along with Shirley MacLaine, for the Nobel Peace Prize.

What is *Titters 101*, and why should you, the reader, read it, other than because every critic worth his bar tab has said, "If you read only one book this year, let it be *Titters 101*"? Well, if your knowledge of women's literature starts with Erica Jong and ends with *Princess Daisy*, then this is your chance to wise up.

Did you know that in Ancient Greece, guys weren't the only ones to use deductive reasoning? Gals did it too, and it was a heckuva lot more fun! Did you know that a woman "marked twain" long before Samuel Langhorne Clemens? Did you know that the Beat writers had wives?

Don't feel stupid—there's a perfectly good reason why you don't know these things. It's called "male oppression," and it accounts for 87.5 percent of the bad things that happen in our lives—and then some! Face it, men don't like women writing because it takes time out from other important things they could be doing, like rolling their husband's socks into balls or putting that blue stuff in the toilet. That's why men have seized control of the media and continue to publish lies and junk about 52 percent of the population. Is this fair? We ask you. Of course

not. But what do you expect from a bunch of bozos who can't even figure out how to stop the arms race?

Nevertheless, women have always expressed themselves through the written word, and we don't mean just grocery lists, although the last one we wrote was pretty interesting. Starting in the Stone Age, they carved pictographs on cave walls with bone toenail clippers; they made room in their ovens to bake the clay tablets on which the first cuneiform characters (later translated as: "Have a nice day") were scratched; in the Orient, where men hid all the pens from women and then bound their feet up so they couldn't look for them, our resourceful slant-eyed sisters dipped their makeup brushes in cuttlefish ink and painted delicate ideograms on rice paper.

Today, women's struggle to communicate has become a little easier, yet a recent survey reveals that for every 200 men who have access to a word processor, there is only one woman, and she is usually the cleaning lady. But regardless of the writing implement, we find the same themes running through all female expression, themes that have often been characterized by men as trivial, frivolous, empty, shallow, insignificant, and of little importance. These themes are life, death, sex, food, money, and dry cleaning.

Of course, there are women writers who are better known than the ones represented here. Erma Bombeck, to name just a few. However, it was our intent to draw attention to more obscure women writers who deserve recognition but whose works have somehow slipped through the bookshelf of history and wound up lying amongst the dust bunnies of oblivion.

In selecting the material for this book, the editors made sure to include an example from every century, except, of course, for the so-called "trash centuries" between 300 B.C. and the Middle Ages. It is truly heartening to realize that there is a continuum of literary endeavor among women which spans thousands of years, dozens of cultures, and scads of hairstyles. In the words of Gloria Gaynor, "We will survive."

So get comfy, make sure you have plenty of reading light, have cigarettes, matches, and an ashtray handy if you smoke, pour yourself a generous tumbler of your favorite beverage, throw a knitted afghan over your legs, persuade your kitty to curl up on your lap, unplug the phone, persuade your kitty to curl up on your lap again, and prepare to climb aboard a magic carpet that will carry you to faraway lands of wonder and enchantment. You are about to begin *Titters 101*.

—The Editors
New York City
Spring Break, 1984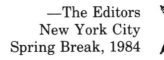

Detail from an Athenian red-figure vase, probably by the painter Exxon, showing Helen of Athens getting a refill. Note the subtle realism with which the artist depicts her excited anticipation. This picture was the prototype for many modern coffee advertisements in which delighted housewives become pre-orgasmic at the first whiff of this mysteriously invigorating beverage. In fact, Helen of Athens was the original "coffee achiever."

Helen of Athens
361–311 B.C.

THE status of women in Ancient Greece was almost as low as it is in the average Greek-American working-class household today; in other words, the wife was expected to do all the housework, bend over and fake orgasm, and help out at the diner.

Under these conditions, it is not surprising that few Greek women were listed in the *Who's Who of Greek Literature,* or even in the phone book. Sad to say, "the glory that was Greece" gave the world only one female philosopher: Helen of Athens (she was the smart one: Helen of Troy was the pretty one). Her philosophical views have been described as provocative, pertinent, pesky, and a lot of other words beginning with "p."

Born in Babylonia, she moved to Arizona, where one of her childhood playmates was a little Egyptian boy, also of an inquisitive turn of mind, King Tut ("Funky" Tut). This was her first contact with another culture in which women were treated a little better, i.e., more like they are today in countries behind the Iron Curtain, where men and women alike get to wear the same unflattering hats and stand in the same lines for the same number of days to get the same potato, which they then share equally.

Helen's family abruptly pulled up stakes and moved to Athens shortly after Helen reached puberty and began asking embarrassing questions, like whether Egyptian boy-kings were circumcised or not. However, there is no doubt that this early friendship stimulated, encouraged, and inspired her to continue asking questions. In fact, as a student at Eros Memorial High, she asked so many questions that her classmates christened her "Miss Curiosity."[1]

---

[1] See *Cupid's Quiver,* Eros Memorial High School for Girls yearbook for the year 359 B.C. (available on microfiche at the Widener Library, Harvard).

Greek girls were expected to marry as soon as they were able to bear children, and sometimes before.[2] Helen was no exception. She married George of Athens when she was thirteen.

At first, she genuinely tried to fill her allotted role of wife, home-maker, and sperm receptacle. But Helen's innate gabbiness soon came to the fore, and she found herself spending more and more time chatting with her girlfriends in the marketplace or in the street or anywhere else where women were allowed to go, which was hardly anywhere.

Her husband, who was a typical Greek male, was unhappy with this state of affairs and was constantly bugging her about it, when he wasn't off buggering someone else. This typical Greek male reaction undoubt-edly goes a long way toward explaining why there weren't more female Greek philosophers.[3]

Other Athenian women, equally bored with their drab humdrum existences in this pre-soap-opera era, congregated about Helen wher-ever she went, until someone got the bright idea that they should con-tinue these discussions at home, where they could sit down and have some coffee.

Dialog = more than one person talking

Like Socrates, Helen communicated her views through dialogues with her disciples, some of whom in later years confided that they had often been reluctant to ask Helen to pass the salt, for fear of setting her off on a long-winded rambling philosophical mishmash, which might have had something to do with salt but never actually got you the salt. This was an especially severe problem when fried chicken was being served.

Those who entertained Helen on a regular basis preferred to serve food buffet-style. As word of these informal discourses spread through-out Athens and attendance climbed, savvy hostesses economized by serving only coffee and cake, with an occasional Kaiser roll. Thus, the origin of the term "kaffeeklatsch."

Fortunately for posterity, a fascinating version of one particular kaf-feeklatsch was recorded by Babo, Helen's most devoted and house-proud disciple. Although Babo did not attend in person, because she

---

[2]Greek high school for girls lasted from ages eight–twelve. It was called high school because it was as high as they went.

[3]Sappho didn't have this problem because she was of the lesbian persuasion, and anyway she wasn't a philosopher, she was a poet, and she didn't know it, but her feet show it, they're Long-fellows!

was home cleaning,[4] there is little doubt that her account gives an accurate picture of this event, or nonevent.

The Kaffeeklatsch takes its place alongside the rest of Babo's writings as a truly impressive oeuvre, not just of philosophy but of literature. It is virtually studded with gems of period detail which sparkle, glitter, and pulsate with freshness and vitality. On reading it, one almost imagines that one is actually in Ancient Greece, reclining at table, listening to the sparkling, glittering, and pulsating conversational gems that fall like gems from the lips of our formidable Greek fore-mothers. So come with us now as we journey into the past and capture Greek women in the hilarious act of being themselves . . .

[4]Although in the original ms. of *The Kaffeeklatsch* itself, Babo cites "shopping" as the reason for her absence, certain historians deduce, on the basis of a letter from Babo to her friend Drāno, that she was actually cleaning but was too embarrassed to admit how compulsive she was.

Coffee was such an integral part of Greek society that ancient Greeks often held their hands as though they were drinking coffee even when they weren't. Greek coffee was especially strong, very much like Turkish coffee (but don't ever say that to a Greek).

The Kaffeeklatsch

I **THINK** I am pretty well word-perfect in what you are inquiring about. It so happened that a day or two ago I was in the marketplace searching for tiny cocktail onions with which to stuff my olives when one of my girlfriends, who had caught sight of me from behind, interrupted my quest by calling out for all to hear, "Yoohoo! Where have you been? I've been trying to get in touch with you for days, but all I get is your servant."

"What's up, Periclea?" I inquired, for she appeared to be in a tizzy.

"Peroxide, the daughter of Ammonia, told someone who told my neighbor that you knew the true version of that *intime* little dinner at which Helen of Athens discoursed about art, architecture, and guys."

"Whoever told you that, Periclea, must have had a kink in their grapevine.[1] It was hardly a dinner, in fact, it was not even a luncheon. It was a kaffeeklatsch."

"What, then, is the difference between a kaffeeklatsch and a luncheon?"

"At a luncheon we serve an entree. At a kaffeeklatsch, it is only necessary to serve cakes and a variety of beverages. And at this particular event, some of those beverages were a tad stronger than coffee."

"But were you not there?"

"Certainly not. I was at the market looking for olives in which to

[1] First known use of "grapevine" as a metaphor for gossip; also, probably inspiration for popular chart-topping tune, "I Heard It Through the Grapevine," by Gladys Knight and the Pips.

This illustration, from a nineteenth-century German text, shows a bunch of Greeks having a good time on the Feast of Aphrodite, the ancient equivalent of Sadie Hawkins Day. Note that there is only one guy for all these women. Some things never change.

insert tiny cocktail onions. But Souvlakia was in attendance, you know she can never pass up free food, and she told Peroxide, daughter of Ammonia, who told the person who told your neighbor who told you. So I'm sure I can give you all the juicy details."

"Oh, goodie! Please do!"

"Okay, but before I tell you that, perhaps I should begin at the beginning as Souvlakia herself recounted it to me personally to my face."

Souvlakia said that she met Helen returning from a visit to the Oracle and couldn't help but notice she was wearing evening sandals. She asked her where she was going all dressed up like that. Helen said, "I'm going to Helen of Crete's for a little get-together. Aren't you going?"

"Well, no one told me about it. But aren't you a little overdressed for a kaffeeklatsch?"

ex: dialog

"Let us consider that proposition. Would you not agree that it is one's duty to please one's friends and, even in some instances, one's acquaintances, especially if they are providing the beverages?"

"Why, certainly, that is so."

"And is not Beauty something we all seek after?"

"Without a doubt."

"And, therefore, are not one's friends pleased by the sight of Beauty?"

"You're darn tootin'!"

"Then it would be appropriate to wear evening sandals even in the middle of the day, would it not?"

"Yes, I concede your point, Helen, but wearing those heels on marble all day will ruin your back."

"You're just p.o.'ed because you're not invited. Why don't you come along anyway? It's not formal."

So after some such talk they started off, but on the way, Helen kept stopping and looking in windows. When Souvlakia came to Helen of Crete's place, the hostess herself rushed up to greet her. "Souvlakia, I'm so glad you're here. Did you bring the skewers?"

"I didn't even know I was invited."

"Oh, dear. This is the third time this has happened this year! My messenger was killed en route, and half my guests never got their invitations."

"Remind me to give you the name of my messenger service. I wouldn't even be here if I hadn't run into Helen of Athens."

"Oh, good, where is she?"

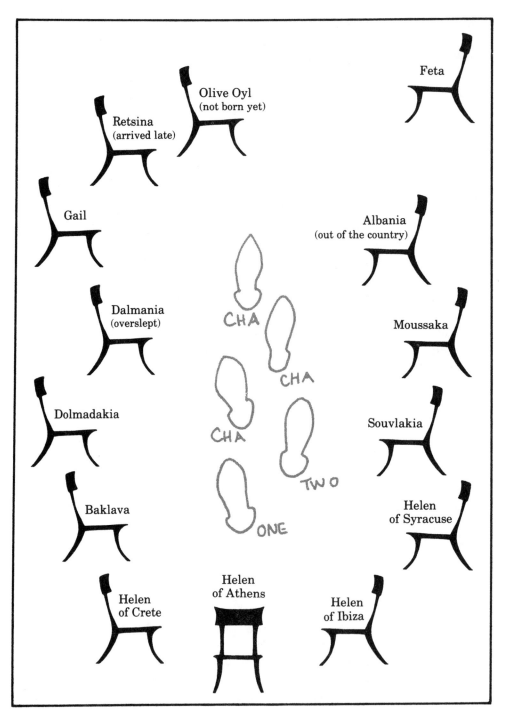

Reconstruction of the original seating plan composed by Helen of Crete for the Kaffeeklatsch. Absenteeism was common at these functions because of the lack of an efficient telephone communication system, such as we had before the AT&T breakup.

"I don't know. She was right behind me a minute ago—she's probably window shopping."

"Oh, no! If she's stopped in at the Feast of Aphrodite clearance sale at the stall of the Hebrews, she'll be at least an hour. Let's start without her. Okay, gals, coffee's perked. Just help yourself to the goodies."

After everyone had helped themselves to macaroons and fruit, Helen of Crete did something that Souvlakia had never seen done before. She presented something she called a seating plan, in which everyone was assigned a place to sit by means of little cards with their names written on them[2] and a cute little drawing of the masks of tragedy and comedy in the corner. This was to everyone's satisfaction, as it is always difficult trying to decide who you want to sit next to.

Just then, Helen of Athens limped in, having broken the heel of one of her sandals. After finding her place, she sat down and said, "What a blessing it would be if wisdom could only run uphill, for then I would be filled with the wisdom of Souvlakia, who warned me not to wear these silly sandals. Boy, I'm pooped! Got anything to drink around here?" Then the Ethiopian servant girl, Beulah, filled everyone's drinking cups with Samian wine.

Thus commenced the true philosophic conversation about which you were so anxious to·know.

Helen of Syracuse:[3] So Helen, what's new? Got any good dish?[4]

Helen of Athens: Did you hear the news about Herpes?

Helen of Crete: No! What's he gotten himself into now?

Helen of Ibiza: Just about every sailor in the port of Piraeus.

Helen of A: But that's not all—

Gail: All we ever talk about is men. I thought we decided last time that we wouldn't do that.

Dolmadakia: What's wrong with talking about men? By the way, did you sneak a peek at Jason and the Argonauts exercising at the gymnasium the other day? Their buns looked so sexy under their cute little tunics.

Helen of C: Cheez 'n' crackers![5] Don't you ever think of anything but sex?

[2]Earliest known reference to the art of seating arrangement. See M. Gross, "The Art of Seating Arrangement," *Titters,* (Macmillan, 1976), p. 23.

[3]The presence of many Helens at any event was not unusual, as during this epoch "Helen" was the Greek equivalent of "Jennifer" today.

[4]First known use of crockery as a metaphor for gossip. The Greeks, who practiced bisexuality, had forty-four expressions for "gossip," yet not a single word for "down vests."

[5]Euphemistic derivative of "Jeez," which itself is a derivative of Jesus Christ; mysterious early reference to the Savior, 337 years prior to His birth.

Gail: Certainly you can't imagine that men are foolish enough to sit around talking about women all the time.

Helen of I: No, they talk about little boys.

Gail: Beulah, you've poured wine at the men's banquets. Tell us what they discuss.

Beulah: They be talkin' foolishness 'bout Truth, Justice, and the Athenian Way.[6]

Gail: What's foolish about that? It is noble to seek the truth—not that I endorse their male-dominated version of the truth.

Beulah: Truth, shee-it! They be talkin' trash, girl.

Helen of A: Now, Beulah, let us always bear in mind that what is trash to one is treasure to another.

Feta: Speaking of trash, have you been to the Acropolis lately? Those new statues are disgusting.

Dolma: They looked all right before they painted in the pubic hairs, but those garish colors—they're just disgraceful.

Moussaka: Who poses for them anyway?

Souvlakia: Henna, Peroxide's cousin, did some modeling for Praxiteles, but she swears she was wearing clothes.

Gail: By accident, Dolmadakia, you have hit upon an important subject: smut. It's disgusting the way men exploit our bodies for their own salacious enjoyment.

Helen of I: But they make statues of nude men, too.

Helen of C: That's different. We have more dirty parts.

Helen of A: Gail's point is, Greek men are always taking off their clothes and hanging around in the nude in front of each other while exercising or having baths. But this is not true of women. Therefore, this is misrepresentation.

Dolma: It's misrepresentation of the men, too. When have you ever seen a man hung like one of those statues?

Feta: Please pass the cheese tray, Moussaka.

Mouss: I will if you open the window, Feta.

Laughter.

Gail: Wait, you guys! Let us not lose sight of this important issue. I feel sure it is one around which we can mobilize a major grass roots action.

Helen of A: Let us ascertain exactly the nature of the proposition

---

[6]Not to be confused with "Appian Way," which came later. We're still in Greece now.

which Gail is endeavoring to put forward. What on earth are you talking about, Gail?

Gail: I'm proposing that we take to the streets and demonstrate our outrage by defacing every example of Greek art in which women are depicted in a degrading fashion. We'll start with subway posters!

Helen of C: We don't have subway posters!

Helen of S: We don't even have subways!

Gail: That's a minor detail. We will one day, and when we do, I'll be outraged. And so will you if you have any brains in your head . . . If we don't act now, we will be setting a dangerous precedent which could affect the image of women for years, decades, maybe even centuries.

Helen of A: Don't be ridiculous.

Mouss: How could that ever happen?

Dolma: And even if it's true, who cares? I like it better when we talk about men.

Bakl: I'll tell you one thing about men . . . if any man had ever tried to clean a house that had Corinthian columns, he would never have built another.

Helen of I: Oh, men are so thoughtless and impractical! Why don't they think of something useful instead of wasting their time on frivolities and homosexual acts?

Mouss: Look at Pythagoras. Why didn't he invent a machine which sucks up dust or something to make our whites whiter?

Souvl: Only a woman could think of something like that.

Dolma: Yeah, and instead of sending men around to collect the tax drachmas, why don't they just send a letter?

Gail: Men would rather go around and beat people up to get the money—it's a typical example of meaningless male aggression.

Bakl: Men are such dum-dums.

Helen of I: *(whispering to Helen of Syracuse)* Baklava's sweet, but she's not too bright.

Helen of A: Well, in my opinion, men could never survive on their own. Most certainly, they would starve. For instance, a man left to his own devices does not understand why there is no food in the snow box,[7] when the reason there is no food is because he has not bought any food. Men just have no concept of shopping. They never make a list. Why is it that a man can walk through the market every day, see lots of food, yet

N.B. Is male domination of our culture hereditary or environmental? YES

---

[7]The Greeks were pioneers in the art of chilling food, due to their fondness for iced potables.

never think to pick up any food? Not even a ham, which is such a versatile meat.

Mouss: *(interrupting)* Helen, where did you get this fabulous dishware?

All Helens: *(in unison)* Who?

Souvl: One might assume Moussaka was referring to our gracious hostess, Helen of Crete.

All Helens: Oh.

Mouss: All that talk about food made me notice your dishware. It's fabulous.

Bakl: It's exquisite, Helen, just exquisite.

All Helens: Thank you.

Mouss: Where did you get it?

Helen of I: 'Fess up. You got it at Two Guys from Turkey.

Helen of C: Well, actually, my husband, Puny of Crete, received it from General Exochiko after the sacking of Sumer. It's Mesopotamian Modern.

Mouss: Well, aren't you the lucky one? The only thing my husband brought back from the Five Day War was a chipped gravy boat[8] and an oversized spoon. He ransacked the whole town, and he couldn't even find the matching ladle. Pillaging just isn't what it used to be.

Gail: Listen to you! You sound like a bunch of chickens cackling in the hen house.[9] I thought the purpose of this kaffeeklatsch was to discuss things of a higher nature.

Bakl: What's wrong with talking about dishware? Dishes are an important part of our everyday life. After all, we look at them three times a day, twenty-one times a week, ninety times a month, and, um, uh, a lot of times a year. And that's not even counting snacks.

Helen of A: You two gals have raised an interesting question, for what is important to one may be insignificant to another. Who is to say where the real truth lies? Things are not always as they seem.

Feta: Baklava, please pass the garlic pita bread.

Gail: *(exploding)* Pita, pita, pita! That's all you ever think about! Helen, please continue.

All Helens: What?

Helen of A: She means me, girls. While we're waiting for Beulah to

---

[8]The Greeks were almost as fond of gravy and sauces as they were of iced potables.

[9]First known reference to women as poultry.

clear away the cake plates and set out the candy dishes, why don't we consider the following parable? Imagine, if you will, a large, spacious, pink room, populated only by women who are seated, each and every one of them, in chairs in a row, all facing in the same direction. Above each head sits a conelike object, from which issues a steady stream of warm air. This strange device, even when no longer in contact with the head, causes the hair to remain neatly coiffed and in place; while, during its use, it prevents those sitting under it from moving their heads from side to side. They can only look directly in front of them.

Bakl: I see.

Helen of A: Moreover, placed in front of this row of chairs is a long reflecting glass in which the women see themselves and those who move about behind them. These people in the background have a curious function. Some carry trays laden with vials of exotic essences, which are used to cleanse and beautify the hair, others bear cylindrical objects which are used for rolling the hair, and still others bring coffee and BLTs to those who sit under the cones.

Mouss: Sounds like a remarkable room. I could spend hours there.

Helen of I: You would, if you could afford the tips.

Grecian coffee cup, circa 420 B.C., depicting Moka, goddess of spring cleaning and irritability, bestowing the precious gift of black gold on the grateful Queen Melitta of the Expresso Isles. Greek coffee cups customarily had two handles, as Greek women drank so much coffee their hands often shook.

Helen of A: Well, imagine that these women have spent most of their adult lives in that room, which I will henceforth refer to as a salon.

Bakl: Why a salon? What's wrong with parlor?

Helen of A: Point well-taken, Baklava. It's true that this hypothetical room about which I keep yammering might be called a parlor by ignorant people who live in the sticks.[10]

Bakl: Oh.

Helen of A: Other than staring straight ahead, the only diversion the women in the salon have is to look through magazines, which are stacked next to their chairs.

Bakl: What are magazines?

Mouss: Are they not like stone tablets, only lighter?

Helen of A: Exactly.

Dolma: Magazines . . . are they not like papyrus scrolls, only heavier?

Helen of A: Yes, only they're not rolled up, except when they arrive in the mail, which, ironically enough, will in the future be delivered by the same person who, in the ideal city-state[11] would bring the letters demanding your tax drachmas.

Gail: Are we not getting off the track here?

Bakl: Are we not men?

All: (singing in chorus) WE ARE DEVO. D-E-V-O.[12] All giggle, except Baklava, who doesn't get it.

Helen of A: But seriously, though,[13] imagine that these magazines purport to publish authentic histories of people who are famed throughout the known world.[14] For example, one magazine, let's call it *Teen Greek Idols,* might contain a dialogue with a well-known Olympic athlete or profile of a blind wandering poet like Homo[15] the Brave.[16] Yet, the unfortunate fact is this: not one word of what they would print would be true.

---

[10]Some ignorant translators who live in the sticks themselves render this as "Styx," e.g., the celebrated river of Greek mythology that separated the underworld, or Hades, from the world of the living. This is just plain stupid. In fact, the Greeks, who were no slouches themselves in the slang department, coined the term "sticks" (der. of Styx) to refer to any remote area of the country, i.e., the pits, armpit of the universe, or Cleveland.

[11]Not to be confused with the fun city-state, Ibiza.

[12]Joke typical of the way-out, offbeat humor much beloved by ancient Greek women (and the young and middle-aged ones, too).

[13]First recorded use of popular stand-up comic segue.

[14]What Alexander the Great conquered all of in 323 B.C.

[15]Pretty low, huh?

[16]*Really* low.

Feta: *(interrupting)* Excuse me, but does anyone else besides me feel like sending out for a double-cheese and anchovy pizza?

Helen of C: Here, Feta, why don't you have some more garlic and onion dip instead?

Feta takes dip grudgingly; digs in.

Helen of I: You mean they make up things and exaggerate, just like in Ibiza?

Helen of A: Exactly. For instance, they might publish a story saying that a famous comedienne had been seen under the influence of ouzo in a posh taverna in the capital[17]—and yet in fact, the story would be a complete fabrication entitling the comedienne to sue for libel.[18]

Gail: That's incredible! You mean they do that to real people? I'm surprised they don't cause more family feuds.

Helen of A: Well, you asked for it, Gail! You wanted to discuss things of a higher nature, so we're discussing the myth of the salon. To sum up, these women, held prisoner by these immobile steel cone-hats, can only perceive life through the images they see in the glass and in the magazines, all of which are illusions. Therefore, the reality which they believe to exist actually exists only in their minds. Do I make myself clear?

Mouss: I get it! I think what Helen is trying to tell us, girls, is that things are not always what they seem.

Helen's phil. of life

Souvl: Why didn't she say so in the first place?

Helen of I: She did, but it didn't seem as though she did.

Bakl: I don't get it.

Helen of A: That's exactly my point.

Retsina stumbles in, drunk, and spills wine on Helen of Crete.

Helen of C: Ye gods, Retsina!

Helen of I: Stewed to the gills again!

Helen of C: Sorry I freaked, but this robe is pure silk, imported all the way from Silkistan.

Dolma: Isn't that always the way the first time you wear a new toga?

Retsina: Toga! Toga! Toga![19]

Helen of A: A surefire way to remove those pesky wine stains is by the application of salt, and plenty of it.

Bakl: What a mind!

RANDI'S PHIL: THINGS DON'T ALWAYS SEEM LIKE THEY ARE!

[17]Reference to the capital city. Not to be confused with the capital on a Greek column, the three types of which are Ionic, Ironic, and Moronic.

[18]Our lawyers have instructed us to state that this should in no way be construed as a reference to Carol Burnett or any of her relatives, living or dead.

[19]Prophetic reference to popular scene in the movie "Animal House." Of course the Greeks didn't wear togas, but who cares?

Metaphorical beauty salon in which metaphorical patron has hair metaphorically bio-waved while reading metaphorical magazine and waiting for metaphorical BLT.

Souvl: You should write a book and call it "Helpful Hints from Helen."

Helen of A: Somehow I don't feel the pressure to publish. I mean, after all, I won't perish. But if another female Greek philosopher wants to capsulize my pithiest hints,[20] I would be happy to relinquish all rights, except for videodisc, of course.

Helen of S: Someone send Beulah to the salt mines, ASAP, before Helen's stain sets in permanently.

Gail: The salt mines are no place for a woman, especially a black woman—she'll stand out too much against the salt.

Helen of C: Nonsense, it's a social situation for Beulah. She gets to see all her friends there.[21]

Beulah picks up pick and shovel and leaves with some reluctance, whistling fatalistically.

Helen of C: *(to Helen of Athens)* Helen, in the ideal city-state, wouldn't they have spot remover?

Helen of A: Why stop with spot remover? This is the ideal city-state we're talking about. Let your imagination run riot.

Retsina: *(riotously throwing cheese at Feta)* Food fight! Food fight![22]

Helen of I: Cool it, Retsina![23]

Helen of C: Tell us more about the dry-cleaning procedures of the future, Helen.

Helen of A: Well, for instance, they would have clean, well-lighted places[24] where you could have your clothes Martinized in one hour.[25]

Beulah enters with an urn of salt. She is somewhat disheveled.

Beulah: Yeah? How you gonna get them clothes home without dirtying them up again?

[20] Ironically enough, centuries later, Heloise did exactly that.

[21] In Greek and Roman times, escaped slaves, when recaptured, were sent to the salt mines. (See "Spartacus." See it with a friend.)

[22] Food fights were a popular recreational activity in Ancient Greece, as well as in American college fraternities and in movies about them. No doubt this is why fratmen are called Greeks.

[23] Retsina, the drink, was often served cold (see Footnote 7) at Greek functions; whereas Retsina herself was often out cold. In this retort, Helen is punning on the phrase "cool it!" which refers to the ancient Greek custom of putting ice cubes on their friends' foreheads until they calm down.

[24] First known and pathetically gratuitous reference to Ernest "Papa" Hemingway's worldview.

[25] Martinizing is not to be confused with Sanforizing, which is a completely different process, and we don't know how long it takes.

Helen of A: Why, they will provide hermetically sealed bags made out of material which is nonbiodegradable and therefore will have a shelf life of billions of years.

Helen of S: I hope they print warnings on those bags so children know not to put them over their heads and suffocate.

Helen of A: *(shrugs)* In an ideal city-state anything is possible.

Bakl: If I lived in an ideal city-state and could do anything I wanted to, I'd give my children animal names—like Robin, Bunny, or Beaver—instead of those names with hard K-sounds in them that my husband always insists on.

Helen of C: Speaking of husbands, I wonder when my guy[26] is coming back from the Macedonian Wars.

Enter a messenger, panting.

Messenger: Ladies, I bring good news. The wars are over. Our victorious armies[27] have been sighted about an hour's march from the city. Thanks be to Athena.

All rejoice, especially Retsina, who throws up on Messenger.[28] They gather their belongings and leave, and the kaffeeklatsch breaks up.

Helen of C: Beulah, I want you to have this place spic and span[29] before Puny gets home. He hates a messy house more than he hates the Macedonians.

Beulah: Yes'm.

---

[26] Earliest known reference to the chart-topping hit by Mary Wells.

[27] The Greeks actually lost the war with Philip II of Macedon, and Greek hegemony was effectively destroyed for all time. The official Greek position was that they had achieved "Peace with Honor," a concept later borrowed by Henry Kissinger to describe American withdrawal from Vietnam.

[28] Throwing up on messengers was a relatively modern and humane practice, as, in earlier times, messengers bearing good news were sacrificed as a thank-you note to the gods.

[29] First known reference to popular household cleaner.

For Further Study

1. Why were so many women in Ancient Greece named Helen? What is its modern equivalent? Isn't it getting on your nerves?

2. Who recorded the dialogues of *The Kaffeeklatsch?* From whom did she get her information? How did the gossip of Ancient Greece inspire such contemporary people as Gladys Knight and the Pips?

3. Compare and contrast the works of Babo with the chronicles of Rona Barrett.

4. In fifteen words or less, describe the difference between a kaffeeklatsch and a luncheon.

5. Who are Jason and the Argonauts? Who was Pythagoras? Who was Puny of Crete, and what was his relationship to General Exochiko? Who was Herpes? Why didn't anyone want to hang out with him?

6. What is the role of the Negro slave Beulah in the dialogues? Why is it that Negroes in literature have a colorful way of getting directly to the point and explaining in memorable jargon what everyone else is trying to say? Why do we have to call Negroes "Black people" now? Why can't we all just get along?

7. Why didn't anyone sit next to Feta? Under the same circumstances, would you?

8. Which member of the Kaffeeklatsch espoused a philosophy which today might parallel the phenomena of women jockeys, the unisex look, and the Virginia Slims ad campaign?

9. Using the time-honored method of deductive reasoning, explain the essence of Helen of Athens' cockamamie parable of the salon. Compare and contrast Helen's salon with Vidal Sassoon's. (If you are not familiar with the Vidal Sassoon salon, you may substitute the salon of your choice.)

10. Who is DEVO?

This medieval woodcut has traditionally been identified as a portrait of the Chaucerian character the Wife of Bath. However, scholars have recently discovered correspondence indicating that Pippa Chaucer posed for the artist at her husband's request—an action Geoffrey Chaucer later regretted when he discovered a series of nude woodcuts of his wife in compromising positions executed by the same artist.

Dame Philippa Chaucer
1331–1410

MUCH has been written about Geoffrey Chaucer's *Canterbury Tales*. It has always been assumed that his wife, Philippa, or Pippa, as she called herself in a vain search for the lyrical, did not accompany him on the pilgrimages but stayed at home recopying manuscript pages which he sent back by messenger from taverns along the route.

The recent discovery, however, of her massive work, unearthed during the excavation of Chillblains Castle, near the medieval village of Bestialbourne, Nightbridge, would seem to indicate that either Pippa Chaucer did, in fact, join her husband on his journeys and kept her own log of the events, or that, while awaiting his return, she penned her own fantastical version of the tales, driven by the boredom and sexual deprivation she felt as a pilgrimage widow.[1]

[handwritten note: did she or didn't she?]

The earliest known records of Pippa Chaucer, daughter of Sir Payne Roet, are in the household register of Elizabeth, Countess of Ulcer, and wife of Prince Lionel the Nag. They state that in December, 1357, Pippa was allowed twenty shillings "for papier on which to wryte jokkes aboute Lionel," indicating that, even at that early date, she was already working for the women of the court, plying her trade as a female humorist.

Her wedding to Geoffrey Chaucer in 1366, at the age of thirty-five, came, as court decorator Lady Sneer wrote in her diary, "nat a momente too soone. Hire biologickal clokke was rustynnge oute," and can clearly be seen as a blatant move to further her career. At that time, she was writing short biographs to accompany the display of portrait minia-

[handwritten note: ONLY HER HAIRDRESSER KNOWS FOR SURE!]

[1]The ancient equivalent of a football widow. There were also Crusade widows, joust widows, and falconry widows.

tures,[2] under the tutelage of Burt of Lancaster, and she was terribly depressed.

Royal Household Accounts indicate that she lied to Chaucer about her age and promised all kinds of kinky sex in return for his proposal and an introduction to the controller of Wools, Skins, and Humorous Writings,[3] from whom she might cadge a contract. Perhaps the result of this contract was, indeed, Pippa Chaucer's *Canterbury Tales*.

Although, at first glance, Dame Chaucer's poetry seems inaccessible, unintelligible, and even impenetrable, at second glance the reader's reaction is, "I can't. No way. I want my MTV." At third glance, however, it proves to be fascinating, richly evocative, and just as filthy as Michael Jackson's glove at the end of a Pepsi shoot. In fact, if the reader reads it out loud, the text becomes instantly understandable. So understandable that one should avoid doing readings for Mom's bridge club, Dad's lodge, or on the Jerry Falwell show.

Yes, in the quiet of his or her locked room, the diligent reader of Pippa Chaucer will be rewarded with many hours of solitary pleasure, and perhaps even an orgasm or two (three, if you eat oysters first). In the final analysis, these tales demonstrate that women in the fourteenth century were almost as funny as the way they spelled things then. Indeed, Pippa Chaucer might be ranked supreme in the backseat driving school of feminist poetry.

—Emily Prager

[2]The medieval equivalent of celebrity profiles. Her tutelage was suddenly terminated when, in a court circular, she described a fistfight that took place between her tutor, Burt of Lancaster, and one Mistress Kidder, a famous danseuse, during the Michaelmas Pantomime of 1367.

[3]Probably John Cheepshott, the Punster, of whose work only this famous line is extant: "Tak my fyfe, pleese."

HELP!!! What's this about?

Two women have escaped from their cruel
Italian husbands who keep them in chastity belts.

Soooo — can they have ORAL SEX?

Not in cold weather 'cause when it's freezing their
tongues stick to the metal. Anyway, they tell this story
of how they happened to be married to Italian guys in
the first place. The whole thing is a flashback. Near their
village this saint died and priests put up a statue of him.

Did he really pop out of the womb talking?

Well, out of the VAGINA, to be more accurate.

That must have been a surprise Was it LaMaze?

Anyway!!! If you're a virgin, you're supposed to lift the stone.

So that leaves you out —

I am as pure as the driven snow.

Yeah - after a lot of people have driven over it!

Forget it! I'm not helping you!

PLEEEESE !!!

OK OK. So, the priests have this hook at the back of the statue and you have to pay them to unhook it — so you can lift it and be pure.

Typical !

Yeah. The women don't know about this and so they can't lift the stone and their village calls them whores. But the Italian guys say they'll marry them as long as they wear chastity belts. They don't care.

Julio Iglesias would care !
Don't talk about the man I love.
He's MINE !!!

Shut up! You're too immature for Julio, and your tits are tooo small! — So, anyway, the Italian guys marry the women and clap them into C.B.s.

C.B. Radios ?
Shut up.

I wish I could understand this Chaucer stuff, it sounds really DIRTY.

That's another thing. you're too dirty for Julio Iglesias.

You wish.

Dame Philippa Chaucer's
Canterbury Tales

The General Prologue—Fragment I

WHAN that Aprille with his shoures dreere
The droghte of Marche hath perced in the ere,
And drenchen al myn hous in swich licour,
Of which mildewe engendred is the flour,
Whan Zephirus[1] eek with his garleek breeth
Inspired hath in every holt and heeth
The meagre croppes, and the doumbe sonne
Hath in the Ram his slough cours y-ronne,[2]
And smale foweles maken melodye,
Til I slepen al the nyght with open ye,
(Wolde slee hem with a knyf, hadde I corage)
Than longen Geof to goon on a pilgrimage.
Myn housbonde thynkes to seken straunge blondes,
In ferne halwes, cooze in sondry londes.
He knoweth wel from evry shires ende
Of Engelond, to Caunterbury they wende,
A joly blisful lechour for to seke.
If they thynke it be my Geof,
They maken greete mystake.
   Bifel that in that sesoun on a day,
In Southwerk at the Tabard[3] as we lay
Redy to wenden on oure pilgrimage

(handwritten marginal and interlinear annotations: "showers dreary", "draught", "pierced", "such a liquid", "caused to grow flower", "wood", "dumb", "slow course run", "birds", "courage/heart/energy", "SPEED", "→ pussy!", "seek strange", "fair blondes / sundry lands", "come", "lechour", "1 day", "it rehearsed season", and bracketed left margin "periodic sentence")

[1]The wind from the west. They called it Zephirus. We call it Maria.

[2]A weird way of saying the last half of April.

[3]The Tabard, an inn that catered to pilgrims and was praised at the time for its musclade of minnows and larded milk, two dishes which bear a close resemblance to the modern Friskies Buffet Seafood Supper and mouldy yogurt.

And bete som lyf into oure mariage, *beat some life*

At nyght was com in-to that hostelrye

Wel nyne and twenty in a compaignye,

Of sondry folk, by aventure y-falle

In felawshipe, and morons were they alle.

Whil that I have nought els to doon

Me thinketh it accordant to resoun — *makes sense*

To telle yow of ech of hem, so as it semed me

And whiche they weren, and of what degree;

For Geof wol tell it wrongge

If the tale be lefte to he.

A KNYGHT ther was, and whot a peese of ers!⁴ *ass!*

[Expurgated.]

Two women ther wer, escaped fro Itallie,⁵

Y-clothed bothe in belts of chastitee. *iron prisons*

Greet y-ron baillyes hadde they round hir hippes *their*

That no man myghte assege hem with his lippes *besiege them* — *oral sex!!!*

Or with his wanger, whan that hir housbondes wer aweye. *penis*

Or so hir housbondes thoghte, but trouthe to seye, *their*

They wolde ley doun with eny parfit knyght *lay down* *handsome*

Who hadde with him a blowtoorche, or who myghte

Bestir himselve to werke a keye, *make* — *get himself together*

⁴Philippa Chaucer's pilgrims are far more vivid and personal than either the Theophrastan characters or the medieval characters with which they have been compared. In fact, they are disturbingly pornographic, which is only a snatch, you should pardon the expression, of this tale is printed here. The full text resides in the archives of the Victoria and Albert Museum, where, of course, they also have Prince Albert in a can.

⁵Whether the Two Women did in fact exist has long been a matter for historical speculation. In *The Oxford History of Medieval Torture of Women and Other Beasts* (Oxford University Press, 1933), Twit makes reference to the Italian practice of clapping women into chastity belts as a way of "belting women without actually laying hands on."

And ope hir legges and set ~~hem~~ *them* free.
It was hir dreme that ~~swich a~~ *such* man
Wolde perce ~~hem with~~ *them* a batterene ram
Of vaste dimenscioun,[6] lyk a Godde
Of Love, ~~thyk eek and~~ *thick also* longe, a magik rodde.
And for this resoun wer they commen
On pilgrimages to seke som funnen. *party*
I hadde no herte to ~~telle hem nay,~~ *tell them no*
Ful many a yere of howe I preye
For ~~swich a oon,~~ *such a one,* and I withouten belt!
And so with hem biforn the seintes I knelte,
In case the Goddes myghte tak on hem ~~pitee,~~ *pity*
And ther myghte ben som leftouveres for me. *SLOPPY SECONDS*
It made me sad to see hem ryde.
The ~~soun~~ *noise* was lyk greete belles innesyde
A chapel ~~tour,~~ *tower* and ~~peyned~~ *hurt* myn hede. *RIDE HORSES*
~~I noot howe~~ *don't know* they wende to bedde.
I asked hem howe it cam to be
Weren they belts of chastitee.
And ~~thinne~~ *then* this tale did they bigan
Of mannes crueltee to wommen. *GAVE HER A MIGRAINE*

OPEN BOOK TEST
FRI
Remember to bring book
!!!

---

[6]Professor Gedda Boner, noted physical anthropologist, has documented that in the 14th Century, the average penis extension at full erection was a meager 5 inches in length. Well, people were smaller then, ceilings were lower. Look at how tiny the armor was. So, when Dame Chaucer talks about a "Godde of Love," she is really talking about an erect penis length of 7 inches tops, a mere inch longer than the present American national average. It seems clear, then, that though her expectations might have been flashy at the time, in modern terms she is not shooting for the moon.

The Tale of Two Women
Wearing Chastity Belts

Heere bigynneth the Tale of Two Wommen Weren Belts of Chastitee

"Oure housbondes be two lordes of Itallie,"
Seyed they as oon. "And we two susters be
From Engelond, verray, a parisshe smale
Wher dyede Seinte Rumald whil infant male.[7]
Lordynges! But coulde he spoke, this seinted ladde,
And cryed oute thryes, 'Christes!', biforn he hadde
Fuly escaped his moders lusty wombe.
Stonden was oure hous wel neigh his toumbe
Wheron was putte of him a stoon image.
A hooly thynge for rites of mariage.
In somer, preestes bringen al the maydes
Of oure village oute to the toumbe and bade
Hem seke to lyfte the stoon, ye see,
And if they coude, it proeved hir chastitee.
Lyte was the stoon as eny maydenes grace
Biforn she wedde and droppeth doun hir face
Fro gravitee. But oftetyme it nolde moeve
The stoon at al, and so wolde certeyn proeve
The mayde hadde loste hir maydenhede precious
and was nat fit for mariage vertuous."

[7]Dame Chaucer has here plagiarized the ancient legend of Saint Rumald and interwoven it into her tale. The story goes that the infant Rumald emerged from his mother's womb preaching of Christ. For three days he wandered, preaching, and on the third day, died, interestingly enough, at a spot near the Chaucer cottage outside Bestialbourne. At the spot, the ancient priests erected a small statue of him. In later times, during the summer solstice, the local virgins were summoned to the shrine, and asked to prove their virginity by lifting the statue. Those who could not lift it were tagged "damagyed goodes," and apprenticed as cage cleaners to itinerant bear-baiters.

Stoppeth the wommen thinne, oon shook hir hede. *head*
Hir neke entwyned was, hire visage rede. *neck twisted / face red*
"Jesu!", cryed she, and shyfteth on hir hors.
A clanken soun oute rangge, both loud and cors, *rang out*
Folwed by a ferte verray smale *very small fart!!!*
"Pardonne me for nature me y-calle."
"How shitteth ye?", asked I and wisshed to knowe.
"With difficultee," seyed she, "Do nat aske mo."
"Wolde take some drugges?", hire suster seyed to hire, *opium*
"Som opie strongge wolde stoppe ye uppe for shure."
"There is nat need," seyed she, "Wher weren we?
Ah, yes, the stoon and belts of chastitee!
   It came to pas oon somer was the tyme *to pass summer*
That we moste lyfte the stoon and drynke the wyn *must / wine*
Of Fortune. For two lordes of Itallie
Hadde journeyed to oure parisshe for to see
What wommen ther wer to take hem for to wyf *marry*
And spende with hem a longe emprisouned lyf. *them*
Loved we two squieres yongge and fair *squires*
Who loved ous, a rude and lusty pair.[8] *us*
But they wer poore, and so oure familie
Preferred alle the men of Itallie.
Ther was a chaunce we coude have hadde oure squieres *squires*
And parfit lyves and alle oure beste desyres
But for the dredfulle fate which did befalle *their cake & eat it too*
Ous bothe, harde by Rumald, the seynted infant male. *near*

[8]No one knows why squires were always "rude and lusty" in those days, but certainly that was their rep. But, frankly, at an average of 5 inches per squire, translate "rude and lusty" here to "unpretentious and retiring."

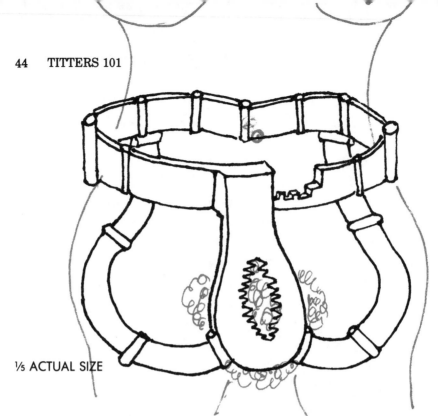

1/5 ACTUAL SIZE

Artist's rendering of chastity belt, evidently designed for a woman who today would wear Number Two pantyhose (5'4"–5'7"). The *American Heritage Dictionary* describes the chastity belt as a sexual device "supposed to have been worn by medieval women to prevent sexual intercourse." Who's the brains behind this gem? How come they don't define "saddle" as "a device supposed to be worn by horses to permit people to ride them?" Nowadays, the only reason someone would wear something like this would be if some fashion designer sold it to them as a New Wave belt.

> That special daye cam we to lyfte the stoon.
> It wolde nat moeve, no matere how we groon,
> Or pusshe, or pulle, or grevous streyne endure.
> And heres the rubbe: we bothe wer certeyn pure
> By Jesu, oure desyres wer nat whetted
> Tho holden handes we hadde, and hevy petted.
> It seemed in bak the stoon ther was a hooke,

(Enfashiouned by oon preeste who was a crooke),
So that ye coude nat lyfyte the stoon biforn
Som gold y-passed hadde throgh chapel doore and
Into the poket of this vilein preeste
Who bothe oure lyves hadde smote atte leeste.
Whan that the parisshe saugh with hir oon yen
We coude nat lyfte the stoon, they demed ous lyen,
And thinne pronounced ous bothe to strompets be
With wikked hertes and noon virginitee.
    The squieres took hir leeve in wretchednesse.
They haten al which ones was gentilesse.
Nat so the lusty lordes of Itallie.
They lyked ous mor withouten chastitee.
Y-giveth hem resoun for oure abuscioun
And so forthwithe cam they to this conclusioun:
That they wolde take ous bothe to be hire wyves
If weren we y-ren nikkeres al oure lyves,
Whan that they wer aweye or oute of syghte.
Oure familie cared nought for oure plyght
Synse that muche gold gave they to oure fader,
And seyed greete plaisanteries to our moder,
That she was kyn to faire Helene of Troye,
Which verrily was a sory, aged ploye.
    But al of this is passed historye.
Ful many a yeere dwelled we in Itallie
With lordes who hadde knobbes upon hir chekes,
And aten oftymes garleek, onyons, lekes.
But happily escaped we hir grypen,
The reste of lyf to gambol and to trippen

On pilgrimages. Pardonnes," thinne ended they, *then*

"Ous bothe, for we be ladies and be lothe *loth*

To give offense or offer speches pithee, *Pithy speeches*

But, knowe ye, perchaunce, a cheepe and competaunt smithee?" *locksmith*

Heere endeth the Tale of Two Wommen Weren Belts of Chastitee

ACTUAL SIZE

Medieval key to medieval chastity belt on previous page. Any fool knows you can't keep the key with the belt. By the way, did you notice that the chastity belt turned upside down bears an uncanny resemblance to Old King Cole's crown? No wonder he was such a merry old soul.

For Further Study

1. What language is this? a) Greek; b) Piglatin; c) Afrikaans; d) none of the above.

2. Where can I get a crib? a) college bookstore; b) frat house; c) baby furniture store.

3. Where can I use this in later life? a) cocktail parties; b) job interviews; c) swing clubs.

4. Reviewing Pippa Chaucer's attitude throughout the Prologue, would you say that Geoffrey Chaucer was impotent? a) Do pigs have wings? b) Is the Pope Polish? c) Only when he was overexcited.

5. When she describes the Knyght as a "peese of ers," what does she mean? a) that his purse is filled with gold sovereigns and he likes to eat out at fancy taverns; b) that he has stood for the bar, owns his own house in London, and is naive about women; c) that he has bedroom eyes, runs with a group of minstrels, and loathes commitment.

6. In the Introduction, Dame Chaucer is described as having spent the early part of her career in the household of Elizabeth, Countess of Ulcer, writing jokes about the Countess' husband. In Middle English, write five jokes about your own boyfriend's weaknesses using the following medieval terms: erly balled-nesse; badde skinne; poore sens of hewemor; stingynesse; prematour ejakulacioun.

7. Discuss why, in medieval times, the person who controlled wools and skins also controlled humorous writing. Could this explain the curious modern practice of classifying humor as nonfiction? What could?

8. What did the "two lordes of Itallie" do for a living? a) welding; b) kneecapping; c) nothing is known except that they were on strike.

9. In the Prologue to the Tale of Two Women, what is the significance of the fact that Saint Rumald popped out of his mother's womb already able to speak? Could this happen in modern times? Do you have any proof besides the *Enquirer*?

10. At one point in the Tale of Two Women, one of the sisters offers the other some opium to stop up her bowels. Discuss this and elaborate on medieval women's use of hard drugs, why they took them and where they would be likely to get them. Using your own experience and names and telephone numbers, expand your discussion to include your own dealers and connections. Do you know anyone in Afghanistan or Tibet? Would you be more likely to get a good grade if you laid some opium on your professor?

The pamphlets of Elizabethan advice-monger Elleyne Gurley Browne helped hundreds of lonely women out of their dating doldrums and into the cozy servitude of wifehood. She herself, however, never married, preferring to nibble at the smorgasbord of life rather than sit down to a real meal. Our suggestion for the lead in "The Elleyne Gurley Browne Story:" actress Betty White, best known for her portrayal of Sue Ann Nivens on "The Mary Tyler Moore Show." (Check your local TV guide for scheduling.)

Elleyne Gurley Browne
1626–1572

THE blazing comet that was Shakespeare tends to obscure the other stars in the Elizabethan literary galaxy. Nonetheless, the sixteenth century was, in fact, an era of creative ferment for everybody except, of course, women, who as usual found themselves in last place in the literary sweepstakes. It's true that Queen Elizabeth herself wrote essays and even sonnets, but then, of course, she was the Queen. She could do what she wanted, and usually did.[1]

However, one outlet available to women writers of the time was the pamphlet. With the rise of the middle classes, there was an increased demand for reading material, and these short booklets, which could be printed and sold relatively cheaply, were the Elizabethan equivalent of *People* magazine.[2] These pamphlets were characterized by the hard-hitting, vivid style with which they dealt with controversial subjects, and the fact that when you read them ink came off on your fingers.[3]

We do not know who the author of "A Tender Trap" was, nor do we know whether or not Elleyne Gurley Browne is using a pseudonym. But historical records from the period indicate that a woman of that name did exist and was apparently married to a well-known and prosperous producer of court masques.

---

[1]Queen Elizabeth, or "Queenie" as she was known among her courtiers, was a notorious prankster, given to shaving her head, wearing bright red "Bozo the Clown" wigs, and mooning the populace from the Royal Coach. Once she bet the Earl of Essex that he couldn't beat her pancake-eating record at the International House of Pancakes. She was right, he couldn't, but what the Earl didn't know was that hers had been only silver-dollar pancakes, and she didn't use any syrup. Another time, she pretended to sentence Sir Philip Sidney to the Tower for life, letting him out a week later with a note that said, "Sorry. Just kidding."

[2]Others were the equivalent of *Us* magazine.

[3]Thus giving rise to the expression, "If they can send an indentured servant to the New World, how come they can't invent an ink that doesn't come off on your hands?"

The first pamphlet, published in 1546 under the name "Mating and the Single Maiden," which, among other things, exploded the myth of the vaginal orgasm, aroused so much controversy in England that Elleyne was forced to flee to the Continent. Later, "When a Man Doth and a Woman Doth Not," a pamphlet that she wrote and had printed while abroad, was smuggled into England, where it circulated widely, even being sold in the streets of London. It came to the attention of the Queen, who, sympathizing with this universal feminine problem,[4] recalled Elleyne Gurley Browne to England in 1571 under a safe-conduct. (Ironically, Browne died of the plague in 1572, several months later.)

Doubtless it was her experience abroad that gave her writing a Cosmopolitan flavor, at its peak in the pamphlet reprinted here. Unlike other pamphleteers, she believed not in simply exhorting her audience, but in giving practical advice. The underlying theme of all her pamphlets, and a theory to which she ascribed fervently, was basically humanistic: even the lowliest mouseburger could, with the aid of her suggestions, transform herself into someone who looked as though she'd had a couple of expensive facelifts.

Modern-day interest in Elizabethan pamphlets is minimal, due to their boring and antiquated prose, but Browne's work is valuable in illuminating the daily concerns of a woman of the period: how to find a man, what to wear while looking for one, what to do when you've got one, and how to get rid of one when you're through with him. To modern tastes, her writing may seem contrived, even cloying, yet there is no question that she makes the Elizabethan era come alive, "lice and all," for her readers.[5]

YOU MIGHT THINK I'M A HORSE BUT I'M NOT. I'M A GRIFFIN.

[4]Sir Philip Sidney doth, the Queen doth not, if you catch our drift.

[5]She also did a roaring sideline business in love potions.

A Tender Trap
In Which To Snare Wild Boar

TO the Gentléwomen of England, health!

I pray you, grant me your forebearance if I set down herewith that which some among you whose wits are sharpest may well have knowledge of: namely how to snare a husband, be it your own, or somebody else's. For do not the philosophers decree that a woman without a man is a thing unnatural and greatly to be abominated, somewhat akin to a fish without a bicycle? Just as the horse or dog shall find a master, so woman shall find a mate, and thence shall proceed her true happiness, for he shall provide for her in the matter of food, shelter, and that with which to clothe her nakedness, and she in turn shall learn how she may twist him about her little finger, so that he shall do all that she asketh, and buy her silk, and oranges, and oils and unguents with which to anoint her body for his pleasure, and cute tops.[1]

The poacher and the gamekeeper alike know where to seek the wild hare, and set their traps accordingly; if you wouldst capture a man, you needs must go where men are. You wilt in no wise meet anyone moping around your chamber. Frequent not a nunnery nor seek out the company of ancient gossips and wrinkled crones. Forsooth, you wilt not find an able-bodied man herein.

At the smithy gather men of all ranks from churl to baron, and there can be no fault to be found in a young maid who of an afternoon's walk chooseth to stroll past the blacksmith's shop and compliment a handsome customer on how well his horse is hung. Bear in mind that a man who stints not to shoe his horse when needful will neither stint in the care of his wife, and the man who is quick to tickle his mare with a whip may likewise choose to tickle his mate.

Ply you the twin tools of wit and imagination and ye will uncover as many opportunities of meeting men as there are blackbirds in a pie.

---

[1] The Elizabethans, both male and female, were fond of cute tops, especially if they had ruffles, but they hadn't figured out how to make proper pants yet, and therefore the men were forced to run around in tights, codpieces, and those silly-looking bloomer-type things which can be seen in pictures of Sir Walter Raleigh on tobacco tins.

A Tender Trap

in Which to Snare thee Wilde Boare
or
Honey Catcheth thee Moft Flies
or
Step into My Chamber

Being an Inftrvment whereby to Engender Paffion

I' the Breaft of that Sex

Wovldft Fain Prefvme Itfelf Svperior

Written by One that Dares Call a Dogge, a Dogge

And a Spade, a Nvbian.

By Elleyne Gvrley Browne.

Empreinted in England by Miftreff Makepenny
to bee fold from 'neath her petticoats
fo long as noone fhall be looking on.

1654.

Go Ye from Movfebvrger to Marvelovs.

Title page from Elleyne Gurley Browne's "A Tender Trap." This pamphlet sold like hotcakes; in fact, it was sold next to hotcakes and later, when it was remaindered, it was sold wrapped around hotcakes, which were the *pommes frites* of their day. *Pommes frites,* of course, are the giant pretzels of France and the Benelux nations, which in themselves are the *pommes frites* of New York City, which is the Atlanta of the North.

Follow after your own inclination; should you love the theatre, many a
fun-loving young gallant can be found at the playhouse of an afternoon,
drinking wine and throwing vegetables at the stage. Fie! If your search
prove useless, you will at least have seen the play. But have a care lest
ye fall in with the players themselves: shun ye those strutting cocks
who preen their feathers onstage amidst a hail of vegetables. As the
saying goes, "Love a lawyer, make your will; love a doctor, spare the
bill; love an actor, come to ill."[2]

But if your perfect match is a man who cares for the good of the
commonwealth, and stands staunchly behind the laws of the realm, and
furthermore is desirous of eliminating diseased persons from the body
politic, as a surgeon would remove your ear if you had an earache, then
get ye to a hanging, for most assuredly those who would fain witness
hangings are possessed of all these qualities in good measure, and
moreover are probably real fun guys who like to live life on the edge.
There's nothing like a good hanging to remind you of your own mor-
tality.

Let me bid you once again, seek out men where men are known to
gather, and you will surely find that which ye seek. A friend of mine is
happily married to a handsome wainwright she just happened to
"bump" into at a bear-baiting—and imagine, she almost didn't go because her wig hadn't come back from the dry cleaner's.

But if ye hanker after a husband, at your peril will you follow behind
those men who go a-soldiering in the wars, for their general desires
bend toward rape and pillage, and as husbands they are apt to prove
unstable. Sailors, on the other hand, are generally lusty while in port,
but liable to be absent for years at a time, which may or may not be to
your liking.

So with a mixture of common sense, confidence, and a ha'penny's
worth of wit, you may yet gather your wheat, that is your Husband,
which will be your bread and butter; and throw away your chaff, that is
those knaves with no thought of matrimony in mind.

Once you know where to fish, you must learn how to bait your hook.
Dress not like a harlot, for if you wish a man to make you his wife, he

[2]The notion that actors make unreliable mates originated not long after the first public performance of a play, when the actor who played the leading role left his wife and six children to run off
with his co-star. This attitude persists to the present-day, perhaps with good reason. Talk to
Debbie Reynolds. Or Eddie Fisher. Or Elizabeth Taylor, or Richard Burton. But don't ever try and
talk to them all at once.

HOT

will surely want to think himself the first to plough your furrow. Do not deck yourself in gaudy brocades and satins or you may affright him by your extravagance, and make him fear that he needs must keep you in the lavish style of a court lady. Just wear a simple full-sleeved bodice and stomacher over one or two corselets, a petticoat, farthingale, under-skirt, paniered overskirt, and, of course, the all-important face-framing ruff. You'll look ravishing, and what's more, your virtue will be well-guarded.

Elizabethans were → dirty! IN MORE WAYS THAN ONE!

It is good to bathe at least once a month, and give yourself a PTA[3] on Sundays and Saints' Days in between. A healthy cleansing regimen makes all the difference in how you look and feel about yourself. Physicians now know that sickness is not caused by bathing, but by going outside before your hair is dry.[4]

If you are scarred from the pox, cover what marks you can. A simple ointment can be made by mixing oil and clay, taking care to choose a shade of clay which resembles the colour of your skin. Fill in the pockmarks and powder with flour to give yourself the fair smooth complexion of a young maid, provided you stay out of the rain.

Go neither unlaced nor unperfumed from your abode, but tighten your corselet to make your waist appear small and your hips well-suited for childbearing, and douse yourself with some fragrance other than your own, such as Yardley's Olde English Lavender.[5] The aroma of lavender is especially offensive to lice, which is another reason why it is appealing to men. Mark the words of the old Welsh drinking song: "Show me a maiden with good skin and no lice; I'll marry that maiden and live without vice."[6]

[3]Pussy, Tits, and Ass. Elizabethan slang for a quick sponge bath, or half-shower, as some gym instructors call it.

[4]It took until the sixteenth century for the medical profession to realize the dangers of going outside with wet hair. Interestingly enough, mothers knew it all along. Statistics show that the risk of illness increases proportionately to the amount of fun you have wherever you intend to go with your hair wet.

[5]This early reference to Yardley products really shook up the editors: we had no idea Yardley's Olde English Lavender was that olde. Subsequent research revealed that the author had taken money from Yardley to help defray her printing costs, and was basically giving them a free plug.

[6]The reference to this song may be a joke on the author's part, since to Elizabethan humorists, the Welsh were the Polish of their day, viz., this popular Welsh joke: "Q. How many Welshmen does it take to screw the Queen? A. Four. One to do the deed and three to turn the chair." This is typical of the bawdy sense of humor of the Elizabethans, who liked to talk dirty, especially about the Queen, in spite (or perhaps because) of the danger of having their tongues cut out if they were overheard.

If your appearance pleaseth and you find yourself alone in the company of a man whose attributes are to your liking, how then do you begin to allure his heart to you? Avail yourself of the qualities bestowed on you by the gods. If they have given you the voice of a nightingale then woo him with a madrigal, for music hath charms to soothe the savage breast. Tempt his palate with dainties prepared by your own fair hands (if they're not, he need never know). Set your table with such dishes as will stir the amorous appetite: pigs' knuckles, smoked eel, and blood sausage. Yet resist the temptation to give him a surfeit of such delicacies, for eating overmuch perchance will induce drowsiness. A man who has just consumed twice his body weight in shepherd's pie is not likely to prove the ardent swain.

Do not overfill his glass with wine; make his drink generous enough to make his blood run warm, yet not so large it taketh two hands to lift. Yea, forsooth, spirits do lighten our souls and enliven our wits, but be advised: taken in too great quantities they rob men of their sexual prowess and vigor. And that's one problem you don't need tonight.

Now that the stage is set, be sure that this is the peacock you wish to skewer; for your ship is about to set sail for the Isles of Matrimony, and there can be no turning back. The journey from dinner (and do not stop to wipe the trenchers)[7] to postprandial activities is nicely accomplished over a flagon of love potion. Remember a good love potion costs a pretty penny and this is no time to pinch pennies. Choose one that has been successful for a friend and comes from a reliable peddler; do not attempt to make it yourself. Setting aside the tragic accidents of paralysis and even death, there are reported cases where the victim of a homemade potion has been afflicted with an overpowering lovesickness for the first object he spies in his euphoria, whether it be an armoire or the mistress' cat. And that's a problem you don't need—ever.

Nature being what she is, in the blink of an eye you may well find yourself with your skirt over your head busily making the beast with two backs.[8] Whilst he is still inflamed by Cupid's dart, seize your moment and exact from your lover a promise of marriage. Should he think it a trifling matter to plight his troth, as he knows he nonetheless may

[7] Dishes. Not to be confused with trench mouth, although some people did get trench mouth from eating off unwiped trenchers.

[8] Shakespeare, who was a notorious thief of other people's material, obviously "borrowed" this line, as well as a loaf of bread and a pair of hose, from the author. The only thing he returned was the hose, and they had a run in them.

evade you in the future and not prove good as his word, you may play your masterstroke. Summon your lawyer, whom you have concealed within your house,[9] mayhap beneath the bed,[10] or in that very armoire I spoke of betimes, and cause him to enact a contract witnessing your intention to marry within a fortnight. It is a crafty fox indeed that can gnaw his way out of that trap. I know well whereof I speak;[11] my husband proved a gentle lamb to the slaughter, and if sometimes he may roar like a lion, why in almost all matters pertaining to domestic life he is a darling pussycat.[12]

So go ahead, ladies, and take up the pursuit of a husband. Fear not, for somewhere in this wide world wandering is one with your initials on it, even if he doesn't know it yet.

[9]Is she kidding?

[10]She's kidding.

[11]She's not kidding.

[12]The Elizabethans were as fond of animal imagery as many of our modern-day magazine editors, who use cats, turtles, and rabbits as heraldic symbols. The Elizabethans would have loved the Playboy Clubs if they could have gone to them.

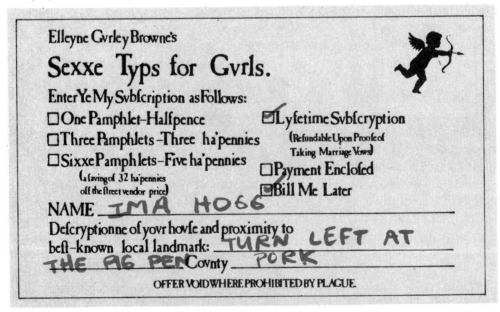

Although she is not known for it, the traditional magazine subscription form was first conceived by Elleyne. However, the idea wasn't very successful, since no one had yet thought of a way to collect money from people who checked "bill me later."

For Further Study

1. What's with all the celestial references in the first sentence of the introduction to this chapter? Doesn't it kind of piss you off and make you want to stop reading? Well, go ahead, buster, fail the course, see if I care.

2. What is the Elizabethan pamphlet the equivalent of in communication today? Do you think people would buy *People* if *People* didn't run photos of people?

3. Explain the derivation of the word "codpiece." (Deduct ten points for jokes about fish.)

4. How does a harlot dress? Does anyone in your class dress like that?

5. Using your imagination, write a short story or skit depicting a visit by a typical Elizabethan to a modern Playboy Club.

6. Do you think this pamphlet actually helped any Elizabethan mouseburgers find husbands, or was it just designed to promote the sale of mail-order breast enlargers?

7. Prepare a short report on feminine hygiene in the Elizabethan Era. THEY STANK.

8. Do you have any idea whether the Elizabethans substituted f's for s's when they spoke or just in writing? If they did, did it make them sound like assholes? Is there any connection between this and the indiscriminate wearing of lace by both sexes during the Elizabethan period?

9. Go to the library. Using the Dewey Decimal System, look up love potions. What were their main ingredients? Do you think it was easy for the average Elizabethan woman to lay her hands on two ha'pennies' worth of bat snouts? Would it be easy for you? If not, how do you expect to get that cute guy from Comp. Lit. to ask you to the freshman mixer?

10. Couldn't the editors have thought of something less tiresome than the old "calling a spade a spade" joke? Does it offend you personally? If so, keep it to yourself because, frankly, in all sincerity, not to put too fine a point on it, we find your carping criticism kind of tiresome, to tell the truth.

A portrait of Lillian Putian from the frontispiece of her book. True to the spirit of her time, Lilly sports an adventurous coiffure which reflects Brittania's emergence as a world power, and Vidal of Gore's emergence as a hairdresser. Lilly discarded this do after discovering that when she walked, she listed slightly to the port side.

Lillian Putian
1700–1769

LILLIAN Putian was born in Dingbatonshire, Wales, in 1700, fourth of a family of ten children. Lillian, better known as Lilly, was brought up in a bookish household and, although she moved her lips when reading, was a voracious reader from the age of eight. The imaginative Lilly produced an enormous mass of unusual juvenilia, including elegies, songs, farces, tragedies, epic poems, and elaborate birthday cards.[1] From the age of twelve, she suffered from bouts of melancholia. During one such spell, Lilly collected her manuscripts together and made a tremendous bonfire to protest the double standard she found her parents inflicting upon the girls in her family.

This battle for basic human rights for women continued throughout her life and was often expressed in her writing. When denied admittance to the Welshpool Seminary for Boys, Lilly stood out front circulating copies of her essay entitled "What God Lacks in Length, He Makes Up for in Height," in which she satirized the male dominance of the church. Horrified, her parents, who had an almost religious respect for the Royal Family, insisted that she accept a post at court as Second Keeper of the Robes to the Duchess of Buckingham.

Although she hated her years of courtly servitude (1721–1726), and although she was often bullied and harassed by some of her fellow courtiers, she found time to keep a diary. Here she was free to exercise her keen satirical wit and her powers of caustic observation, as well as to develop her journalistic style. Her diaries are full of interesting

---

[1]One such birthday card, which escaped the bonfire because it was preserved in the home of its recipient, Lilly's great-aunt Elsie Putian, is currently on display in the Putian museum in Dingbatonshire. (Open daily from 2–4 P.M., admission 2s., cream teas with crumpets 12s. 6d.) It reads: "Dear Auntie Elsie/It's too bad you live in Chelsea/It's too far away/To see you each day/Especially when I am not wealthy/Happy birthday anyway/Your loving grand-niece/Lilly"; and is decorated with a motif of suns, moons, stars, and what appear to be flying pigs.

details of the court life in which she was embroiled, written with a strange combination of cool vision and hot rage as to "what foolish creatures abound within that animal called man."

Unable to contain her outrage at the hypocrisy of the times, Lilly Putian penned a pamphlet entitled "An Humble Proposal." A blistering attack on the brutality of the English, it suggested that dissenting women should be eaten by the members of Parliament.[2] Later acclaimed as the greatest short satire in the language, "An Humble Proposal," published under the assumed name of Don B. Cruel, caused great confusion at the time of its publication. A warrant was issued for the arrest of the author, and when the offender was discovered to be a woman at court, Putian was forced to return to Wales.

While in exile at her father's home, Lilly Putian became involved with a group of coal miners' wives who were concerned with the conditions in the mines. "From My Tub" is a scorching satire on the hardships of living a coal miner's life, emphasizing the difficulties of keeping one's husband, children, clothing, and finally, one's tub clean. She submitted it to the *Aberdale Gazette* under a pseudonym and only when her mother had heard it praised by her friends did Lilly admit to her that she was the unknown author.

Putian now became a hero to the women of Wales and was offered an editorial job at the *Gazette,* which she happily accepted. Thus began a long and productive relationship between Lilly Putian and her publisher, the handsome Harold Halfpennysworth. We are not concerned here with idle chatter about the private lives of great writers: after all, it is no one's business if it was rumored that he used to poke her in the print shop after hours. It is by his or her works that we know a writer.

Lilly Putian was a progenitor of editorial writers. She was an artist first and foremost, but she also had what she used to call "a nose for news." When an unusual occurrence happened in some remote place, she developed the habit of traveling to the spot to investigate and write up the incident. Quite like a modern *Enquirer* reporter (but with more talent and integrity than most of them), she would interview the natives, take notes, then return to her home base, where she would order her notes into an artistic model of news reporting for the *Gazette*.

It is not, however, as a journalist that we remember Putian, but as

[2]This pamphlet was so influential that it occasioned an X-rated parody, "An Immodest Proposal," suggesting that dissenting women should be eaten out by Members of Parliament (*Royal Lampoon,* "Funky Parliament Issue," August 1727).

the author of *Robin Caruso*. For the mature reader, it is a satire on humanity, expressing Putian's abhorrence of the traditional Christian views and of society in general, with subsidiary attacks on the evils of human pride, especially as exhibited through fashion. For the young reader, *Robin Caruso* is a heck of an adventure and a lot more fun than watching reruns of "Fantasy Island."[3]

Putian's novel was first published anonymously, purporting to be the true adventures of one Robin Caruso. The opening creates an air of authenticity through its details of Caruso's past life and the circumstances of her voyage and shipwreck, all told in the most matter-of-fact way. After several years of being alone on the island, Caruso suddenly finds herself with a talking horse, but again, the narrative moves with such directness and ease and with such attention to minute detail that it becomes almost plausible in its absurdity.

No doubt it was during her years at court that she developed both her grim vision and her fetishistic obsession with clothing. As Second Keeper of the Robes, it was Lilly's responsibility to care for dozens of heavy velvet and brocade court garments which were worn repeatedly without being dry cleaned in between. In a deodorant-free society, this must have been a nightmare.

It is a little-known fact that Lilly Putian, besides inventing the modern novel, was the inventor of the steam iron, almost a century before James Watt.[4] Unfortunately, she never patented it, and died penniless but with a closet full of perfectly pressed clothes.

Lilly Putian is buried in the Welsh section of Westminster Abbey, right next to a plot that is reserved for Engelbert Humperdinck. She lies beneath the epitaph which she composed herself at the age of ten,[5] "Would that there were as few spots on my soul as on my garments." There were, however, no spots on her writing.[6]

---

[3]This also holds true for most of "Gilligan's Island," but not the episode in which Ginger sings "Happy Birthday" to the professor.

[4]Scottish engineer and inventor (1736–1819) who invented the steam engine, thus paving the way for the steam iron, steam kettle, and steamroller. Not to be confused with James Watt, Secretary of the Interior under the Reagan Administration, who was ultimately forced to resign, not because he sold hundreds of thousands of acres of Federal land to coal mining interests, but because he told a bad joke about a woman, two Jews, a black, and a cripple.

[5]She burned this epitaph with the rest of her work at age twelve, but she never forgot it, and wrote it up again just before she croaked.

[6]Although she did dot her "i's" with circles.

The Life and Strange, Surprising
Misadventures of Robin Caruso

(SUMMARY)

The narrator, Robin Caruso, was born in Grimsby, England, in the year 1652. Fourth child of a Polish immigrant, Robin Caruso (the name Krczkwsky was mispronounced by Englishmen) was not the prime interest of the family, and being the second girl child, her formative years were spent in her sister's hand-me-downs. Her father, who was a wise and sensible man, saw that she had sufficient learning, as far as house-education generally went, the ultimate end of which was to make her a good wife. "Conceal whatever learning you attain," he advised her, "with as much solicitude as if you were a crook or a gimp, for the parade of it can only draw upon yourself envy, hatred and, perhaps, an occasional pervert."[1]

But Robin is not satisfied to settle for a husband, and takes to disappearing from home when suitors come to call. During these absences she disguises herself as a young man and wanders about the docks of Grimsby, hoping to find a dock sale.[2] On one of these adventures, she is terrified by a drunken sailor who nearly beats her up because of the way she is dressed. The sailor contends that her choice of a pink vest on white makes her look like a magpie. Caruso fears for her life, viewing this incident as God's judgment on her for disobeying her father. She is determined to repent and return home when her beating is over, but suddenly the sailor relents, insisting that they become drinking companions, and she joins him in the consumption of sailor's punch—soon forgetting her fears, her promise to herself, and for a short while, her name. On returning home, she learns of an arranged marriage her father is planning, from which she is determined to escape.

Caruso's father summons her to his chamber to counsel against what he foresees as her design. Angry that women were forbidden actions that

---

[1]The original definition of the word "pervert" was a man who was attracted to educated women.

[2]Dock sales were the equivalent of today's garage sales.

men were free to commit and resolute in her commitment never to marry, Caruso plots and carries off her escape.

(EXCERPT)

MY FATHER'S good counsel lost upon me, I hurried on with my plan and blindly obeyed the dictates of my fancy; gleeful in acting the rebel to my father's authority, not to mention that of England and God, so anxious was I to avoid having to marry the buck-toothed, mealymouthed cabinetmaker whom my father wished me to wed. I bade my parents sweet dreams, and went to my room as if well-satisfied with my lot, but when the house grew quiet, I donned one of the outfits I had worn to the docks: a well-fitting pair of turquoise knee-breeches over white stockings, a pale green blouse with lace and ruffles, a long, brown vest, black floppy boots, and a three-cornered hat edged with braid. I drew my hair back into a queue tied with a black riband; I longed to use a bright colour, but black was the current rage for ribands among the men. Being that I was not a shapely girl, I looked quite convincingly to be a young sailor boy; I wrapped some extra clothes into a bundle and stole unnoticed into the night; consulting neither father nor mother, nor saying goodbye, not even leaving a note, much less getting a goodbye kiss. With little thought to what ill might befall me, or where I would have my clothes cleaned or pressed; and God knows, at a ridiculous hour to boot; on the first day of October, in the year of our Lord, sixteen hundred and seventy-nine, I stole into the night.

The evil influence that led me to leave my father's house, that hurried me into the wild and indigested notion of independence and adventure, and that shouted those conceits upon me so loud as to deafen my ear to all good advice, I say, the same influence, whatever the dickens it was, now lured me on board a vessel bound for the islands of the Caribbean, heeding not the fears of my first voyage, nor the warning of the raggedy, peg-legged man who stood near the gangplank, repeating, "Beware a wounded dove in the sails!" I continued to act the fool.

Our vessel was what the men vulgarly called a "beast of burden,"[3] and carried six rather frightening guns and thirteen men, as well as the captain, his boy, and myself. I was pleased when, after only one day at

[3]Sailors' slang for a heavily laden ship; originally from the Bible, where it means "donkey." Centuries later, however, when Mick Jagger sang, "I'll never be your beast of burden," he didn't mean he didn't want to be a ship or donkey, he meant he wouldn't carry the groceries in from the car, or marry Jerry Hall.

sea, the mate told me he would show me how to steer the ship, and, admittedly, I was not strong enough to do so without the aid of the mate, who stood behind me and helped me hold the ship on course. Anxious to do well, I was delighted at the end of the day when he complimented me on my ability, and suggested that we go to his cabin where he wanted to show me how to use his sextant. Never any young adventurer's misfortunes began sooner, for the instant the mate closed the door to his cabin, I suddenly felt aware of the motion of the boat, and of the closeness of the room; I was inexpressively sick in body in a most frightful way, for it seemed as though my stomach fell to my feet and the room spun uncontrollably—all this while the mate was trying to show me his sextant. In a word, I vomited. What followed immediately I cannot recall for certain, except to say, no sicker dog has ever been. I began to reflect on the advice of my parents: my father's wisdom and my mother's nagging came now fresh into my mind, and my conscience, which had not been talking to me much of late, reproached me with the breach of my duty to God and my father, and the ill breeding I had just displayed by throwing up in front of the first mate. In the agony of my mind I made many resolutions, praying to God that if he would spare my life and let me put foot on solid ground again, that I would, absolutely, no way I'd forget, go sciddily-scat right home, no detours, to my father.[4]

(SUMMARY)

Once Caruso's seasickness abates, she joins her shipmates in the drinking of "the Devil Rum." The next day she is plagued by a terrible hangover, which once again sends her to the depths of despair. She spends the day hanging onto the side of the ship, crying, "Lord be merciful! I swear I shall never again touch another drop, so long as I live!"

On the third day out to sea, a tornado strikes. It buffets the ship for ten days, driving it out of the usual sea lanes. Caruso, violently ill, attempts to jump overboard to end her misery. One of the crew, sensing her hopelessness, ties her to a mast "for yer own good." Finally one morning, the lookout cries "Land Ho!" But, alas, he is too late, for the ship makes a jarring thud as it runs aground on a sandbar. Fearing the boat will split

---

[4]Although Caruso puts forward propositions of this kind repeatedly during the course of her adventures, it doesn't seem to have occurred to her that God himself is notoriously reluctant to accept this type of deal. In fact, even people who keep up their end of the bargain find that God frequently welshes on His.

under the heavy winds, the crew decides to abandon ship. In the panic that ensues, poor Caruso is left behind.

NOTHING can describe the sinking feeling (no pun intended) that I felt as I watched the men row off in the dinghy; although I shouted and screamed and pounded my feet upon the deck, they could not hear above the roar of the storm. My strength too depleted to loose myself from the mast, I could not deliver myself from the swell so as to draw breath, till that wave having swept over me, and having spent itself, went back and gave me a moment to breathe. "This outfit will never be the same," I thought, as again and again the ocean came upon me, buried me in its soul; the onslaught continued till I felt my clothing would be worn to shreds, when, to my relief, the fury of the sea lessened. With some time, I caught my breath and noticed that the salt water had removed that pesky wine stain from my doublet, and with that, found new courage.

Casting my eyes about, I realized gradually that my position was by no means hopeless, inasmuch as the ship had already weathered the worst of the storm, and seemed to be rather solidly settled on the sand. As the rain pounded on my head, it began to knock some sense into me. I prayed to God for deliverance, and swore that once rescued, I would return directly home to my father and mother. I committed myself to God's mercy, and that of the sea, for though the storm was beginning to let up, it churned something dreadful, and might well be called *den wild nd crazee zee,* as the Dutch call the sea in such a storm. Accepting my situation as being in the hands of God, I resolved I was best off lashed to the mast, where, at least, I would not be washed overboard; and being excessively weary, fell fast asleep, and slept soundly as, I believe, few in my position might have done, and found myself the more refreshed when I awoke, although a bit on the stiff side.

When I waked it was daylight, the weather clear, and the sea calm, so that the horror of the night seemed far behind. Undoing myself from my binding took much labour and aggravation, for I found myself to be completely famished, and, as my stomach grumbled, so did I. When I finally stood on deck, and got the blood circulating in my legs once again, I began to kneel in prayer, but found my breeches much too stiff and, therefore, stood in prayer and thanked God that my life was spared; and urged Him to keep up the good work. Then I noted an incredible thing; the sandbar was such that at this low tide, I could walk to shore! I cannot tell you the joy I felt when I thought of my two feet planted squarely on solid ground; then, just as suddenly, I was paralyzed at the thought of having to face this strange island on my own—me, Robin Caruso from Grimsby, England, deserted! For the first time since the storm, I wondered at the fate of the men who fled the ship; there was no sign of a vessel and no evidence of anyone along the shore. I was frightened by the prospect that I might have to face savage animals or beastly men, or that I might find no food or water, much less any clothing store of any kind. But after all, I had my health, and so long as that was true, Providence would grant me a way to survive until help and new outfits arrived.

My mind now cleared of negative thoughts, I addressed myself to the problem at hand. I had to be honest with myself (after all, if you are not, who will be?); I had to consider the possibility that I could be on this island a long time, maybe even a couple of weeks. Therefore, it was of the utmost importance that I take to shore with me anything that would be of benefit to my stay. But I decided it best to first turn my attention to food; for I knew well that a good breakfast is wind in your sail,[5] not to mention that I thought I would just die if I didn't get something to eat.

After a fine meal, my next order of business was to get me something else to wear, for admittedly, no one would rescue me if they saw me looking so worn. I had always admired the captain's wardrobe, so I decided to look through his cabin first.

In the first trunk I looked into, I found some lovely linens, as well as the proper tools to make up a sewing box. At the very bottom of the heap, I found the captain's fine silver; certainly not Queen Anne's, but not a bad pattern. In his clothing trunk, I found the captain had a rich array of short-waisted doublets and several pair of breeches, and one especially nice pair of blue velvet, with ribands up to the pocket holes. I found him not to be lacking in shirts, waistcoats, nightshirts, or stockings. I spent a pleasant hour trying on his various uniforms, although, to my dismay, none were suited to me; the captain's shoulders being twice my width, the breeches so wide that I was able to put both of my legs into one compartment.

Most surprising to me was that the captain had an assortment of

---

[5]First half of the sailor's maxim which ends: "And a bad breakfast is bilge in the fo'c'sle." No doubt Lilly Putian omitted the second half of this saying because she didn't know how to spell fo'c'sle.

women's clothing, suitable for a very large woman, indeed, just about the same size as the captain. This I deemed a great find, for with a little of my time spent tailoring, I could have myself a going-home dress.

I thought I had rummaged the cabin so effectually as that nothing more could be found, but yet I discovered a locker with drawers, in one of which I found several garters, a woman's bodice, and a rubber petticoat; in another, a beautiful diamond-studded tiara.

I smiled to myself at the sight of these jewels. "Oh, drone!" said I aloud. "What are thou good for, anyway? Thou art not worth the taking, no, I say thou are but a stingless honeybee, performing no work, and producing no honey. One of those forks is worth all your sparkle; ever remain where thou art, and find yourself on the head of Neptune, as you are an object whose weight is not worth carrying." However, upon second thoughts, I said to myself, "Self, don't be a putz," and wrapping the crown in a piece of linen, I began to think through what else I needs might do.

I determined that I would need the rest of the afternoon to organize, then wait till low tide the next afternoon to attempt to move my cargo; timing was of the essence for this plan, as I could not swim, and was, therefore, frightened to enter the water unless it was very low. Upon this thought, I remembered my father's words: "Don't you realize, my child, how foolish you are to think of such adventures which would take you about, sailing the high seas, when you cannot even swim!" But, alas! For me not to listen that never listened before is no great wonder. I resolved that I would give my ears a good de-waxing[6] for Providence, once I was off this forsaken wreck.

Caruso works until dark, collecting things she will need: casks of food, several vests after the Persian mode, some bedding, spools of rope and twine, and all the pieces of sail she can detach from the masts. She also collects the cook's pots and pans, which were rather the worse for wear, and a few cups and plates. Also on board with Caruso, she finds, is a large black cat, which she names Cat, and some frightened farm animals in the forward hull. After a generous meal of biscuits and dried goat's flesh, Caruso falls into an uneasy sleep, waking at daybreak.

[6]Not to be confused with leg waxing, a painful process involving pouring hot wax on your legs, allowing it to cool, and then ripping it off, thus pulling out the tiny hairs by their roots and making your legs soft, smooth, and attractive to men.

Captain was transvestite?

"...I spent much labor and aggravation, fashioning a raft of sorts by tying about, and began assembling my caravan. I put the hens and roosters into sacks quickly learned that an animal of the feathered persuasion does not like to be put

DIRECTLY after feasting, I dressed for my exodus, tying my shirt tails up about my waist; I added a three-cornered hat, just to give that sense of jauntiness I needed. I made a last search of the ship, looking for items of use which I might have overlooked; I found some paper and pens, and grabbed a small chair which went with the captain's desk and two pillows, as I have a very hard time sleeping unless I have two pillows.

Having collected my cargo on the deck, I spent much labour and aggravation, fashioning a raft of sorts by tying the hogsheads together on top of which the other items rested. I then gathered the animals about, and began assembling my caravan. I put the hens and roosters into sacks and tied these over the back of the cow; this was, pardon my French, a bitch of a task, as I quickly learned that an animal of the feathered persuasion does not like to be put in a sack. Speaking of animals that don't like to be put into a sack, Cat was at her most unpleasant, and I still have a couple of scars as proof of just how unpleasant she could be. Anyway, I tied the sow atop the raft, as I had a

sheads together on top of which the other items rested. I then gathered the animals
these over the back of the cow; this was, pardon my French, a bitch of a task, as I
k . . ."

horrible image of its tiny little legs being too short to keep its head
above the water at this depth (all night I had dreamed of a pork sausage
sinking like lead into a pot of boiling water). I tied the raft behind the
horse, leaving plenty of slack, then tied the other animals, two goats
and four sheep, in a line behind the raft.

Just as I felt the tide was near its lowest, I lowered the gangplank
into the water and led the horse, whom I named Ed, into the water.
Once Ed had a good footing on the ocean's bottom, I tightened the slack
in the rope leading to the raft, and slowly we pulled until the vessel was
down the plank and afloat. As we moved toward shore, the rope pulled
the other animals into the ocean. This might have been a humorous
sight for one who has no feelings for animals, as the surprised beasts
were quite comical in their reactions to their fate, but I, who was so far
from civilization, and didn't really feel like laughing, felt a kind of
camaraderie with my four-legged friends.

I need not recount the horror I had to overcome when I was forced to
enter the water; feeling the power of the waves rush past my legs made

me dizzy, not to mention the water was awfully cold and sometimes came as high as my belly button; once I walked into some seaweed and nearly died from fright,[7] but I kept moving my caravan toward shore, until, at last, all were safe on dry land.

After thanking God for her deliverance, Caruso gleefully sets all the animals free. With night coming, she fears the approach of unknown beasts or savages and therefore spends her first night sleeping on the back of the horse. The next day, a slightly bowlegged Caruso decides she must put on something more appropriate and make a quick survey of the area. Caruso wears leather buckskins, for their sturdiness in these wild surroundings, a simple blouse, and her boots. She ascends a steep hill and discovers that she is on an uninhabited but fertile island, with no other land in sight. Caruso determines she should remain near the beach, where she can watch for a rescue ship. To deliver her mind from despondent thoughts, Caruso sets about altering a dress for her return trip to England.

Two weeks after Caruso first set foot upon the island, a storm blows up. The next day, the ship is no more to be seen.

concern
w. →
clothing
-was
Putnam
really
transvestite?

IN THE morning when I looked out, behold, the ship was gone with the wind. I was somewhat distressed at its disappearance, as a vessel sailing a ways off might notice the wrecked ship, whereas they were not like to spy me, but I regained myself with this thought, viz., that I had everything out of her that could be of use to me, especially all the best articles of clothing; that if I was to be deserted on this lonely island, at least I would be the best-dressed person on a deserted island.

Caruso's thoughts now turn to providing herself with a more comfortable dwelling. She follows the stream uphill to its reservoir, which is located on a hillside with a grove of trees, so abundant and green that she describes it as "more beautiful than the garden at Versailles," although she admits she has never seen the garden at Versailles. The grove provides an abundance of orange, lemon, lime, and citron trees, as well as cocoa, coconut, coco-crispy, and cocoa-puff[8] trees. Along the side of the grove is a field where Caruso decides to set up her new home.

---

[7]If you think she was scared then, imagine how frightened she would have been if she'd seen "Jaws."

[8]She was cuckoo for Cocoa Puffs.

A T THE top of the hill, on the flat of the green, between an orange and a coconut tree, I decided to hang my tent. The tall grass spread out beneath the trees like a field of grain, and the quiet reservoir was a pleasant change from the roar of the ocean. I contemplated with great pleasure the pleasantness of the situation here, the security from storms, the water and wood, the fruitfulness; I concluded that when you consider that thousands of babies starve to death every day in a place like India,[9] I was really pretty lucky. I tended to believe my island was, in many ways, a paradise; yet, I dare say it was a paradox of a paradise, for if it was a beautiful and peaceful spot, so was it the most boring place I've ever been.

Caruso constructs a sledge from boards which wash ashore and, with the help of Ed, spends the better part of a week moving her many possessions. Then Caruso determines to create a dwelling as comfortable as possible within her situation. She stretches a hammock between two trees, beneath which she sets up a shelter on the ground, so clever and inventive that, "should a stranger happen upon my little home, he might well think its inhabitants Swiss." There follows a lengthy description of the construction of her home (including a large closet with lots of shelf space), to which she adds a characteristic finishing touch. "I put a piece of sail on the ground to make a floor, then I made a rule that no one could wear shoes in this area. I had once heard that the Japanese people did that, and I always thought it would be fun."

I T COST me much labour, and several splinters, before all these things could be completed. Cat was interested in all the activity, and had become my main source of amusement, as well as my best friend who slept with me.[10]

I found food was plentiful on the estate; I worried that I might be putting extra pounds on, as I seemed to eat so much, and this led me to devise a way in which I could watch my weight. I took a piece of mast and found the center, using a piece of cord to measure. I tied a rope to

---

[9]Despite the fact that through the ages, including the present day, children have starved to death in many countries besides India, India still gets all the publicity.

[10]As Caruso was quick to discover, when bereft and alone on a desert island, the cuddlesome nature of cats can be of great comfort. No doubt this is why so many single people in modern society sleep with their cats. They also attend plays and buy books with "cats" in their titles, as well as purchasing T-shirts, bookbags, mugs, stationery, and barbecue aprons with cats on them.

". . . I worried that I might be putting extra pounds on, as I seemed to eat so much, and this led me to devise a way in which I could watch my weight. . . . I wished for a companion to help me utilize this crude invention, for it was a cumbersome task to get in and out of the cask as I removed coconuts, one at a time. My first weighing was 93 coconuts, and I am proud to say, I never went over 99."

the center, then threw the rope over the branch of a sturdy tree, and tied it to Ed, the horse, who pulled until the mast was up on top of the branch. Next, I attached two casks of equal weight, one at each end of the mast. Into one cask, I piled a hundred coconuts; then put myself into the other. I wished for a companion to help me remove the coconuts from the other cask, until my weight and that of the coconuts balanced out and the mast rested horizontally to the ground; for it was a cumbersome task to get in and out of the cask as I removed coconuts, one at a time. My first weighing was ninety-three coconuts, and I am proud to say, I never went over ninety-nine.

Having now fixed my habitation, I found it absolutely necessary to find some kind of oil for my skin, for the many months of exposure to salt air and sun had truly dried it something terrible. But I must first give some account of my thoughts on life at this time, for, as you may well guess, I spent a lot of time thinking now.

I had spent a good deal of my time depressed and contemplative, wondering were it not the determination of Heaven that I should end my life in this desolate manner, and I would cry myself sick at the prospect of this destiny. I would expostulate with myself, why in Heaven's name Providence would go to the trouble to create mankind, and then do nothing but make his creatures miserable, depressed, and abandoned; it could hardly be rational to be thankful for such a life. Now I truly understood what my father meant when he used to say, "You think life is a big picnic. Wait until you're on your own and have to buy your own candles and lard."

But something always returned swift upon me to boost my spirits, and one day in particular, when I was smashing a piece of coconut between two rocks to see if I could get any oil from it, I was very melancholy about my situation, when Reason, as it were, expostulated with me t'other way. "Okay, so this is the pits, so you are stranded on a deserted island, so you will not likely see another person for the rest of your life; you are liable to be torn limb from limb by wild beasts; if you fall sick there is no one to make tea and cinnamon toast; but pray remember, you could have been in a bad marriage, and who is to say which is worse."

I now began to put the state of my affairs in writing, not so much with the intention of leaving them for anyone who would come after me, for I was a one-woman show on this island and not like to have any heirs, but I wrote to clear my mind of these hounding thoughts. I stated it as clearly as I could, setting the good against the evil; and I stated it very impartially, as I imagined a gentleman in the House of Lords might, making a list weighing the comforts I enjoyed against the miseries I suffered, thus:

EVIL

GOOD

I am horribly lost, void of any hope of rescue, singled out and made example of, as it were, to wallow in misery for the rest of my life.

But I am singled out, too, from all the starving babies in India.

Mel Gibson
~~CLINT EASTWOOD~~

There is no soul here with whom to talk.

But I cannot say anything which would embarrass me.

I can buy no new clothes.
NO ONE TO DELIVER PIZZA

But I will save a lot of money I would have spent on clothes. I WON'T GET FAT FROM NOT EATING PIZZA.

And so it was that I, the most miserable wench in the whole, wide, entire world, consoled myself and turned myself around; which goes to show (wouldn't you know) that in every grey cloud is a fluffy white one. It was from this day forward I stopped staring out to sea, that is to say, I gave up the idea that I might spy a ship for my rescue, and I began to care more about the quality of my time spent on the island.

Now I began to apply myself to the business of keeping a journal, and meticulously recorded how I spent each day's employment, for when I first arrived, I was in too much of a dither, what with all I had to do to set up housekeeping, not to mention that my self-possession was at a minimum; and, I am sure, a journal written at that time would have been a real downer. But, having gotten over these things, and having about me beauty and comfort, I began to keep my journal, of which I shall here enclose as much as there is; for, having writ the last of it with an ink I made from berries, the goats ate those pages one day.

THE JOURNAL:

This chapter marks the beginning of a major division in Putian's novel, for now she relates the story in diary form. Much of what we have just read is retold to us, probably to emphasize the intense boredom of Caruso's life. However, the last few entries in the journal are not told to

the reader earlier in the book, the following excerpt being immensely
important to the story.

JUNE 18—Rainy season being upon me, I spent much of my time in the tent, trying to weave a pair of shoes from tall grass. Found some mushrooms growing plentiful under a nearby tree, and heated some up in butter churned last week. Very tasty.

June 19—Woke up very ill, and hallucinating. Everything appeared distorted and wavy. Colours seemed intense. You could say I was giddy.

June 20—No rest all night. Had a terrific urge to listen to music, so I rummaged through my sea chest and pulled out the lute I had salvaged from the ship. Considering I have not played for several years, I sounded surprisingly good.

June 21—Better; having no victuals in my tent to eat, picked some more mushrooms for my breakfast and heated them up with some turtle's eggs.

June 22—The ague again so violent that I stayed in bed most of the day. Prayed to God for the first time since my arrival, but scarce have the slightest idea what I said, or why, or how, for that matter, my thoughts being so confused. I believe I did nothing for several hours, till, the fit wearing off, I fell exhausted to sleep. When I awaked, I found myself refreshed, but still in a somewhat confused state. I thought that I was sitting in my bed, but realized I was stretched out on the taller grass. How I got there I never knew, but I returned to my bed and went to sleep again. In this second sleep I had this dream.

I thought that I was standing on the beach, on the spot where I had first come upon the island, and that I saw a great black cloud move swiftly toward me. Just as the cloud was above me, a figure in a white, flowing robe descended from it, so brilliant that I could just bear to look towards it. Its countenance was most unexpressibly odd; at first I imagined it to be a man with a Chinese hat, but then I recognized the figure to be a giant mushroom.

It was no sooner come upon the earth, but it moved directly toward me, to kill me I imagined; and when it came directly in front of me, I heard a voice so strange, that it is impossible for words to describe. All that it said was this: "Mellow out."

No one who shall ever read this account will ever understand the love I suddenly possessed for this giant mushroom; I mean, that even while I

*poetic
license
or
Caruso
actually
"high"
???
• • •*

knew this to be a dream, I actually felt love; nor is it possible to explain the impression left upon my mind when I awaked.

I had, alas! no mushroom knowledge; but I knew now of the divine power within them, and from this day forth, honored and worshipped the mushroom, making it a part of my daily diet.

June 23—Caruso finds a Bible among her goods and opens it to the words, "Let him who is on the housetop not come down," paying particular attention to the phrase "top-knot come down" and interpreting this as a message to wear her hair long and flowing.

At this point in her journal, Caruso begins using the berry ink, the pages of which are subsequently destroyed by the goats. She returns to her narrative.

THE following days I began to make good order of my time. I read from the Bible three times each day; spent three hours collecting, preserving, or processing my food; and the rest of the day I spent working on various projects. I employed myself to the task of sewing beads in gay patterns upon my breeches, and experimented with ways to apply the colours of nature to my face to express my newfound intoxication with life. I determined it would be pleasant to attach the feathers of birds to my hair and decided to explore the interior of the forest for unusual plumage. I gathered some nourishment to take along for my adventure, mounted Ed, and proceeded to follow a path made by the wild goats. This led to a brook, which, in turn, led us to a juncture at which I found several very beautiful, colourful feathers, which had an unusual pattern, not unlike a large eye. I dismounted to collect my treasures, when I spied several animals in a nearby field. Their physical attributes were very singular, and they were unusually shaped and apparently deformed. Having never beheld such a disgusting animal, I hid myself behind a bush within a stone's throw to observe them better.

The heads and bodies of these strange creatures were covered with a coarse, dark hair, except for their faces, feet, and bottoms, which had a thick skin of brownish buff. The features of the face were extremely grotesque, with beady little eyes set deep in the protruding brow, and an unusually wide, flat pair of nostrils, which flared in a threatening manner with each breath. The pudenda of these surprisingly agile creatures were distastefully large and had an annoying way of swinging when they walked. Upon the whole, I daresay I have never in all my

*exagg.
portrayal
of humans
2*

travels beheld such a disagreeable animal, or one against which I naturally conceived so strong a feeling of aversion and opposition.

Having seen enough and feeling full of disdain and repugnance, I
returned to the spot where I had left Ed, but found him to have wandered off. I assumed he had headed back to the estate and turned to do
the same, but was surprised to find one of the ugly creatures full in my
way. I carefully attempted to sidestep him, but the beast imitated every
move I made and would not allow me to pass. Mimicking my frustra-
tion, he distorted his face into hideous contortions, then stared at me as
if at an object he had never seen before. Suddenly he raised a forepaw,
whether out of mischief or anger, I could not tell. But I drew forth one of
my feathers and tickled his underarm, for I didst not know what else to
do. When the beast felt the feather, he withdrew a foot and let out a roar
so loud that the herd from the field came flocking about me, screeching
and making abhorrent faces and rude gestures; but I leaned my back
against a tree and swung my feather as if it was a weapon and thereby
kept them off. A few of the cursed brood climbed the tree and placed
themselves above me so that they were able to release their excrement
upon my head; this attack I was mostly able to dodge, but the stench
was so horrendous that I thought I might be suffocated by it.

In the midst of this harassment, as sudden as the onslaught had
begun, the beasts all ran away as if in fright. Looking about I saw that
Ed had returned. Then what occurred was a most remarkable thing; Ed
walked directly up to me, looked me squarely in the eyes and said, "You
look like shit," then burst into a most annoying laugh.[11]

For a moment I was most sure I must be mad, or in shock, to have
imagined such a thing, but as Ed gained control of himself, he said, "I'm
sorry, I know it's not funny . . ." then again lost himself in his whinnying laugh.

*After a quick bath in the brook, Caruso and Ed return to the estate.
They talk well into the night, Ed explaining that he comes from a land
called Nneeeee, from which he had been captured by some Portuguese
sailors. Caruso wonders why Ed had not spoken to her earlier, and he*

---

[11]"A horse is a horse, of course, of course, and nobody talks to a horse, of course, unless that horse
is, of course, the wonderful Mr. Ed." This, of course, was the theme song of the popular television
show, "Mr. Ed," which featured a talking horse. The creators of this show obviously read *Robin
Caruso* in college and borrowed the idea years later, thus proving that a liberal arts education can
occasionally be good for something.

explains that until he had seen Caruso up close to the diddywahs,[12] he had thought her to be one of them and that, in his country, diddywahs are not worth talking to as they possess no quality of reason nor a sense of humor. In fact, since his capture, Ed had not found any rational conduct or sense of fun from any of the others of Caruso's type.

Caruso is appalled by this mistake and explains that her species are known as humans and describes to Ed her native land of England. She expresses her uneasiness at being called a diddywah and begs that he not apply that name to her. Ed graciously complies.

ED WAS curious to know more about human behaviour. He was especially interested in my clothing, and why humans went to such an extent to cover their bodies. I explained that clothing helped to protect our skin from the excessive heat of the sun in the warm weather, and kept us warm in the cold weather. He found this particularly difficult to understand,[13] as it was not rational that our bodies could not bear these natural hardships; and it seemed tedious to put a covering on and take it off each day. I explained that I enjoyed selecting various colours and styles of habit, that this form of dressing up was a way to express one's emotions. Ed said that in Nneeeee, people expressed their emotions by rubbing necks, laughing, or having sex, although laughing while having sex was not usually successful. He did not comprehend anger or hate, and when I tried to explain these feelings, he thought I was telling him a joke, and although he did not understand it, he would laugh, because Nneeeeeans are also terribly polite.

In the course of their conversations, Caruso learns of the ideal state in which the Nneeeeeans live. They are a peaceful and fun-loving society, with no concept of money, because they have no use for it; things are so arranged that every Nneeeeean has his share of the necessities of life. Therefore, when Caruso explains that in England, poor men labour most of the day to provide luxuries for those few who have enough money to

[12]The beasts from the forest. Today certain savvy Midwesterners have adopted this term to refer to anyone who's from a town smaller than the town they're from, i.e., hicks, hayseeds, rubes, shitkickers, crackers, yokels, and clodhoppers.

[13]However, Ed did understand the concept of being a good sport; in fact, every year on Robin's birthday, Ed donned a festive party hat.

[handwritten margin: Putian's ideal soc. possible or ? imp. similar to hippie phil.]

[handwritten: — READ "Electric Kool-Aid Acid Test" for extra credit]

possess these items,[14] Ed rolls in the grass with laughter at what he considers to be one of Caruso's best jokes.

These eye-opening conversations which Caruso has with Ed force her to view her former life and England through the superior moral vision of the Nneeeeeans. Meanwhile, Caruso is finding more parallels between humans and diddywahs, and one afternoon her curiosity takes her back to the forest to observe the creatures, from a safe distance.

I WAS struck dumb with amazement and horror when I viewed these creatures again, for I observed in these repulsive animals a perfect human figure; the face of it, indeed, was broad, the nose flat, the lips a bit thick, the mouth wide. But these variances are common to many primitive nations, and, in fact, are characteristics of many a good horn player. The forefeet of the diddywah varied little from mine, except that I had coloured my nails with a dye I made from berries. There was the same likeness in our feet, except that I had the need to wear shoes; the same with every part of our body, except that a female's dugs hung almost to the ground, as did the male's dong.

It is a great shock to Caruso to conclude that a human bears a closer physical resemblance to the diddywahs than to her beloved Nneeeeean. Caruso then makes every attempt to disassociate her physical resemblance from the beasts. She shaves off most of her hair, leaving a row of hair long from the middle of her forehead to the nape of her neck.[15] She spends several hours a week finding quartz rocks and grinding them into fine particles consistent to a powder, which she wears on her forehead in the shape of a blaze. Ed finds these changes most becoming, and the two of them live a life of peace and contentment.

MY ISLAND now so arranged to my liking, I often fancied myself to lead a life better than a queen. We wanted not for any of the necessities of life, and enjoyed some luxuries as well. Ed

[14]Today things have really changed! Now illegal aliens toil in sweatshops only fourteen hours a day in order to produce Calvin Klein underwear at $6.99 a pair for anorexic models, who probably get it free anyway, to wear while eating angel hair pasta with caviar that they're planning to throw up later.

[15]Centuries later Jason of Antenna claims credit for this coif, popular among contemporary urban youth and bejeweled musclebound black TV stars given to repetitive verbalizing. In fact, just last week, one of the editors paid through the nose for one of these peculiar do's and hasn't ventured from the house since. We pity the fool who dates that editor.

Did she & Ed "do it"? Ed idealized vers. Harold Helppenaysworth

"Caruso spies a ship . . ."

and I had planted a beautiful and productive garden, and at the end of
the day, we would take a leisurely stroll among the flowers, then watch
the sun set over the ocean. By conversing with Ed and learning the
superior ways of the Nneeeeeans, I found that I looked upon him with
great contentment, and I fell to imitating his gait and gestures; tossing

my head and stamping my feet, even reproducing the vibrato of his voice.

In the midst of all this happiness, when I looked upon myself to be in the most ideal state of life, a most disastrous thing occurred. One morning, as we worked in our garden, I stopped for a moment of rest, and gazing out to sea, my eye plainly discovered a ship sitting at anchor, not a league's distance from our shore. By my observation, I could see it flew the flag of England.

I was struck with the utmost confusion and despair. What business did an English ship have in this part of the world? This was not their trade route, and I knew there had been no storms to set them off course; most likely it would be a ship full of thieves and murderers, perhaps rapists and horse beaters! I had not been long on this train of thought when I saw the ship set to water its shore boat, with eleven or so men in her, and head toward shore, to the same spot where I had found myself deserted, just seven years last fall. So full of fear and overcome by a sense of futility was I, and being unable to support these agonies, I gave one last cry to Ed and fell into a swoon.

When Caruso comes to, she is on the ship. Her fellow Englishmen view her strange appearance with uncertainty. Upon realizing what has happened, she runs to the side of the ship to jump overboard, but one of the crewmen restrains her. And so it is that on January 7, 1686, Caruso sails away from her island, ironically, under the preventive measures of a sailor, just as fate had forced her staying on the ship that led her there in the first place. Ed stands on shore until the ship is out of sight, and the sound of his whinnying laugh floats across the waters, as Ed thinks Caruso's departure to be an uproarious prank.

ex: irony

When the crewmen speak to Caruso, she is horror-stricken by the unfamiliar sound of human speech. In addition, when she attempts to plead with them to return her to the island, the strange, neighing tone of her voice convinces them she is mad. In keeping with the captain's orders, they treat her with decency and kindness.

After an uneventful voyage, the ship arrives in London, and arrangements are made for Caruso to return to her family. Although her mother and father are dead, her brother agrees to let her live with him. He greets her with joy and is filled with compassion for his sister, who is obviously mad and suffering greatly. However, to the now-demented Caruso, her brother is only a diddywah.[16]

ex: grim vision

[16]Do wah diddy, diddy dum, diddy dee.

For Further Study

1. Why did Robin Caruso change her name? Would you read a book called *The Life and Strange, Surprising Misadventures of Robin Krczkwsky?* Why not? Don't you like Polish people? What about Lech Walesa? Do you think the Solidarity Movement would be more effective if it were led by Lech Wales?

2. Until the seventeenth century, literature consisted of poems, odes, ballads, sonnets, verse plays, and dirty limericks, but no novels. Discuss the importance of *Robin Caruso* in the development of the novel genre. Doesn't it blow your mind that it took the human race thousands of years to figure out that they could tell a story without making it rhyme? Were they retarded or what? The case is open and shut.

3. One of the recurring themes of *Robin Caruso* is her obsession with dressing up. Does this parallel Lilly Putian's own attitude toward clothing, or was her intent satirical? Perhaps she is just another fashion victim? Dress up and discuss.

4. Write a brief character description of Robin Caruso. Note that she frequently makes promises to herself she doesn't keep. Is this one of the ten warning signs of alcoholism, or is it just a woman's prerogative to change her mind? Forget it, we don't want to know the answer anyway.

5. Much has been made of Lilly Putian's use of detail to add verisimilitude to an otherwise bald and uninteresting narrative. Explain how this technique is employed humorously, for instance in the section where she describes bringing the animals to shore. Round up all the animals at your immediate disposal and try and re-create Caruso's exodus from the ship. If sacks are not available, use triple-ply lawn and leaf bags. Be sure to poke holes in the bags so the animals can breathe.

6. Do you feel that Lilly Putian was successful in describing Robin Caruso's emotional state on being marooned? How would you feel if you were stuck alone on a desert island with no moisturizer, not even the cheap non-hypoallergenic kind?

7. Do you think our dependence on modern technology would make it harder for someone from this

century to survive alone on a desert island? Make up your own list of the comforts and miseries that you might experience in these circumstances. Would the absence of drugs, sex, and rock 'n' roll be on your list? What about cars, electricity, Valium, and Stouffer's Lean Cuisine? If you had a headache, which one of the above would you take for it?

8. Stylistically, *Robin Caruso* is divided into two parts, the second part starting with the visit from the giant mushroom. Describe the metamorphosis of Caruso's character and estimate how many 'shrooms she was gobbling up per day. Do you believe that a horse was really talking to her, or was she just wiped out of her gourd? Have you ever had any experience like this? Describe it satirically.

9. What do the diddywahs represent? Fess up, didn't you think at first that they might be Negroes? Even for just a second? Admit it. What did this tell you about yourself and your perception of black people? Aren't you ashamed? If you are a Negro, you need not answer this, and we want you to know that we have nothing but respect for you and your people. Really. In fact, we'd like to go on record that we always believed that Martin Luther King's birthday should be a national holiday, so get lost, Jesse Helms, you diddywah!

10. Try writing the story of a journey to an imaginary country in which you satirize practices of modern life. For example, you might satirize New York, Los Angeles, or stand-up comedians who insist on telling you the difference between them.

This portrait of George Brontë was engraved by his devoted sister, Leek, on the occasion of the Gothic novelist's twenty-eighth birthday. Although physically a male, George's attitudes, traits, and clothing were those of a woman (or, in George's own language, a "wo'-per-own"). During the nineteenth century, this was considered unacceptable; yet today, with or without a shave, George could have a flourishing career in many areas of the creative arts, from omelet chef to Broadway playwright to proprietor of an imaginatively named flower shop such as Stamens and Pistils. But fortunately for the Gothic novel fan, George Brontë sequestered himself in an attic, where only his mirror could tell him he needed a shave, and he still didn't listen.

George Brontë
1801–1834

THE Brontës were one of the most extraordinary literary families *Before the Pill* ←
who ever lived. The fifteen children—Charlotte, Emily, Edwina,
Ernestine, Frances, Victoria, Samantha, Leek, Leslie, the twins
Chastity and Felicity, the triplets Slut, Whore, and Filth, and George—
lived during the early 1800s in an isolated Yorkshire Village on the
moors.[1] As the Brontës were the only family in the tri-county area, the
children were unable to associate with their peers and thus led a
rarefied existence in which they were each other's only friends and
playmates and, as they entered puberty, of course, editorial con-
sultants.

For those were the years when each Brontë child put pen to paper and
told the stories that were burning within them. With the exception of
George, the writing Brontë siblings[2] produced several shelves' worth of
manuscripts detailing the bleak life they all endured at the oppressive
family manse known as "Cardigan Sweater." Their father, Hoofmouth,
an austere man with an eye for a sixpence, saw to it that the works of
his offspring were published by his lifelong friend, Parson Elihu Tithe,
of the Anglican Church Never Has Enough Money Publishing House.
So popular were the Brontë books that they were soon translated into
every language whose native country featured bad weather, and even
today have been included along with Chuck Berry records on the most

---

[1]This section of the moors was once thought to be sparsely populated because it was haunted by
werewolves. But recently, a crack team of Japanese exorcists discovered that the area inhabited by
the Brontës was plagued not by werewolves, but by the ghosts of Alistair Cooke's ancestors, thus
leading to the undesirability of the region.

[2]Not to be confused with the Flying Yglesias Family or the Amazing Wallace-Wallechinsky
Family, who, respectively, have glutted the publishing world with different versions of the same
novel, or tedious books of interminable lists that are only of interest to people with severe bowel
disorders.

recent Viking mission into outer space, as a result of the idea put forth by the librarian at NASA headquarters, who said, "There might be women on other planets, and if there are, they're probably pretty depressed."[3]

Today, the editors excitedly present the autobiographical and byzantine work of the fifteenth writing Brontë, George. Unlike other women writers named "George," George is actually a man. So why are we publishing the work of a man in a book devoted to women? you probably find yourself asking. The answer is simple. George Brontë, for all intents and purposes, lived the life of a woman. Although there is no physical proof of this,[4] we have learned from obscure diary entries of the Brontë girls that George bore the physiognomy of a man, or at least their idea of what a man looked like; for it can be safely said that these girls never actually laid eyes on a man, except for their father or the occasional time-traveler who stopped by, searching for the holy grail.[5]

However, physical evidence to the contrary, George believed himself to be a woman. Fortunately for the literary historian, many facts about George were recorded in the diaries of his sisters, particularly in the chronicles of Leek, an unfortunately named girl who, according to the diaries of the Brontë triplets, Slut, Whore, and Filth,[6] bore an uncanny resemblance to the popular soup green. "Daddy never wanted a boy," Leek wrote in one of her journals. "Even though he said that girls were the yams of evil, boys were far worse because they were the Devil's gardening tools. Until the birth of George, the good Lord had listened to Daddy's credo. But then Cardigan Sweater was struck by chaos. George entered this world."

It is not clear whether in fact Agnes and Hoofmouth Brontë realized that Agnes had actually given birth to a boy. George's mother died

---

[3]Possibly because the dry cleaning process of Hollanderizing requires more oxygen than most atmospheres contain. Or maybe they're depressed because John Chancellor has the flu. Who knows with women?

[4]We don't really know that Jesus Christ, for example, was a man either. Oh sure, there's that shroud and everything, which supposedly bears the imprint of a man's face, but why don't they have the thing dry cleaned and see what happens? Shouldn't the face of a man, and not just any man, for Chrissake, stand up to carbon tetrachloride? So what are they waiting for—Christmas?

[5]See Monty Python's "The Holy Grail" and/or "Time Bandits." See them with a friend.

[6]A trio also unfortunately named. This was because in the eyes of their father, a superstitious man, the birth of female triplets could only be viewed as an evil omen, suggesting, as it does, an unholy trinity of giggling, fun, and disrespect.

during the long and arduous delivery, and his father was outside in a downpour engaged in one of his favorite pastimes, being pelted by hail-stones.[7] But the wet nurse, Bonnie McAllister Moran,[8] knew that her master would not be pleased by the arrival of a tiny boy.

There was only one thing to do. As soon as George was weaned, his sisters took him to secret quarters in the attic, where they raised him as a girl. This was partly due to the fact that they had no boy's clothing in the house, and they were afraid to ask Hoofmouth to buy any, but it was also because they felt that someday, just once in their lives, they'd like to see a really good drag show. And so George became a girl.

At first George eagerly joined with his sisters in the creation of their own fantasy world. They staged tea parties for their pet kitties, made friendships with pieces of furniture, and wrote playlets in which they took turns playing each other.[9] Needless to say, this confused George. He had been confused before, but this really confused him. Like his confused sisters, he also wrote. And like them, he employed a female voice in his work.

[handwritten margin note: voice = persona in which work is written]

By the time George was seventeen years old, he had become so much of a woman that he perceived injustice everywhere. He couldn't under-stand how his sisters tolerated their plight in the world.[10] Leek ex-plained to George that it wasn't that bad after all; their father didn't beat them—he only forced them to perform tasks such as narrowing the

---

[7]For some strange reason, it was always raining when Mrs. Brontë gave birth. In fact, it was always raining during any momentous occasion. In general, it was always raining. It is said that the Brontë family didn't know what it was like to not have a cold and didn't believe that heavy sneezing and coughing weren't a part of everyone's waking hours.

[8]She hailed from a long line of wet nurses. As the need for wet nurses declined, Bonnie's family miraculously availed themselves of the process of natural selection and evolved into a family of tugboats.

[9]This presaged modern encounter-group therapy methods in which practitioners assume their partner's persona and then proceed to cause each other to experience a nervous breakdown. It is said that the Brontë children themselves cracked up, but no one knows whether it was a result of the constant exchanging of roles or the fact that they were forced to sleep standing up, alone, in their own individual armoires.

[10]Not unlike the modern cinematic character "Tootsie," a man who put on a skirt and proceeded to tell women how oppressed they were, or even Alan Alda, a man who tells women how oppressed they are, without even bothering to dress up like one.

[11]Hoofmouth Brontë, in fact, was once investigated for operating a Gothic novel sweatshop, but the charges were dropped when George, the only witness for the prosecution, showed up to testify in a beard and dress.

[12]Not to be confused with Curious George.

shoulders of his hair shirt, flossing his teeth, and signing over all of their book royalties.[11] Furious, George[12] began to detail his thoughts on life at Cardigan Sweater in what he hoped would someday become the most celebrated work of the Brontë children, *Warrensville Heights*.

Alas, the entire 678-page manuscript was written in a bizarre language that George, in his rage at the inequality women suffer, invented in order to eliminate discrimination from English. He called it Feminish, and the rules were as follows, as George himself explained in a pamphlet circulated surreptitiously at Cardigan Sweater.[13]

"We begin at the most obvious point. The very word that man long ago decided to call his counterpart was woman. Why *woman?* Because it was merely an extension of the word *man!* We have no moniker that is truly our own! Therefore we must take the next logical step on the road to real self-definition, delete the second syllable *man* and insert temporarily the less unfair label *person,* so that *woman* becomes woperson (pronounced wo'-person). The word *person,* however, has for its second syllable the exclusively male noun *son,* and is therefore unsuitable, so *son* must be replaced by the truly nondiscriminatory noun *one,* so that person becomes *perone* (pronounced per-own'). Thus *woman* becomes *woperone* (pronounced wo'-per-own). This new label will be hard to get used to, but after several months' usage, I am quite comfortable with it. When alone, I practice: 'I am a *woperone,* she is a *woperone,* and we 'women' are all *wo'-people.'*"

To read *Warrensville Heights* in Feminish was a difficult task indeed, and only George's sister Leek rose to the occasion.[14] Parson Tithe refused to publish it on the grounds that it was "pure gibberish." Meanwhile, as his sisters became more famous (even Filth penned an impressive little potboiler called *The House*),[15] George sank into a deep depression and died one night in the attic. His terse burial instructions ("Headstone inscription: 'A woperone's work is never done.' Outfit: crushed velvet gown, pumps with silver buckles") were ignored, although they were the talk of the countryside for days. But, thanks to the editors, George Brontë will be ignored no more.

[13]Decades later, "The Feminish Dictionary: A Guide to Defining Ourselves" surfaced at a meeting of feminist dictionary monitors. After many seminars and votes, these gal word patrollers adopted Feminish as their official language, even though "When push came to shove, George had a penis."

[14]Sort of. "Jeez!" she wrote in one of her private journals. "I didn't know I had a *hymen.* If I do have a hymen, am I a traitor to my sex if I don't call it a 'hything'? George doesn't have one, anyway. I don't think he's rowing with both oars in the water."

[15]Later burned down by the Talking Heads.

Cast of Characters

(IN ORDER OF APPEARANCE)

GRAVESEND - Dark, cold manor containing many depressing people and secrets.

GRIMHEATH - Dark, cold manor containing more depressing people and secrets.

MRS. HEADSTONE - Retained by the wealthy to interpret the secrets of their inbred families.

HEATHER MOORDEAD - Chatelaine of Gravesend.

EMMA FORCEMEAT - Housekeeper at Gravesend; thought to be related to everyone, but no one knew exactly how.

UNCLE STILLWATER - The man of Heather Moordead's stepmother's dreams.

GATELOCK - Former caretaker of Gravesend; love of Heather Moordead's life; also, her son.

EDWARD EDWARD - Obscure resident of Corpse Hall.

AUGUSTINE GRILLÉE-SLOWBORN - Obscure daughter of Jonas Slowborn and Langoustine Grillée.

JONAS SLOWBORN - Father of Augustine Slowborn.

LANGOUSTINE GRILLÉE - Creole mother of Augustine Slowborn, imaginatively named after a Caribbean crayfish.

CRAGDEATH - An old estate whose riddle was confused with the riddle of Gravesend, until Mrs. Headstone set the record straight.

LOCKGATE - Second son of Heather Moordead; convincing argument for enforced sterilization of the upper classes.

LOSTSOUL - Grim-faced master of Grimheath; Heather Moordead's brother and husband.

BLOCKHEAD - Houseman at Grimheath.

ELIZA FANNELLI - Popular tavern singer of the period noted for big emotions.

DR. BOBB-WHITE - The local physician and child molester.

RICHARD OF HEARTGROG - Ancestor of Heather Moordead.

PROFESSOR REHNQUIST- DEPRESSING INSTRUCTOR + CHILD MOLESTER

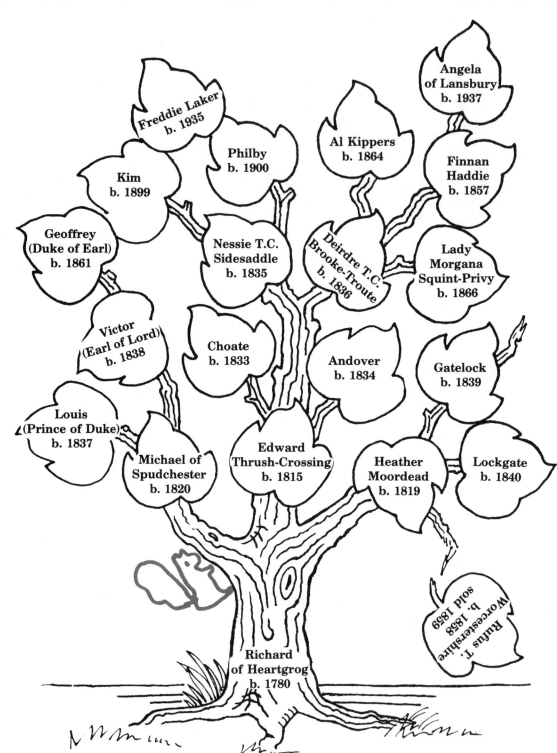

Richard of Heartgrog family tree.

Warrensville Heights

A BRIEF SUMMARY

Warrensville Heights *is perhaps the best example of the Gothic novel. In other words, everyone is related to him- or herself, and houses explain things that the author couldn't. Set during the claustrophobic 1800s, the story closely parallels the author's. The main character, Heather Moordead, tells the story. It unfolds at Gravesend, a lifeless mansion on the moors with a lot of skeletons in the closet, relatives in the hallways, and spiders in the basement. It is here that Miss Moordead falls in love with the mysterious caretaker, Gatelock. One night during a heated argument, Gatelock storms out of the house. Weeks go by; then years. Lostsoul, the widower across the way at Grimheath, proposes. But Heather Moordead sequesters herself in the attic, awaiting the return of her beloved Gatelock, while subsisting on a diet consisting primarily of boiled moss.*

In the attic, our heroine begins to learn the secrets of Gravesend. One afternoon, the house reveals what seems to be its most bizarre riddle—but actually, it's a red herring. Years later, Gravesend deems it fitting to explain things to Heather Moordead. The man for whom she yearns is actually her son. The news changes nothing, and she resolves to wait for Gatelock. In the interim, she agrees to marry Lostsoul and move to Grimheath, but only if he promises to let her sleep in the attic by herself. Lostsoul readily assents, as he finds the idea of a man and woman sharing the same storey of a house repellent.

One day, Gatelock returns in a strange incarnation, then disappears again. Heather dies shortly afterwards in a dramatic, weather-related accident, joining Lostsoul, who died several months earlier while choking on a blanched pig snout during dinner. But our heroine does not rest; her ghost haunts Gravesend, where it is often seen in the attic, scaring people and uttering cryptic messages.

Editor's note: To make this important work more accessible to the reader, only a small selection is reprinted in the original Feminish. The most important passages of *Warrensville Heights* are excerpted on these pages, translated back into English.

PERONE, OH, PERONE, OH,
PERONEISCHEWITZ!

Chapter 3

WHY was I cursed with the body of a woperone? Why was half of the huperone race peroneacled by the physiognomy of a feperone? Was it the same for the other half of huperoneity—did men, too, feel as if physical characteristics coperoneded their every move?

Alas, I did not have the answers to these questions, as I stood before the mirror in my lace peronetilla. I only knew that in my heart of hearts, as I noted the daily transactions of life here in this cold and dark peronesion, the inequality between men and wopeople haunted me like the ceaseless drops of rain atop the peronesard roof, did not let me slip comfortably back into the peronesuetude which was my peroneifest destiny, made me wonder what it would be like to be a woperone and live on the Isle of Perone!

Craving sexual eperonecipation, I deeply lapeopleted this sad state of affairs. And it was sad! It was indeed an unfortunate state of affairs that huperoneity really wasn't huperone at all, that after marriage, for example, when a man penetrated the hything of a woperone, she was respected as a wife, but should her hything be lost before legal union, a result, perhaps, of sitting astride any item that vibrates, or wopeople-struation, or both, she was forever ridiculed as a woperone of the street . . .

Chapter 22

THERE was no possibility of leaving the attic that day. I had been wandering, indeed, in the dark hallways since breakfast time; now, dinnertime had brought with it clouds so dark that I refrained from descending the dark stairway into the chill of the dark drawing room here at Gravesend where Mrs. Headstone was entertaining a depressed band of guests from Grimheath,[1] the dark manor across the way with which we shared the same relatives and cliff.

Let them make merry, I thought! Let them have a gay time! For soon, should providence hear my loudest and innermost cries, I shall be dead, dead as this cold, dead field on which sits this dead, cold house of death, dead as—

"Miss Moordead! Miss Moordead!" It was Emma Forcemeat, for the third time that day, at my chamber door. "Are you dead?"

"No."

"You will be soon, if you do not eat something."

"Yes."

"I have brought you something very special."

"What?"

"Boiled moss, boiled parsnips, and boiled entrails."

"Leave me the moss, and go away."

"As you wish."

The moss, I realized, would provide me with enough sustenance to exist for perhaps another three months. By then, perhaps they would all be dead, and I would become the chatelaine of Warrensville Heights.[2] Or perhaps I would marry Uncle Stillwater, the man of my stepmother's dreams, thus simultaneously becoming my own niece and aunt. Or—dare I say it?—perhaps Gatelock would return, bring with him the energy, the fuel, the hot meat injection for which my heart never stopped pounding.

Chapter 35

ONE afternoon during my attic solitude, I was disturbed by the cry of a newborn infant. The sound had come from below, and in an effort to ascertain the gender of this toddler, as well as the identity of its progenitors, I pried up a floorboard and peered through. But there was no one there! I quickly replaced the floorboard, and as I did so, I spotted a yellowed scroll that an erstwhile inhabitant of this household had evidently deposited there. So much time had I spent buried within the walls of Gravesend that it was now telling me its deepest, darkest secrets! I excitedly unfurled the parchment.

It bore the unmistakable seal of Deare Abbey.[3] Beads of sweat formed

---

[1]Not to be confused with Coldgrange, the manor that was two cliffs away.

[2]Thus prefiguring the establishment of the suburb of Cleveland, Ohio, which bears the same name. However, there are no chateaux in today's Warrensville Heights, only subdivisions. But a girl can dream.

[3]A church named after the expensive, Presbyterian advice columnist whose personally calligraphed advice flyers enjoyed a brief fad among the wealthy. Today, the tradition lives on in the person of Abigail "Dear Abby" Van Buren, popular newspaper counselor. The old abbey, however, has since been replaced by a new wave shoe emporium.

above my upper lip, my hands quivered, and my loins grew moist with excitement as I anticipated the document's heretofore hidden message. It stated the following: "This affirms that on Arbor Day, the 20th of October AD, 1702, Edward Edward, of Corpse Hall in the county of Edward, and of Rottingham Manor in Edwardshire, England, was married to Augustine Grillée-Slowborn, daughter of Jonas Slowborn, oarsman, and of Langoustine Grillée, a Creole, at Church of the Wayward Pirates, Spanish Town, Jamaica."

Who were these people? The knowledge escaped me. And Mrs. Headstone, whose innate ability it was, according to my mother on her deathbed, to interpret the secrets of inbred families, was of little use either. "Too bad," she intoned when I summoned her to my attic chambers and she had read the affirmation. "This explains the riddle of the old Cragdeath Estate, not Gravesend. You might as well stay up here forever."

There was only one thing for me to do. I must wait in the attic for another sign.

Chapter 47

GRAVESEND must have been impatient, for the message came twenty years later. It came during a stormy night. I was dreaming. As the word "gklotcea" swam before my eyes, I again heard the cry of an infant. Days later, I realized that "gklotcea" was a subconscious spelling of "Gatelock."[4] Why was Gravesend trying to tell me about Gatelock, the erstwhile caretaker of this dark, cold house, the man whose unexplained departure drove me to the attic, where we had spent so many afternoons locked in wild embrace, talking about our hearts, and my clothes?

"He's your son," a voice whispered, and it compelled me to believe it. "Your son."

Although I had no recollection of this pregnancy, or subsequent birth, or any other pregnancy, or subsequent births, but as I did remember a nine-month period during which I gained a great deal of weight, I decided that it was right to wait for Gatelock to return, for sons always

---

[4]It also spells "Lockgate," Gatelock's retarded half-brother, whose birth Miss Moordead could not recall either, although when pressed, she did remember a four-and-a-half-month period during which she gained a great deal of weight.

do, and in the meantime, I would take the widower Lostsoul[5] up on his longstanding offer to reside with him at Grimheath as his betrothed.

Chapter 66

A STRANGE event occurred one day in my career at Grimheath. Lostsoul and I had been entertaining for weeks, as a torrential downpour had flooded the one road leading to and from our house, thus making it impossible for our guests, the Headstones, the only other people besides lower forms of help now living on the moors of Warrensville Heights, to leave. We were finishing off a bottle of port, toasting our houseman, Blockhead, due to the fact that we had run out of toasts, when the front door flew open and in walked what appeared to be a rain-soaked woman who seemed to closely resemble Eliza Fannelli, a popular tavern singer of the time.[6] Blockhead took her coat, threw it out the door, and invited Miss Fannelli to join us for dinner.

As everyone drank up and expressed themselves convivially, I could not remove my eyes from the eyes of our guest, who, in turn, could not remove her eyes from mine. This was no woman, I then realized; this was Gatelock, my son and my beloved! What happened here at Warrensville Heights that drove this once-virile young man to don the clothing of a woman?

I started to ask, but then I bit my tongue, as I had done so many other times when I had to restrain myself from speaking, realizing that if my husband had had the slightest inkling that this guest was Gatelock, he would surely have locked him in the cellar until it stopped raining, then taken him into town and sold him to a pin cushion factory. As it was, "Eliza" was the highlight of the evening, regaling us with good humor and song.[7]

[5]Unbeknownst to the narrator, Lostsoul was her own brother, if the family tree as set forth in this book is carefully studied.   Had she known, she probably would have moved to Grimheath much earlier, in an effort to make life on the moors more varied than it already was, thereby missing the opportunity to become hopelessly involved with her son, whom she rarely saw but dreamed of for thirty years.

[6]Thus living up to a Fannelli family tradition but, hopefully, with a happier ending. Eliza's mother, also a singer, died at an early age of an overdose of ale. In tribute, Eliza performed for pub denizens, singing the songs her mother made famous, and wearing too much lipstick.

[7]Another edition of *Warrensville Heights,* found during a dig at Stonehenge, where George liked to play, stated that at least one song crooned by Eliza that evening was "Ding dong, the witch is dead." This edition also had it that with the collapse of Grimheath and entombment of Miss Moordead, servants rejoiced by singing this song.

Chapter 110

change of voice but not tone

HEATHER Moordead died at age fifty-six.[8] Some say it was of a broken heart, but Dr. Bobb-White, the family doctor and child molester, diagnosed it as a severe case of moss poisoning, which was known, every now and then, to make people look very sad. Of course, there was also the fact that at the moment Miss Moordead expired, she had been struck by a lightning bolt which she had willed to find her by spending her last remaining days outside in the rain, dressed in a suit of armor that once adorned the figure of her great-great-grandfather, Richard of Heartgrog.

And so it came to be that Heather Moordead was buried next to Lostsoul, in the family duck blind, that being the only ground at Warrensville Heights not already in use as a cemetery. Every now and then, the ghost of Miss Moordead can be seen wandering the moor, to and fro, pacing, unable to sleep, as always, unable to rest. And the same can be said for Warrensville Heights, for our rest, too, is disturbed, interrupted by the mournful plaint which the ghost of Miss Moordead seems doomed to utter: "There once was a man named Gatelock."[9] Perhaps one day, Gatelock will return to those bedevilled heights and restore symmetry to a world of chaos by marrying me and impregnating me with child, thus continuing this tired legacy.[10]

---

[8] As George Brontë could not figure out how to end this book when the narrator died, the remainder of the story is told by Emma Forcemeat, the housekeeper and everybody's favorite relative. (In fact, she was everybody's relative.) Some critics speculate that this is the way George really wanted it anyway, as he really didn't like Heather Moordead, as she reminded him too much of his tutor, Jayne Gruel, preferring the thinner Miss Forcemeat, whom he supposedly modeled on the family henkeeper, Gwen Mashbanger.

[9] Fortunately for anyone listening, this pathetic specter was never able to complete the limerick.

[10] And sparking the need, years later, for Geritol and mood elevators.

1. If you were a boy and had fourteen sisters, how would it affect your writing style? Your clothes? Your lifestyle? What if, on top of that, your name happened to be George? Using these ideas, compare and contrast young George Brontë with Boy George.

2. What is Feminish? (For further reference, see *Titters,* Macmillan, 1976.) What on earth possessed George Brontë to write in Feminish? If you had to spend your whole life in an attic, what other things could you do besides inventing a language: a) translate Feminish into Chinese; b) annoy everyone downstairs by learning how to tap dance and practicing all the time; or c) devise a time-consuming game based on everything you've ever heard and call it Trivial Pursuit.

3. Make a time chart tracing the influence of George Brontë from the 1800s to the present, culminating with the queens of the modern-day romance novel, Judith Krantz, Barbara Cartland, and Quentin Crisp.

4. Who is Lostsoul? How was he related to Heather Moordead? Who is Heather Moordead? How is she related to Gatelock? How is she related to herself?

5. What do you think Heather Moordead smelled like after all those years in the attic? Can you blame Gatelock for waiting so long to return and, when he did, wearing a disguise?

For Further Study

6. In Gothic novels, houses often reveal secrets of their past inhabitants to those who currently live there. If your house talked to you, how would you react? a) pack up and move; b) talk back; or c) call William Peter Blatty.

Ex: anthropomorphism ←

7. What do we learn about the nineteenth century diet from Heather Moordead's eating habits? Do you think that the people who lived downstairs existed on a diet consisting primarily of moss, or is that a decision generally made by a deranged individual who lives in a small, dark, and clammy little cubbyhole?

8. Is it your personal diagnosis that Heather Moordead died of a broken heart or moss poisoning? How much moss can the human body ingest before the organs cringe in disgust and write thirty to the whole thing?

9. If you were a female impersonator in the nineteenth century, which woman would you impersonate? a) Marie Antoinette; b) St. Joan of Arc; or c) Wallis Simpson. If you chose c), you should transfer out of this class immediately.

10. In George Brontë's selection of names for his characters, was he trying to tell us that everybody in Warrensville Heights is either dead or dying, or did he just get the names from a phone book? WHERE DOES THAT LEAVE PEOPLE WHO ARE UNLISTED?

This early photograph, taken just after Emily Davenport won the Barnstable Academy mother-daughter bake-off, catches the poet in a rare festive mood. "I'm sure this is as happy as I'll ever get," Emily observed. Prophetically enough, it was.

Emily Davenport
1833–1865

EMILY Davenport is unique among American literary figures of the nineteenth century in that nobody really knew she existed until the twentieth century. True, a smattering of her poems had been published in the newspapers of her day, but only the fish that were wrapped in them came in contact with her name long enough to remember it,[1] and dead fish tell no tales. Or as Mick Jagger[2] once put it, "Who wants yesterday's papers? Who needs yesterday's girl?"

Merely appearing in print seldom if ever makes an author's reputation. It usually takes a juicy court case. Emily was no exception. Following her precipitous[3] death, her father, Edgar Davenport, no doubt feeling guilty about sex after all the deaths in the family arising, whether directly or indirectly, from his interest in it, declared her work obscene and suppressed it.[4]

It was not until 1942, when Edgar's grandniece, Augusta Couch-Tufted, irked by a pain in her back that felt "exactly like a shoe box, or maybe a shoe-tree box, pressing into it right about here, no, lower," decided to purchase a Sealy Posturepedic, that the lost hoard of poems and poem fragments was discovered. Augusta was on the verge of using

---

[1]We bet you can't remember the name of the author of one of those poems they use to fill up the space at the end of the columns in *Rolling Stone,* and if you can you're either cheating or the author in question, in which case write to us, we'd like to meet you. We've always wanted to know if anyone actually wrote those things or whether they just let the computer typesetting machine make them up as it went along.

[2]Mick Jagger is the lead singer of the Rolling Stones. What an amazing coincidence! (See previous footnote)

[3]No, she didn't die by falling off a precipice. If you must know, she stifled herself with a small feather bed, giving rise to the expression, "Oh, go stifle yourself," later popularized by Carroll O'Connor as Archie Bunker in the hit television show, "All in the Family."

[4]Oddly enough, her poems were suppressed, or actually pressed, in two shoe boxes and one shoe-tree box, under the very same feather bed beneath which Emily had breathed her last. Will coincidences never cease?

them to clean the oil lamps which she used to save on electricity when her sensitive Portuguese cleaning lady, Agua Caliente, read them and wept.

Augusta, who could be as tough as nails when she had a mind to, at first dismissed Mrs. Caliente's all-too-genuine emotion as "a transparent ploy to get out of hard work." Then she had the poems assessed and discovered that not only were they authentic, they had considerable literary worth.

Augusta was of two minds as to what to do with them; on the one hand, she could publish them now and have enough money for electricity and a new, less-weepy cleaning lady, maybe even one of those new-fangled vacuum cleaners. On the other, she could hold on to them until the Women's Movement came along, by which time their value would have appreciated considerably.

Lust for modern appliances won out over traditional New England thrift, and Augusta had the poems published by Little, Brown and Company. They were greeted by resounding critical acclaim and a whopper of a lawsuit, involving the Couch-Tufteds, the descendants of Mademoiselle Chaise-Longue, who made it into an international *cause célèbre* by claiming that Emily had been secretly married to their grandmother, and just about everyone in New England with an item of furniture for a surname. The pie was divided three ways, with the Couch-Tufteds and the Chaise-Longues each getting a piece and the lion's share going to the Tufts library, due to legal error. It was a blueberry pie, as far as anyone could tell after seventy-seven years in a shoebox.

The entire literary estate, on the other hand, was awarded to Dr. Fenwick "T.T." Trestle Table, a millionaire peridontist descended from dentist Ezekiel Trestle Table, on the basis of the poem "Remorse," in which Emily expresses her regret at having been so unbending in refusing Ezekiel's proposal and wishes that she could give him "all her worldly goods" instead of just her plaque.

In the end, it was the reading public[5] who became the richer, thanks to the attention the courtroom custody squabbles had drawn to Emily's work. In fact, the reading public were 1,643 poems to the good, since amazingly enough, that was the total of Emily's output during her short lifetime.

When the first collection of her work appeared, people flocked to

[5]And the lawyers.

campus bookstores to purchase it, though subsequently many were dis-appointed, since they had been hoping for something more juicy and less depressing.

Dr. Ernest Smith-Corona, the noted Davenport scholar and cousin of Dr. Fenwick "T.T." Trestle Table,[6] compiled a <u>concordance of Emily's work</u> in which he discovered that the depressed bard <u>used the word "white" over 2,000 times.</u> After years of study, he formulated the the-ory, expressed in his book *Yankee Specter* (Tenure Press, 1953), that in Emily Davenport's unique cosmology, the word "white" could be equated with "<u>death.</u>"[7]

Comp. w. Melville's ← "Dick"

Yet perhaps Dr. Smith-Corona sums up Emily's work best when he says, "Far from being a dreary old raisin, Emily Davenport was as full of the juices of creativity as one of her mincemeat pies."[8]

[6]In reality, Dr. Smith-Corona despised the work of Emily, whom he called "that dreary old raisin." His cousin bribed him to publicize it in exchange for free periodontal work, which Dr. Smith-Corona couldn't afford on a professor's salary, and two weeks at his summer house in Chilmark.

[7]Hardly surprising, since white was her favorite color and death was her favorite subject.

[8]Dr. Ernest Smith-Corona, *New England Wraith,* Tenure Press, 1956.

EMILY DAVENPORT—A CHRONOLOGY

1818   Marriage of Edgar Davenport of Barnstable, Massachusetts, to Lavinia Settee of Stablebarn, Massachusetts

1829   William Davenport born, April 16.

1829   William Davenport dies, April 24.

1831   Roger Davenport born, February 9.

1831   Roger Davenport dies, February 11.

1832   Thomas Davenport born, December 30.

1832   Thomas Davenport dies, December 31.

1833   Emily Davenport born, November 10.

1833   Emily Davenport almost dies, November 10.

1834   Emily considered old enough to visit brothers' graves.

1835   Emily says first word, "tombstone."

1837   The Davenports visit the Couches at their family home in Boston, where Emily's precocity and morbidity are remarked upon by Mr. and Mrs. Couch.

1840   Emily starts school September 6, comes home in tears, having pulled her own hair "because nobody else would do it."

1843   Emily goes to Boston to visit the dentist, August 8.

1845   Sometime during this year, Lavinia Davenport takes Emily to tea at the home of her great-aunt, Emma Hutchbench, who comments, "My, what a sallow little thing the child is, and sickly, too. It's a shame you lost all the boys."

1850   Emily graduates from the Barnstable Academy and spends the summer taking private French lessons from a Mademoiselle Antoinette Chaise-Longue.

1850   Mademoiselle Chaise-Longue leaves Barnstable for good, September 11. Emily is inconsolable, writes first poem, "I speak the language of the heart."

1850–
1854   Emily attends the Mount Mary Seminary for Peakish Young Females in Barnsiding, Massachusetts.

1856   Publication of her first poem, under the title "A Valentine," simultaneously in *Boston Herald* and the "Personals" section of the *International Herald Tribune*.

1858   Emily goes to Boston to visit the dentist, May 18, and, while under the ether, hallucinates that he is Mlle. Chaise-Longue.

1858   June 1, the dentist, Dr. Trestle Table, comes to visit Emily in

1956   Mel Gibson born.
1986   Mel Gibson marries Caryn Blackstein
1987   MEL GIBSON ARRESTED FOR BIGAMY.
BAILED OUT BY DENISE GAGLIANO.

Barnstable, proposes. Emily turns him down, writes poem, "How inconsequential is mankind," published as "Thoughts Upon a Table" in the *Boston Courier,* October 14.

1860   Emily goes to Boston to visit the eye doctor, refuses anesthetic.

1861   The Civil War begins, April.

1862   Emily's pie wins second prize at the annual Cattle Show.

1863   Emily's mother dies in childbirth, June 18; Emily's pie wins first prize at the Cattle Show.

1864   Emily's poem, "Had she but lived to taste it," published under the title "Memento Mori" in the *Smithfield Plain Dealer,* September 9; Emily fails to enter Cattle Show due to nerves.

1865   Emily enters pie in Cattle Show, doesn't win. Commits suicide, November 3.

Photo courtesy of Augusta Couch-Tufted.

TERM PAPER
DUE NEXT WK.!!!
Buy paper
brads
NO DOZE
KITTY LITTER

This photograph of Emily's mother Lavinia Davenport (née Settee) was taken on a visit to Boston in 1860 shortly before her death in childbirth in 1863. By our calculations, Lavinia would have had to have been about 62 when her fifth and final child was stillborn. No wonder she died.

Selected Poems

XXXIII

I never saw a Moor—
Nor yet—the bold Chinee—
New England holds not with such folks—
If human folks they be[1]—

But I know how Aunt Jemima[2] looks—
And whence—proceeds our tea[3]—
My narrow cupboard's—world enough—
For simple souls—like me.

[1]Emily Davenport reflected the prejudice typical of her age, which was thirty-two at the time.

[2]Typical! Why can't we all just get along?

[3]Not marijuana.

LXIV

I dress in white[1]—and mope about—
Among—the lipless dead[2]
I dare not fuss—or scream—or shout—
Lest it appear ill-bred—
I keep—my feelings—locked—up tight—
And scribble little rhymes—
For—Sappho's passion—scarce seems right—
In such—Presbyterian times
Yet—oh—my soul's—a-bubble—
Like porridge—on the hob
And—love my heart—would trouble—
Were I—not such a snob—

CLXXV

*note use of
dashes - char.
Davenport
style*

A butterfly—is very fine—
And one could well—do worse—
Than scatter—bluebells every line—
When one—is making verse
To pearly stiles—and unseen moors[3]
My readers aren't adverse—
I craft my—patchwork—metaphors—
But mostly—keep it terse.

---

[1] Reference 1,342.

[2] According to Dr. Smith-Corona in his concordance, *Davenport Unraveled* (Tenure Press, 1946) the phrase "lipless dead" occurs twenty-three times throughout the Davenport oeuvre and refers specifically to skeletons, i.e., dead people whose lips have decomposed. However, Dr. Marcello Olivetti, Italy's foremost Davenport scholar, maintained that it meant "just any dead people." This controversy reached a boiling point during a conference at the University of Verona, which resulted in Dr. Olivetti throwing a cannoli at Dr. Smith-Corona and knocking off his toupee, to the general amusement of all.

[3] A moor is a broad tract of open land, with patches of heath and peat bogs; not to be confused with the other kind of Moor, which Emily had never seen either.

CCCXXII

A clever fellow—is—the worm
Of—infinite resource—
Heeds he—not pomp of government—
Nor—traffic in the Bourse[1]—
Instead—he studies—carpentry—
As—our dear Lord once did—
The—angle—of the coffin's lie—
The thickness—of its lid—
The—architecture—of—the soul
Goes—all—ignored by him—
His chief ambition—and his goal—
Is—measuring limb by limb—
Needs—must he take our measure—then—
As—we lie 'neath[2] the sod—
And make us food—if not for thought—
For—one small son of God—

[1]French for stockmarket. Not to be confused with Boursin cheese, a favorite of French stock-brokers and people who give book parties.

[2]Poetical abbreviation for beneath. Not a typographical error for heath, which, as you know, if you've been paying attention, is found in patches on a moor (not the black guy).

MDCXLIII

While we were fearing it[1]—it came—
And—robbed us of our peace
So we—accepting—gave it—room
Upon the chimneypiece—

Wherefrom it quickly tumbled down—
To give—the world the lie—
In—broken crockery—lay the crown[2]—
Long eaten—was the pie

"I'll bake another," vanity said—
And thus—redress the fault[3]
To what—dire straits[4]—ambition led—
Pride—left out the salt

The struggle—to be human
Must—make the welkin weep
If—existence—is this daunting
Methinks I'd rather go to sleep[5]—

[1]"It" was evidently the first-prize trophy awarded Emily's pie at the Cattle Show in 1863; probably an ornamental china teapot.

[2]Not literally a crown; rather, a broken ornamental china teapot.

[3]Breaking the teapot.

[4]Inspiration for name of chart-topping British rock group, influenced by Bob Dylan. We like them because they're the Sultans of Swing.

[5]After writing this poem, Emily went to sleep for two weeks. When she woke up, she wrote three more poems before joining the lipless dead in the big sleep.

MVXCIVXIII

I died for beauty—but was scarce—
Adjusted—in the tomb—
When one who died for taste—was lain—
In—an adjoining room—

He—questioned—softly—why I failed—
And how—I lost the prize—
I said—though perfectly the crusts were glazed—
You could not eat my pies

In seasons past—I'd laurels won—
But—careless grown—forgot the salt—
Then—my companion—shame put on—
He too—in cookery—was at fault—

For his pies crumbled at a touch—
Though flavorful—and sweet
Alack! That two such epicures—
In common clay—should meet

For Further Study

1. Why was Emily Davenport's work suppressed, and by whom? Do you find her poems obscene? Do you think the remaining 1,637 poems are obscene and we're suppressing them? Do you often feel persecuted? Is it because no one wants to talk to you, phone you, or hang out with you? As long as you're spending so much time alone, why don't you do something constructive, like writing poetry?

2. Write a short essay on Emily's relationship with her father. Do you think your father is guilty about sex? Does this question make you nervous? If it does, talk to your father about it and see how nervous he gets. If your father is dead or out of town, talk to a male psychiatrist.

3. What does it take to establish a literary reputation? a) a court case; b) a sensitive cleaning lady; or c) a shoe box full of cocaine.

4. Select your favorite Emily Davenport poem and set it to music. If you can't, send $5 and we'll do it for you. If you believe that, please remit $10, and we will send you this amazing zirconium pendant with genuine silver-plated chain and snatch-proof safety clasp for a 14-day trial period, absolutely free. You pay nothing! That's right, you pay nothing!

5. Why do you think Emily Davenport was so preoccupied with the subject of death? Could it be connected to the fact that her three brothers died in infancy? For extra credit, if you have brothers, have you ever wished that they were dead? Be frank.

6. Was Emily a genius, or just a kook? Be candid.

7. What do you think really went on between Emily and Mlle. Chaise-Longue? Be kind.

8. Emily Davenport defined her world as "a narrow cupboard." What other dark, airtight containers did she use to symbolize her universe? How could the invention of Tupperware have altered her perspective?

9. Could it be said that Emily Davenport's work was "as American as apple pie"? Was it as good? Do you think Emily had to go to the dentist so often because she ate too many desserts?

10. If Emily Davenport's poetry is your cup of tea, you might like to read one of the following works and prepare a report analyzing the writer's treatment of Death: *Death of a Salesman, Death in Venice, Death on the Nile,* or the scripts of "Deathwish," "Harold and Maude," or "The Big Chill."

In this photograph of legendary frontier humorist Clementine Samuels, the author sits in front of the home she claimed to have been born in when her mother worked there as a vegetable slicer in the kitchen. Or maybe it was a house where her father had delivered some pants. The fact that she was the progeny of an itinerant rag-cutter and a human Veg-O-Matic may have accounted for both her wanderlust and the fact that she had a tendency to julienne everything in sight.

Clementine Samuels
1845–????

C LEMENTINE Samuels, the original frontier humorist, was
born on the Mississippi Delta in the 1840s. The daughter of a
Negro mother, who was a runaway slave, and a Jewish father,
who introduced, unsuccessfully, corned beef to the West, she was renamed Marcia Twain in order to mask what was then considered a
peculiar lineage.[1] But as Marcia entered her teenage years, she
changed her name back to Clementine Samuels. To the world, she
ascribed the name change to pride in her heritage, but it is now believed that the real reason was that being called Clementine Samuels
provided her with more opportunities to talk about her favorite subject:
herself.[2]

As a singular kind of half-breed, Clementine was twice blessed, having acquired two of the skills often associated with Negroes and Jews:
cooking and satire. Moreover she was able to employ these two skills
simultaneously, an unusual ability that was first recognized in high
school homemaking class. It was the day students were asked to prepare Creole rice with crayfish, a popular dish of the region. As Clementine served her carefully prepared meal to several classmates, she also
recited a wry benediction. This was partly to entertain her teacher, who
had not given her the grades she deserved,[3] but mostly because Clem-

[1] And also to avoid being referred to as a "Jewgro," an unfortunate although vaguely amusing
term coined by an intolerant Delta denizen named Sot Sumpinerother. He also boasted that he was
the source of many other pejorative references of the time, such as "mosquito-brain," "pig-face,"
and "horse-nuts," but he was probably just telling a "tall tale." (Evidently, frontier residents were
incapable of telling tales that were short.)

[2] People invariably commented on "Clementine" or "Samuels" or both, but they never said anything about Marcia. Years later, however, when Clementine learned that "twain" was steamboat
jargon for two fathoms of river depth, she considered changing her name to "Clementine Twain,"
but by then someone else was using the surname.

[3] Probably because she was half-Jewish or half-black or vice versa. Or both.

entine herself was so infatuated with her predilection for colorful jargon. "Crack the tails and pop the eyes," she said cryptically, pulling her turtleneck over her head and snapping her hands together like pincers. "Now get outta here, you knuckleheads," she continued. "There's a crayfish loose. Quick! Cover it with melted butter."[4] Her classmates laughed heartily at this charming bit of backwoods humor. They proceeded to consume the crayfish with gusto,[5] and it was then Clementine realized she could parlay cooking and satire into a career, although nobody had ever heard of anybody getting paid to cook and tell jokes.[6]

A kind-hearted riverboat captain gave Clementine her first break. Watching her entertain and serve dinner to a weary group of travelers in a Mississippi tavern,[7] he immediately offered her a job on board his steamboat, the Jubilee II (he lost the first one on a wager about river currents). "Good grub's hard to come by," he reportedly[8] said, "and jokes, too—well, that's the goldarndest thing I ever heard. But keep the jokes down to a minimum, cuz it's hard to chow down and laugh at the same time without choking yer guts out."[9]

Clementine quickly became known up and down the Mississippi for her finely honed combination of skills. She was soon asked to cater large riverboat parties and act as the toastmistress of ceremonies. As word of her keen social eye traveled across the land, she was recruited by the editor of the *Atlantic Monthly,* who said, reportedly,[10] "There'll never be another Ambrose Bierce, but why don't you give it a shot?"

---

[4]The test of a good joke is whether it weathers time. On the bell curve, and even other scales, although not the Stanford-Binet Aptitude Test, this particular routine gets an A. Today, the actor/comedian/writer/father/husband Bill Murray does the same joke with a new twist. He's a lobster!

[5]But not the rice; it was too sticky. Clementine got better at it later, but she was never as good as Uncle Ben, a relative of hers.

[6]There are several cases on record of people being paid *not* to cook and/or tell jokes, but that's another story.

[7]Later, it turned out that this was the ill-fated Donner Party. It was their last real meal, and an amusing one it was.

[8]The reporter in this case was Clementine Samuels, who described this interesting encounter in her pointed essay, "An Interesting Encounter."

[9]Also, as the Heimlich Maneuver had not yet been invented by Henry "Heimlich Maneuver" Heimlich, it was pretty dangerous.

[10]The reporter in this case was Clementine Samuels, who described this encounter in her razor-sharp essay, "I Hear from an Important Editor."

Unfortunately, the editor of the *Atlantic Monthly* was right. Clementine's acute reports were all rejected by the prestigious periodical. However, upon hearing of her plight, a publisher from Natchez printed several of her essays in his ambitious little *Big Muddy Gazette.* He would have published all of them, but one day after a particularly bad storm, Big Muddy itself rose up over the sandbags, flooded his tiny, self-built office, and carried him off without a trace. Naturally, this affected Clementine, and she expressed her emotion in an essay entitled, "To Hell with the Human Race." It doesn't sound that way, but actually she was sad.

Still, enough people now knew of Clementine that she was referred to as "the Delta Scream" and "the culinary cutup." Some river wags even had it that she "used a lot of vinegar in her cooking." Others never believed a word she said or wrote, but Clementine rejected the notion that she was just "yarn-spinning," caustically telling one critic, "Honey, if I wanted to spin yarn, I reckon I'd have a spinning wheel."[11]

The Samuels oeuvre was recently discovered under an old skillet and some stale hors d'oeuvres at a flea market in St. Louis. Careful reading of Clementine's essays indicates that she parted the waters, as it were, for such currently popular wits as Art Buchwald, Russell Baker, William Safire, and Andy Rooney, although they don't cook.[12] She may in fact also have been a predecessor of such contemporary cooks as Julia Child, Craig Claiborne, and the guy at the B and H on the Lower East Side,[13] but, alas, we will never know, as Clementine did not record her recipes (see essay herein, "Why Recipes Are a Waste of Time, Which Doesn't Wait Around").

It is not known what became of Clementine Samuels. Some say that she got tired of the river and took to trains instead, where she became a regular on the whistle-stop circuit and once got to insult a Presidential candidate. After that, the story goes, she was so happy that she died. Others contend that she took up with a half-breed comprised of the same halves, only his skills were singing the blues and nagging, a

why don't they cook — RESEARCH

[11]The critic is said to have been mightily humbled by this barb. At least that's what Clementine herself claimed in a ripping essay called "I Give a Critic a Piece of My Mind."

[12]Or if they do, they keep it to themselves, which is what they should do with their so-called humor, but it's too late for that, isn't it?

[13]Who is known for his own witty aphorisms, such as "I heard you the first time," and "This is a dairy restaurant. You want meat, go to a stockyard."

combination which ultimately drove Clementine insane. Still others report what have come to be known as "Clementine sightings," placing her over the years in breadlines,[14] wartime factories,[15] "freedom rides,"[16] and even Van Halen concerts.[17]

The story that persists, though, is the one about the raft on the Mississippi. Every now and then it appears, drifting through the swirls of mist. It bears a very old woman, who, if you make eye contact with her, will tell you an amusing tale, make you a cake from scratch, if you want one, and "head 'round the next bend to fix dinner for some hungry folks, make 'em chuckle, and put pen to paper to tell everybody about an interesting experience."

[14] Of course, Clementine was not *waiting* for bread, she was serving it, in an amusing fashion.

[15] Where she supposedly enjoyed a brief stint as "Clementine the Riveter."

[16] A term that originated in the 1960s, referring to school buses that carried protesters south of the Mason-Dixon line to express disapproval of segregation. Aren't you ashamed you didn't know that? We just don't understand kids these days.

[17] Thus indicating widespread belief in the notion, "Old humorists never die, they just do a lot of stupid things."

Mrs. Mel Gibson
Caryn Gibson
Caryn Bleckstein Gibson
Caryn B. Gibson
Caryn Bleckstein-Gibson
Mel + Caryn Gibson
Caryn + Mel Gibson
Mr. + Mrs. Bleckstein-Gibson

Representative Essays

An Interesting Experience[1]

I FIRST saw a cypress tree when we stopped for a day at New Orleans to pick up some musicians. I mean I had seen cypress trees, there were more of 'em down there than you could shake a stick at, but I never really paid 'em no never mind. The day we stopped to pick up these upstanding representatives of jazz, I truly took note of the cypress.[2] The one I took note of hung so low over the river that it made me think it wanted to go for a swim, just for a minute, then it would return to its rightful place faster than you could say jackrabbit. But it just stood there like a tired army lookout, too fatigued to talk, and therefore it would divulge no secrets. Ever since that day,[3] I have regretted my childhood forays into the swamp, when I used to carve my moniker on cypress bark, but always ran out of space because my name contains a brimful of letters.

[1]In the Samuels lexicon, "interesting experience" refers to any encounter that when capsulized, is fraught with symbolism of American life. In case you're interested.

[2]Historians suspect that after hanging out with the musicians for several hours, Clementine stumbled to the kitchen and, in a creative haze, concocted several notorious dishes subsequently referred to as "Musicians' fodder."

[3]"Ever since that day" is a good example of the "literary signpost" or "traveling segue," not to be confused with traveling salesmen.

I Play a Trick on a Foreigner[4]

WHEN I saw my first riverbank from the deck of the Jubilee II, I pitched a biscuit that I had baked to the main shore. This was in the middle of a banquet for a so-called explorer from France. I figured he'd figure that he had discovered an American custom and would go home and tell everyone about biscuit-pitching.

The river swallowed my biscuit faster than he did, even though it was not very wide or deep at that point, and my biscuits are not made to go down quickly, 'tho they are light as a feather.

It wasn't until later, when I served the steamed porcupine, that an expression of distress registered on his foreign face. From what I could gather, and I repeat this conversation word for word, the main dish was news to this supposedly worldly fellow.

"What do I do with the quills?" he said.

"Them's what you use to pick up the spuds," I told him.

"Spuds?" he replied.

"You know—carrots," I said mischievously, and our guest proceeded to remove a porcupine quill and stab the boiled carrots.

Meanwhile, the rest of us used the quills to spear the taters, to the explorer's evident chagrin. We all enjoyed a silent laugh at this man who had claimed to have been around the world "once or twice."

---

[4]Playing tricks on strangers was a time-honored frontier habit. Clementine delighted in trick-playing and often boasted about how she once got a queen to eat a field mouse, all the while believing it was a tiny game bird.

ex: →
xenophobe
(look
up)

A Satirist's Needs

THE science of satire has peculiar requirements, especially when it is executed in conjunction with cooking. Nothing short of perfection will do. There is always that critical moment when the storyteller thinks, "Should I go on, like Old Man River? Take it ten degrees to the starboard side? What if I run out of steam? What if nobody laughs, and I'm caught in a crosscurrent of silence?"

It seems to me that a satirist needs two faculties. These faculties are eyesight and hearing. There are no blind or deaf satirists, far as I know, 'tho I heard of one who lives up in the Ozarks somewhere. Mebbe I'll look 'er up some day. In the meantime, I'll try to remember to proceed with caution.[5]

Why Recipes Are a Waste of Time, Which Doesn't Wait Around

FOLKS always ask me to write down my recipes so they can go home and try to rustle up the same kind of victuals. I don't think this is wise, as nothing ever turns out the same way twice.

A piecrust that's the same every time is no different than a man who has only one story to tell. A stew with the same number of turnips each time you prepare it is like a river without any bends. A servin' platter decorated many times over with the same garni is like—well, mebbe that is okay, but every capillary in my body doubts it.

---

[5]Clementine reportedly lost both her sight and hearing in a kitchen explosion on board the Jubilee II. She herself reported this in a moving essay called "I Can't See or Hear." Fortunately, this proved to be only a temporary handicap, as we are informed in the rousing essay "I Can See and Hear Again." Later as Clementine became even more of a literary sharpshooter, she recalled the episode in a no-holds-barred essay entitled, "I Can See and Hear Again, But What's the Use?"

The other side of the story is that I am the possessor of a well-known weakness for watercress, a decoration sold to me by a vegetable vendor when we ran aground near Cairo, Illinois. "It's a versatile legume," said he, although not in so many words.[6] It was a fortuitous accident, as I use the watercress frequently.

As for why recipes are a waste of time, I rest my case, Your Honor.

The Davy Crockett Birthday Speech[7]

". . . and it is an honor to serve and sup with and entertain all of you assembled bellowing bigwigs, and this is certainly an occasion that demands the digging up of reminiscences of certain politically minded folk standing here before this assembled mob of stuffed shirts. I recall the time we stopped to pick up some bituminous coal, tho' it could have been anthracite now that I ponder it . . ."

[6]The actual words were, "Here, lady. Two coppers." They appear in the essay, "Puzzling Lessons," which was published in a newsletter about employees of the Jubilee II Steamboat Company.

[7]Too long-winded to reprint in its entirety. Anyway, Clementine never got the chance to deliver it, as the self-styled "King of the Wild Frontier" never showed up. The distraught humorist later discussed this incident in a biting essay called "Stood Up by a King."

Ethiopians and Hebrews

WHO are the Hebrews? Why do they do so many stupid things? People often pose these queries in my presence, probably because I'm half a Hebrew myself. Or maybe I just look wise. Some say the Hebrews are the ones who possess big noses. Others contend that they killed the son of God. Shakespeare's only Jew is known for extracting flesh in exchange for shekels, and as for yours truly, well methinks that the Hebrews have not been properly considered.

It's true that they have done a lot of stupid things. But the first stupid thing the Hebrews did was not to look funny, nor was it to commit the greatest crime the human race has ever known. And it was not to loan money to people whose only collateral was their body and soul. No, it was the far more irreversible error of turning left at the Euphrates. Evidently, everyone else turned right, of course, but these flashy, know-it-all types with the funny *chapeaux* on their heads had to go in the opposite direction, just to show how different they were. Well, where did it get them, really?[8]

The next stupid thing they did was flee Egypt in order to start their own ghettoes in the metropoli of Eastern Europe, places that already contained enough people who reeked of mandrake root and carried pellagra. And then, once they were there, instead of trying to mingle and get lost in the crowd like every other Tom, Dick, and Harry, they invented a strange new language that no one else could understand because it sounded like they were always coughing up balls of phlegm. What kind of government permits this to happen?

But by far the stupidest thing the Hebrews did was befriend the Ethiopians,[9] a group noted mainly for the gymnastic trick of inserting crockery underneath its lips and leaving it there for an indefinite period of time. The only by-product, as I see it, of this Hebrew and Ethiopian merger has been yet another form of exclusivity, to wit: the underground railroad. Why was it that only runaway slaves were allowed to avail themselves of this transportation? Doesn't a train that travels

---

[8]It's not clear. Some say that the Hebrews have produced the greatest minds of recent history, including Einstein, Marx (Karl and, of course, Zeppo), and Henny Youngman. However, it is Frank Sinatra, another garlic-scented although unrelated ethnic, who sings the chart-topping standby "My Way." But perhaps the lawyer who made the deal is of the Hebrew persuasion.

[9]Can't we all just get along?

underground sound like a heck of a lot of fun to you? Well, did you ever try purchasing a ticket on this so-called train to Freedom? I did, thus prompting the stationmaster to threaten me with a lynch mob. So I ask you: what kind of people would invent a train that only a certain type of person can find or ride on? And where is Freedom, anyway? Now, I hear this train doesn't even exist anymore! But maybe that's what happens when you're a half-breed. Twice condemned, you miss out on everything.

For Further Study

1. Was Clementine Samuels half-Jewish and half-Negro or vice versa? Was this a double handicap or a double advantage? How would you feel if people thought you were a miser with a good sense of rhythm or a comedian who squandered her tips on shag carpeting and customized chrome fixtures for her flashy new Jew canoe? What about the U.N.? Why can't they do their job? Is it because there are no "Jewgroes" on the Security Council? Investigate.

2. Why was the American frontier rife with lessons? Did everybody on the frontier learn them? Are there any places we can learn these lessons today? Should we learn these lessons? Why can't we all just get along?

3. What's long, muddy, and wet, and is the main character in the Samuels sampler? Can you spell it backwards?

4. Do some of us lead more colorful lives than others? Please refrain from making cheap references to skin color, as that is the editors' domain.

5. Did Clementine Samuels die? If so, where is her ghost most often sighted? Do you believe in ghosts? Do you believe in reincarnation? Is it conceivable that Clementine Samuels has returned as any one of the following people: a) Sammy Davis, Jr.; b) Dinah Shore; c) Dinah Shore's baby; or d) Moses Malone? Explain.

6. In her essay "An Interesting Experience," Samuels makes a reference to meeting jazz musicians. Do you think they had marijuana then, and if so, would that account for her famous dish, "Hep Cats' Munchy Gumbo"?

7. Why do you think Clementine Samuels never wrote down recipes? Was it to avoid the meaningless and time-consuming chore of writing down the ingredients and cooking instructions on unwieldy little index cards which you then have to file in those stupid little boxes decorated with disgusting decoupaged hearts and flowers? Not to mention those mindless busybodies who have nothing better to do than bug you to swap index cards and then return them splattered with unsightly sauce stains, thus reducing your life to one endless recipe nightmare. Was Clementine Samuels smart, or what? We ask you.

8. If all it takes to be a satirist is a pair of eyes and ears, how come most people are so boring? Explain in twenty-five words or less. Try not to be boring.

9. Why did Americans of the frontier era take such delight in playing tricks on foreigners? Was the trick that Clementine played on the French explorer a small-time dress rehearsal for the high-level hijinks that America practices on foreigners today, e.g., the invasion of Grenada? For extra credit, find a foreigner, invite him over for dinner, and make fun of him.

10. If Clementine Samuels is responsible for Andy Rooney, how can we stop this from occurring again?

In this photograph of Tekka Maki, she demonstrates the time-honored skill of pouring tea, a feat she accomplished in one graceful, fluid gesture, which could actually be broken down into 433 separate infinitesimal movements. The sensitive poet had a violent streak which she sometimes expressed in her haiku and sometimes in person. Once, when a friend who had just returned from America asked Tekka to serve Lipton's tea, Tekka bowed politely and then proceeded to pour scalding hot water on her friend's

Tekka Maki
1880?–1939

THE historical place of the Oriental woman has been extremely subservient until recently. Today, with Japan thoroughly established as a modern, industrial nation, women are slowly moving up the social ladder. Whereas a woman once walked ten steps behind her man, today it is only two or three. Yet it is not until recent times that we find the first real seeds of change in the Land of the Rising Sun.[1] Through an unusual turn of events, we have been introduced to the moving poems, known as haiku, of a nineteenth century woman named Tekka Maki.

Tekka's story is brief, as is a haiku. Born around 1880, she led the traditional life of a wife and mother. To have expressed a desire for more than this would have made her a slut and a whore. But secretly she was a poet, and she shared this secret with her daughter, Kappa Maki, reciting her poems to the little girl at bedtime. Tekka never learned to write, but Kappa did, and she lovingly handprinted her mother's haiku. Not wanting to dishonor her mother, she hid the pages away until one day, when her own little girl was studying for a haiku test, she showed them to her.

Tekka's granddaughter, Onago, kept the secret for a time, too, but as she saw women breaking into new fields and creating a new self-image,

[1] Have you ever seen their flag? It's impossible to tell whether the sun is rising or setting. There are those who contend that such an indecisive symbol could only have been designed by a woman. Of course, the Japanese insist that it's rising, but it wouldn't be the first time those zipperheads have lied to the American people, would it? What are we, some kind of paper tiger? Where do they get off making those tiny fuel-efficient cars? Sure, they get ninety-three miles to the gallon, but by the time you get where you're going, you're so cramped up you need a shiatsu massage. And guess who's volunteering to walk all over your back with their tiny yellow feet? Don't get us started. Now they have us tying rags around our heads and wearing those stupid t-shirts with seams on the outside. Before you know it we'll all be eating Tofu McNuggets and Seaweed McMuffin! And what about the dolphins? All they wanted was to be our friends. Whose side do you think they were on in Pearl Harbor?

she felt it was time for Japan to appreciate and acknowledge the works of her grandmother. In 1951, she compiled the haiku into a proposal, which she sent to all the major publishing houses. But only form letter rejection slips returned. Next, she sent copies to all the major literary figures. Dr. Kazuo Munakata, Professor of Haiku Studies at Tokyo University, sent this reply: "This woman's poems may imitate the structure of haiku, but her lack of respect for preserving the sense of Nature, to show how it has moved the poet, is unacceptable. Her work is nonsense and garbage and so is she!"

Hurt and angry, Onago changed her name to California Roll and took to hanging out in sushi bars and overindulging in saki. One night, she overheard some customers discussing the International Haiku Convention being held at the Imperial Hotel. In a moment of madness, she burst upon the convention and blasted the Japanese literary world for ignoring the works of Tekka Maki.

In her now-famous statement, California said, "The exclusively male literary world has never wanted Maki's haiku published because they can't come to terms with the fact that they are little men and they'll always have little peenies." Needless to say, California offended everyone and was arrested for public drunkenness. Unable to pay her fine, she was thrown in jail[2] and publicly humiliated.

But the disturbance did capture the interest of Susie Yawao, a highly respected *geso* (gossip columnist) and, as fate would have it, a haiku enthusiast. Susie sent one of her aides to interview California in jail, and he returned with Kappa's final remaining proposal. Susie was immediately impressed with the genius and significance of Maki's haiku. The next day Susie ran an item about California's ordeal and included one of the haiku in her column.

That very afternoon, hordes of haiku-loving teens converged on the jail, set up their transistor radios, and began "doing the haiku," a new dance craze consisting of five hops and seven skips, followed by five jumps.[3] Despite police attempts to disperse them with tear gas, fire

---

[2]The Japanese practice the barbaric custom of putting drunks in jail, instead of just letting them sleep it off on the sidewalk or drive home.

[3]This dance traveled all the way from far-off Japan to Far Rockaway, where it was renamed "the pogo," and popularized by the short-lived but legendary punk group, the Ramones, in a simplified version which left out the skips and jumps and was easier for people who were lobotomized by drugs to learn.

hoses, and firecrackers, the teens, chanting "Sex and Haiku and California Roll," refused to leave until California Roll was released and all charges dropped.

Taking a cue from the nation's youth, Susie Yawao ran one of California's mother's haiku in her column every day for a week. Maki's poems, once branded "flaudulent haiku," finally received the praises they deserved, and California got a book deal for her own story. Today, both are respected Japanese writers.

Photo courtesy of the Wheaton, Illinois, Chapter of the VFW.

The popularity of haiku is widespread in the United States, as well as Japan, due to the influence of Tekka Maki. Here, a typical haiku club grapples with the problem of diagramming a haiku. The most promising student will receive the highly coveted VFW "Hands Across the Water" Haiku Scholarship.

Eleven Haiku

ABOUT HAIKU

Haiku[1] (hi'-koo)[2] are very brief, highly structured Japanese poems. In Japanese form, a haiku[3] consists of three lines with five, seven, and five syllables respectively. It is often impossible to preserve the syllable count and properly translate the images and symbols of the Japanese version into English. The translator, Sake Tume, has attempted to preserve Maki's unique images while maintaining a sense of formal structure. In haiku,[4] every word counts.

[1]Gesundheit.

[2]Ge-zoondt'-hīt.

[3]God bless you.

[4]Have you seen a doctor lately?

Slice raw fish bellies
Squish cooked rice in patties
Dinner is ready

Sumo[1] be gentle
I'm afraid you're just too fat
to sit on my lap

You may have big guns
Mister Commodore Perry[2]
But you have b.o.[3]

The sad geisha girl
With powdered tear-streaked face
Should have been a mime

Do not cry my child
Daddy will find the bad man
Who popped your cherry blossom

Samurai,[4] stop killing
Pummel your sword limp, useless
Like your small peenie

Mount Fuji like drunk
One day very nice . . . next day
A flaming asshole

[1]Japanese wrestlers who gain vast amounts of weight and are idolized by the normally petite Japanese. Due to their enormous bulk and stress-filled profession, they are as likely to die of heart disease as the average American citizen. The motto of Sumo wrestlers roughly translates as "Live fast, die young, and leave a whole lot of corpse."

[2]Commodore Perry was an American naval officer who visited Japan in 1853–54 and persuaded the Japanese to sign a trade treaty, thus ending Japan's long centuries of isolation from foreign powers. If it were not for Commodore Perry, we would never have become so dependent on silk stockings for American women and thus would not have been forced to invent rayon when the war with Japan cut off our silk supply. The invention of rayon was followed by the invention of dacron, orlon, and the popular singing group, the Chiffons. So for those of you who got knocked up in the backseat of a convertible listening to the Chiffons on the radio, blame it on Commodore Perry!

[3]Abbreviation for body odor. Orientals consider that people from western cultures have a distinctly unpleasant odor as a result of eating dairy products. This may explain the emergence in the mid-nineteenth century of the phrase, "Who cut the cheese?" in response to a bad smell. Yet another debt we owe to Commodore Perry.

[4]Member of aristocratic warrior class of feudal Japan who followed Bushido as a code of conduct. Although Sid Caesar sometimes did a samurai on "Your Show of Shows" in the late fifties, it was not until John Belushi created his memorable samurai on "Saturday Night Live" that America took the samurai to their hearts as a comedic character. For some reason, television audiences seem to find these aristocratic warriors very laughable, which would probably drive them to hara-kiri if they knew about it. So don't tell them.

You eye my fine threads
And plot your wicked revenge
My silkworm is squished[5]

Don't talk to sister
She is stricken with the curse
She might bite your head off

A roar like thunder
Rape, loot, murder, destruction
Feudal lord is home

Life is a circle
It goes round and round and round
So you want to fuck

[5] An approximate translation of a Japanese word which could mean either "squished," "smushed," "stomped," or all three, depending on the tone of voice in which it was said. It was one of Tekka Maki's favorite words, especially with reference to cooking. She was renowned for her frozen apricot smush, a recipe which she passed down to her daughter, who in turn passed it on to her daughter, who successfully franchised it to the Loy Logers chain of family-style fast-food restaurants.

1. In your opinion, was the over-whelmingly negative reaction of the Japanese male literary establishment to Tekka's work valid, or were they just mad because they had teeny peenies?

2. In view of the subsequent critical acclaim that greeted Tekka's haiku, do you feel Dr. Kazuo Munakata's judgment was premature? Or just inadequate? Expand.

3. What do you think would have happened to Tekka's work if she had only had sons? Do you think any of her sons would have saved their mother's writing? And what about their sons? Do you think any of them would have become writers? Or were they more likely to be baseball players or manufacturers of microchips? Could any of them conceivably have broken Roger Maris' homerun record or invented the Sony Watchman?

4. Is it unusual for a poet such as California Roll to attract groupies? Is it true that rock 'n' roll songwriters are the poets of our day? Who has more groupies, Robert Lowell or Robbie Robertson? Which of them said that he got more pussy than Frank Sinatra?

5. Common themes of Tekka's work are violence and shame. What does this tell you about Japanese culture? Have you ever felt so embarrassed you wanted to plunge a sharp sword into your stomach? Wouldn't it be more embarrassing to die leaving a mess? Who cleans it up, anyway? Do they have harakiri clean-up crews? Merry Christmas, Mr. Lawrence.

6. Try writing a haiku of your own. Remember that the first and last lines must have five syllables, and the middle line must have seven. What does the structure of haiku have in common with the average height of most Japanese people? Explain in three words or less. IT IS SHORT

7. Did reading these haiku make you want to go to Japan? Or would a Japanese restaurant suffice? For extra credit, go to a Japanese restaurant. For extra extra credit, go to Japan.

8. Why is Chinese food cheaper than Japanese food? Which one do you feel hungrier after faster? Why don't Japanese people run laundries?

9. Are people who write haiku lazy, or just yellow? Are the editors racist, or just lazy?

10. Do you think that haiku as an art form has influenced new wave music? New wave haircuts? New wave clothing? What was wrong with the old wave? Do you think you're turning Japanese? Do you really think so?

* FOR FURTHER STUDY

Photo courtesy of Raoul Heywood.

Wearing her signature polka-dotted silk scarf, Dot Benchley, the hash-slinging wiseacre of the 1920's, was four sheets to the wind when this photo was taken at a bon voyage party for her arch-rival Mae West aboard the S. S. *Vuitton*. Later, Dot observed with characteristic generosity: "I won't say she's built like a truck—but I notice nobody ever passes her on the right."

Dot Benchley
1897–1951

IT WASN'T for nothing that the American 1920s were nicknamed "The Roaring Twenties," as they were years highlighted by an intense desire to drink, do the Charleston, and toss off pithy witticisms about such important topics as methods of suicide, telephone calls, and haberdashery.

Nowhere did this tradition flourish more than at Frank's Coffee Shop, an unassuming eatery across the street from the notorious Algonquin Hotel.[1] Many self-styled wits met every night for coffee at Frank's. This group included the doorman from the Algonquin, the bellhop from the Algonquin, the hatcheck girl from the Algonquin, the assistant manager from the Algonquin, the janitor from the Algonquin, and even several Algonquin guests who were trying to sober up after a rigorous evening of roast capons and bathtub gin at their favorite speakeasy. But whether drunk or sober, the counter at Frank's was more fun than the lobby at the Algonquin, if the stories that have been passed down are any indication. (Also, the burgers were better, and if Frank really liked you, he'd punch out anyone who took your luncheonette stool, no matter how clever they were.)

Among the engaging diamonds-in-the-rough at Frank's was one polished gem: Dot Benchley, the longtime head waitress. Night after night, she took the spotlight with her sparkling rejoinders; never once did she fail to shine with cleverness.[2] The few remaining survivors of

---

[1]The Algonquin Hotel, of course, was the site of the groundbreaking "Round Table" discussions among leading wits of the time. However, the crowd across the street was infinitely wittier; they just weren't sleeping with the right people.

[2]Actually there was one time. After pouring coffee to a hung-over patron of the wee hours, Dot greeted his slurred "Thank you" with a somewhat tired "You're welcome." The regulars laughed uproariously, so accustomed were they to being amused by Dot's every utterance. Years later, the Algonquin janitor realized this remark wasn't really very funny and tried to set the record straight by telephoning the rest of the gang. But they all had new phone numbers, and after a while, he just gave up.

those scintillating sessions at Frank's do not remember what Frank's was like before Dot. "It seems like Frank's was Dot," recalls one alumnus. "Or maybe Dot was Frank's—you're the writer; which sounds better to you?" This vivid recollection of Frank's is offered by the head hashslinger at the Algonquin, "Chucko" Marx.[3]

Still, when reports of the period are pieced together, it seems as if most people agree on at least one fact: Dot felt she had reached the pinnacle of her career at Frank's. This gives credence to the rumor that she was doing something less interesting during her pre-Frank's days, to wit: bussing tables at Al's, on the other side of town, where the wittiest thing anyone ever said was, "I don't believe there is an Al. If there is, how come he's never here?"[4]

Dot's clever aphorisms and well-calculated insults quickly made her the wry toast of the midtown greasy-spoon crowd. Patrons felt as if they had been certified as insiders whenever they were on the receiving end of such deftly snarled remarks as "I'll be right with you"; "I think we're out of seltzer, but I'll check" (the title of Dot's unpublished memoirs); and "Can't you read? The sign in front of your nose says no substitutions. But in your case, I'll make an exception. I'll leave, you take my place."

However, "Battling Benchley," as she was fondly called, is most remembered for the quick, humorous manner in which she always defended herself. There are many anecdotes about Dot's legendary public behavior, but perhaps two in particular serve to illustrate this notorious side of her personality. Once upon a time at Frank's, it was three in the morning. Frank was getting ready to close, and Dot was pouring the last round of coffee. Fetlock Dunne III, of Southampton and Palm Beach, the noted polo player and heir to a vast pinking shears fortune, stopped in, as he often did, to mingle with the hoi polloi. "Say," he said, after swigging down some coffee, "how's about some Kaiser rolls for the gang down at the Polo Grounds?" Dot replied without missing a beat: "Eighty-six on the Kaiser rolls, bub. Let 'em eat cheesecake." As soon as Dunne realized that the crowd at Frank's was laughing at him, he and

---

[3]No relation to Round Table habitué Harpo Marx, for whom Chucko cooked. Chucko, by an amazing coincidence, was the great-great-step-grandfather of Erin Fleming, the last girlfriend of Harpo's brother Groucho. Uncanny, isn't it?

[4]There was indeed an Al. However, embarrassed that his coffee shop didn't inspire more charming conversation, he frequented Tony's, an intimate pizzeria known for its glittering late-night payphone patter. Yes, Tony was always there.

his pals beat a hasty retreat, never to be seen again, except in photo-graphs in *Vanity Fair* magazine.[5]

Then there was the time that Dot Benchley encountered Dorothy Parker entering the Algonquin Hotel as she herself was also entering (to make a call; the telephone at Frank's had been disconnected). As the two stood paralyzed before the entrance, neither wanting to defer to the other, Benchley leveled her famous rival with a well-timed, "After you, hon."

In her private life, alas, Benchley did not fare as well as she did in public. Her tumultuous love life was long rumored to be the source of her sardonicism. As one marriage after another failed, lover after lover walked out, phone call after phone call went unreturned, dinner after dinner was consumed alone, the feisty little waitress grew hopelessly embittered. Her work took on a deeply self-deprecatory tone that in fact makes Joan Rivers[6] seem like Rebecca of Sunnybrook Farm.[7]

Later in life, Dot turned to Jesus and often quoted from the Bible but, unlike others new to the fold, only to provoke arguments. Once when a customer complained that his scrambled eggs were too runny, Dot looked skyward and retorted, straight from the *Book of Irritations and Running Sores,* "Scorn not the fruit of the hen, for thou wast once an egg thyself, pal." This unique use of religion did not endear her to many, but as Dot herself said at the time, "Be not high-minded, but fear" (*Book of Spanky,* VIII, 4:3).

Over the years, Dot recorded many of her nagging self-doubts on napkins and matchbook covers at Frank's. Some luncheonette veterans were so jealous of her writings that they made a point of throwing out anything bearing her caffeine-shaky scrawl. Fortunately for literary historians, though, there were those who recognized a genius in their midst and were thoughtful enough to save various bits and pieces of Dot Benchley's work.

It was only recently that this work has come to light, with the death of Raoul Heywood, a onetime lover of Dot's who washed windows at the

[5]But only when they ran out of photographs of first-class passengers on the *Normandie,* or of Salvador Dali.

[6]Can we talk? Joan Rivers is the popular comedienne known for such self-deprecation as, "The last time I took off my makeup my dog threw up."

[7]The original Rebecca was the eponymous heroine of the book by Kate D. Wiggin, whose cheer-fulness made her synonymous (not to be confused with eponymous; see Glossary) with optimism in the face of adversity; for instance, stocking your fallout shelter with Tab.

Algonquin. Inside a trunk of Heywood's mementoes, a junk dealer discovered a sheaf of papers marked, "Here are flowers, for whom had asked only weeds." Examination of the contents revealed that Dot herself had written that inscription, for the included work painted a picture that, however amusing, wasn't very pretty.

Nevertheless, it is an important testament to those times. Some of these flowers are reprinted herein, with the kind permission of Edith Benchley, a bus driver in Dot's hometown of Weehawken, New Jersey, and her only surviving relative.

"She should have never gone to New York," Edith lamented recently to the editors, referring to the caffeine overdose that caused Dot to one-liner herself into a coma. "If she had stayed here, she would have stuck to simple things, like iced tea. Would you like some more?"

In this candid photograph, Zoë Thurber and Adelle Perelman enjoy a laugh with Dot Benchley (center) at the expense of Dot's cousin Edith. Edith had committed the unforgivable gaucherie of wearing a long skirt, and Dot had just devastated her with this sally: "If I was you, sister, I mean cousin, I'd take that extra material and cover up my face."

Photo courtesy of Edith Benchley.

The Extremely Portable Dot Benchley

Her Wit and Wisdom: A Sampler

On Marriage

It's a great little institution, if you like living in institutions.[1]

Love, honor, and obey
Olé!

> ROSES ARE RED
> VIOLETS ARE BLUE
> THIS CLASS IS BORING
> AND SO ARE YOU

On Being a Smarty Pants

That's what we did best, the gang at Frank's, goddamn it, we were smarty pants.[2]

On Regrets

Regrets lead to drinking, which they want me to give up. I have no intention of giving up regrets, or drinking, which I'll probably regret, but maybe somebody will quote me on it some day. And live to regret it.

---

[1]This standard Borscht Belt refrain may not have actually originated with Dot Benchley. But she's taking credit for it and, to the editors' knowledge, is the first openly to do so. So who cares?

[2]Ironically enough, years after Benchley uttered this remark, Woollcott Alexander, a longtime member of the gang at Frank's, started a line of brightly colored children's underwear called "Smarty Pants." In 1983, fate struck a cruel blow. A large underwear shipment bound for South Korea plummeted to a soggy end in the Pacific Ocean, when the plane carrying the colorful cargo was shot out of the sky by the Soviet Air Force. Subsequently, the underwear washed up on a primitive island in the South Pacific, where the ignorant natives now sport the underwear on their heads. Actually, it looks pretty good. So we ask you, who are the real smarty pants here?

Phone Bill

Hello, is Jack back?
Hello, is Ring around?
Never mind, I'll call them later;
I'm sure they've got dates for some the-a-ter.

Valentine

Bartender, pour me a drink
I'm not exactly in the pink.
My husband, of whom I'm quite fond,
Is out with a sprightly young blonde.[3]

Banner Headline

Men always make passes
At girls with nice asses;
But not if they've glasses
Or are known for wise sasses.
Yes, I envy you masses
From here on Parnassus;
So here's to the lasses
Who are slow as molasses.

Heart Song

Sometimes I'm Carmen Miranda;[4]
Sometimes I'm Helen of Troy.[5]
Then I'm out on the veranda—
Alone, and I sigh "Oh boy!"

[3] An example of poetic license. Dot Benchley didn't know for sure whether her husband was actually out with a blonde. He could have, in fact, been out with a middle-aged brunette or a geriatric redhead. But, then, who would care? In western culture, blondes traditionally take the blame for stealing husbands. In our opinion, this is because blondes are generally fair-skinned and do not like to spend much time outdoors in the sun, preferring to stay indoors, in bed.

[4] Latin American entertainer famed for singing and dancing with fruit on her head and nothing under her skirt. Not to be confused with Miranda Carmen, who does it the other way around and is currently headlining at Bottomless World, Count 'em, 143 Girls, 143, Count 'em, Complete Performances, 8, 10, and 12 Nitely, Including Thanksgiving.

[5] The pretty one; not the smart one. See Chapter One, *The Kaffeeklatsch*.

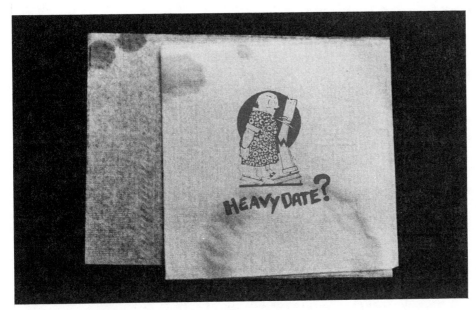

Photo courtesy of Raoul Heywood.

Dot Benchley often combined her witticisms with clever drawings on luncheonette napkins, which she then presented to lucky patrons. This paved the way for the multi-billiondollar-a-year joke cocktail napkin industry. Oh boy! If Dot had only remembered to copyright that one!

Epitaph

I'm stretched out dead;
And now you're here.
"Something came up," you said,
"Can't you be a dear?"
But still I toss in my (dusty) bed
Uncalmed by your crocodile tear;
I'm sure it's late and you haven't been fed,
So go have your nice, foreign beer.

Novel

I fix his coffee
He switches to tea.[6]

---

[6]And that wasn't the only thing "he" switched to. Shortly after Dot penned this plaint, the man in "Novel" married the person who served him his first tea, Dot's second cousin, Edith Benchley.

Aria

O life is a rising sun, you know;
A Matisse that's a thrill to be seen.
And love is the thing that makes you glow,
So I sling hash, like all beauty queens.

Psalm

You love me, you whispered today
(Why certainly, why not?, well sure)
Now dump me—a wilted nosegay
(Don't worry, I'm young, I'll endure).

Dance Card

Oh, splendid was the first love, throbbing and sublime;
The second was forever and it was oh so fine;
Or was that the third or fourth—for them I often pine;
The human race is rotten, and soon I shall resign.

Matchbooks were an appropriate trademark for Frank's, a coffee shop with a counter full of people who smoked so many cigarettes that they sounded like Lauren Bacall on those Fortunoff's commercials.

For Further Study

1. Did Dot Benchley work at Frank's, Al's, or Tony's?

2. Was there really a "Frank"? Who is "Al"? Is "Tony" the name of a permanent, or what? If so, which twin had it, and was it long-lasting with plenty of body?

3. Is there such a thing as "the right people to sleep with"? Would these be people who live in the same zip code as we do? Do they have any social diseases? Make a list, check it twice, and send it to the editors. Does your list include Rod Stewart? Don't ya think he's sexy? If you do, go on along and tell him so.

4. Do you think that the iced tea that Edith Benchley served the editors was made from scratch or instant? Can you tell the difference? Is all your taste in your mouth, or what? Who's talking here—the editors or Dot Benchley?

5. A time-honored Las Vegas lounge song is "Let It Be Him." Another one contains the lyric "One less egg to fry." Are these chart-topping laments derivative of Dot Benchley? Should there be a sand-wich named after her at Caesars Palace? *YES, AND A PIZZA TOO*

6. What foreign beers were available in New York during the 1920s? Don't you wish you had a nice, cold Heineken right now?

7. Dot Benchley obviously used humor as a way of dealing with pain. In your opinion, is this effective, or is it better to just go out and a) punch out somebody; b) kill yourself; c) punch out somebody and then kill yourself; or d) punch out your pillow?

8. If you chose b) or c) in the preceding question, what method would you use to kill yourself? a) razors; b) rivers; c) acids; d) drugs; e) guns; f) nooses; or g) gas. What are some of the unpleasant side effects of these methods? On the whole, wouldn't it be better to continue your existence, however drab and humdrum it might be?

9. Is there any percentage in being a smarty pants? Would you like to be one? Would you like to swing on a star? Carry moonbeams home in a jar? Be better off than you are? Or would you rather be a mule?

10. What's it all about, Alfie? If you have the answer, please write the editors immediately, so we can start our own religion and stop writing about Dot Benchley.

Photo courtesy of Nate 'n' Al's Celebrity Wall, Beverly Hills, California.

Despite the fact that Eskimo writer Noona remained unpublished throughout her life, she was not unappreciated. During the filming of "The Call of the Wild," she was a regular on the 20th Century-Fox lot, and often cadged a free meal from the commissary by posing as an actress.

Noona

????–1978

THE rediscovery of Noona's writings in the dawn of the eighties was perhaps the biggest feather in the editors' collective cap.[1] This lone Eskimo voice crying in the wilderness of Hollywood captured the attention of the most discerning critics following the 1932 release of her only published work, *White Is a Color, Too* (Little, Brown). Unfortunately, most of the small first printing remained unsold, as the public apparently didn't believe that white actually was a color, until migraine-beset modern ironist Joan Didion convinced them that it was.[2] The wave of critical acclaim quickly receded, leaving Noona stranded on the beach of obscurity for the following five decades.

Finding herself alone and impoverished, yet with an incurable lust for baubles, bangles, and bright shiny beads, Noona quickly fell into the buy-now, pay-later Hollywood lifestyle and ran up bills in every store in town. She was bailed out, literally, by the young, aspiring agent, Swifty Leibowitz, then working as a bail bondsman. Swifty later represented Errol Flynn, Jackie Robinson, and more recently, Meatloaf.

Swifty was charmed by Noona's talent and accessibility. In his turn, he had a great understanding and tolerance of the ways in which

[1]The editors are not literally wearing the same cap, although they do have the same taste in headgear and frequently borrow each other's hats, sometimes not even realizing it until they get home.

[2]Or was it the Beatles? And who was the walrus anyway? Obviously the walrus motif derives from Noona's writing, to which we suspect the Beatles were no strangers. In fact, Yoko Ono recently admitted, in a private phone call to one of the editors, that John Lennon was a great admirer of Noona's work. Yoko also claimed that she was the walrus.

Eskimo culture differed from our own, especially sexually. Over the years, Swifty not only encouraged Noona's talent, he also supported her financially and got her what little work he was able to drum up on the basis of her fading reputation. In the fifties, she enjoyed a fleeting resurgence of prosperity as the only Eskimo "front" for blacklisted writers, but blew her entire earnings, doubtless in a nostalgic spirit, at a white sale at Neiman-Marcus.

Once again, Swifty bailed her out, allowing her to take up residence in the pool cabana of his lavish Bel Air estate until her death in 1978. Her last years were marred by bouts of alcoholism, depression, and kleptomania. When she was arrested for trying to steal a snow shovel from a Bakersfield K-Mart, Swifty bailed her out again. Shortly before her death, she became obsessed with the fact that she had never been used to do a Blackglama ad. "I know fur," she kept repeating over and over. Some people thought she was saying, "I know her," and kept asking, "Who?" which only added to her confusion (and theirs).[3]

Her tragic death occurred in unusual circumstances. It seems she had taken to frequenting a Van Nuys ice-skating rink. On October 2, 1978, she stepped out directly into the path of the machine that clears off the ice,[4] with fatal results. Noona had finally gone to join her ancestors. Perhaps in her muddled state, she perceived the ominous machine as one of the mythological monsters which populated the folktales of her youth in her native Alaska.

Despite her manager's assiduous efforts to sell Noona's work based on the idea that it was now posthumous and therefore more valuable, it remained unknown to the public for years. One summer, however, one of the editors rented Swifty Leibowitz's cabana while the Leibowitzes were vacationing in Israel. Unwittingly, she made a significant discovery. Hidden under some very old cans of salmon was Noona's most important work, "The Ballad of the Canned Salmon," published here for the first time. According to her acquaintances, Noona had always kept these cans for good luck. Upon close examination of Noona's manu-

[3]Ours too.

[4]If you know what this machine is called, please contact the editors.

IT'S A ZAMBONI, IF YOU REALLY WANT TO KNOW AND MY UNCLE INVENTED IT.
[VITO ZAMBONI, INV. 1932]

script, it became apparent that these cans of salmon had once belonged to her beloved Uncle Ano.

When "The Ballad of the Canned Salmon" was brought to the attention of the editors, they began an intensive search for Noona's remaining work, which led from the bistros of Hollywood to the frozen wastes of northernmost Alaska. After interviewing scores of Eskimos from Noona's birthplace, the editors learned that her work was not widely read among her own people. In fact, it was not read at all. This was undoubtedly because, as the first Eskimo to write in English, her work was unintelligible to those who would most appreciate it. Alas, such is the bed the tortured genius makes for him- or herself.

What little we know of Noona's early life is that she was an independent, rebellious spirit who vowed she would not settle for the traditional lot of the Eskimo woman, which involved a lot of chewing and sewing.[5] Her elders ridiculed her mercilessly in an attempt to discipline her in the customary Eskimo way.[6] But their efforts proved futile, for as soon as Noona had saved up enough out of her salary from the local supermarket, where she worked as a cashier, she headed for the glittering Southern lights of Los Angeles, California.

Perhaps it was her stay in L.A. that provided Noona with the distance to reflect upon her Eskimo experience, thus enabling her to create a vivid panorama of native life from the time of the first white settler to the age of the twist-off cap and the Jane Fonda workout tape, both of which are currently available in the same supermarket where Noona once worked. Noona's writing was an ingenious amalgam of such Southern voices as William Faulkner, Carson McCullers, Lillian Hellman, Tennessee Williams, and Colonel Sanders. Sadly, her Eskimo

[5]Eskimo women not only chewed when they ate their food, they were also required to chew hides in order to soften them, so that they could be sewn into clothing. As a fringe benefit for their husbands, the women's highly developed jaw muscles doubtless enhanced their conjugal happiness, and also that of strangers who dropped by, since it was in the tradition of Eskimo hospitality to invite guests to sleep with your wife.

[6]Eskimo parents laughed at their children when they did something wrong, instead of spanking them or making them feel guilty, like normal people.

Photo courtesy of Steve Beshakes, long-time mailman on Noona's route.

In her later years, the author seldom left the house, but was often spotted peering through her living room window. Some friends attributed this habit to the fact that Noona believed good luck would come her way with the first snowstorm. Unfortunately, it snowed only once during the forty-six years that Noona lived in Los Angeles, and Noona slept through it.

influences are unknown due to the fact that the Eskimos don't believe in the star system.[7] Nevertheless, Noona remains a brilliant and shimmering supernova in the female literary galaxy. She is our first authentic Northern voice.[8]

[7] Neither does rock star Sly Stone, as exemplified by his chart-topping tune, "Everybody Is a Star." In fact, his hairdresser recently admitted in a private phone call with one of the editors that Sly is a great admirer of Noona's work, and of Eskimo ways in general, especially their sexual mores.

[8] Jack London pretended to be the first authentic Northern voice, but he wasn't an Eskimo, so he doesn't count. And anyway, Jack London's literary executor admitted in a private phone call with one of the editors that Jack was a great admirer of Noona's work and on more than one occasion said he wished he could write like her.

The Ballad
of the Canned Salmon

AT a breakfast meeting with my agent, Swifty Leibowitz, at a place across the street from Nate 'n' Al's, because Nate 'n' Al's had a forty-five-minute wait and Swifty is a busy man (I wouldn't have minded waiting; we Eskimos are used to waiting; imagine how long it takes to catch a fish through a hole in the ice), I ordered bagels and lox. The salmon color of the smoked salmon struck me as a little too salmon-colored to be believable, and I thought to myself, "These people know nothing about salmon." My people know salmon. The real salmon. The good salmon. The salmon that will leap forever across my memories.

Swifty took a long drag on his cigar, and behind the haze of smoke, his sweaty face began to resemble the sweaty face of my Uncle Ano. Uncle Ano understood salmon. He knew their leaps, and how high they could leap, and when they would not leap because they were depressed. When the Old Salmon was depressed, Uncle Ano was depressed also.

"Don't you know there is no Eskimo word for depression?" my forth-right grandmother, Anok, would ask him, chucking him under the chin with a piece of intricately carved whalebone, which happened to be lying around the igloo. But he only rubbed her nose with his affectionately.

My brother Koonan snatched up the whalebone. "You use my good carving to chuck an idiot under the chin, grandmother?" he said, pretending to be angry. My brother knew whalebone, and also soapstone, for he was a carver who carved those substances well and interminably.

My grandmother responded to this new challenge by throwing both Uncle Ano and my brother Koonan out of the igloo. Outside the igloo it was so cold that Uncle Ano lost several toes, and my brother had to catch two fish and slit them open and wear them on his hands as mittens in order to protect him from frostbite. His hands were important to him: without his hands he could not carve.

My Uncle Ano fed his toes to the Old Salmon, because he said they belonged to the Salmon anyway. The Old Salmon was so old there wasn't anyone left to know how old it was. And that's pretty old for a salmon. When the people of my tribe had a problem, they went to a hole in the ice and sang, "No Kan Kee/O Salmon, Come talk to me."

Sometimes the Old Salmon would come, sometimes it wouldn't. For that reason there are those who thought the Salmon was a woman. When the Salmon did appear, they would ask it questions. The Wise Salmon would leap in the air—one leap for yes, two leaps for no; or so my people believed.[1]

During The Time When It Is Cold,[2] not as cold as in The Really Cold Time,[3] but before The Time When It Is Not Nearly As Cold As It Is During The Cold Time,[4] my brother Noonak returned to our igloo from the land in the south where people give other people metal discs in exchange for food. As always he arrived in his luxury sled, which recently had been reupholstered. It made a big impression on me because I was at an impressionable age, an age when one could be easily impressed by such things as newly upholstered sleds.

However, perhaps I was not so overly impressionable after all, since the grown women in our tribe were also impressed by my brother Noonak, no doubt as a result of the quaint Eskimo adage, "You can always judge a man by the length of his sled," which they were fond of repeating to one another, accompanied by much giggling. I, of course, understood nothing of this and am not sure that I do now, or that it matters. But I set it down because it seemed important to everyone else. Eskimos are funny people. I can say that because they're my people, but don't you try it, or I'll bite off your fingers and your toes, too, and feed them to the Old Salmon.[5]

[1]This method of soothsaying prefigured our modern "8-Ball," but fell into disuse because, while you can pick up an 8-Ball at any five and dime, for this you had to be outside and it required a live salmon.

[2]Spring.

[3]Winter.

[4]Summer.

[5]Noona felt very strongly about this issue, as exemplified in an incident that took place at Musso and Frank's, a well-known Hollywood watering hole, when a successful producer told an Eskimo joke to a large table of showbiz types, who all laughed loudly. An enraged Noona hurled a plateful

THE REALLY, REALLY COLD TIME

On this particular occasion, Noonak picked me up, rolled me in the snow, dusted me off, rubbed blubber on my cheeks to make them shine, and exhorted me to express my affection.

"Well, my little merganser duck, you've really grown. Last time I saw you, you were knee-high to a grasshopper."

Brother Noonak was like that; he was always using expressions I didn't understand, but that held a considerable fascination for me. When he said the word "grasshopper," I had a vivid picture of something hopping over something else, which made me feel connected to a whole world of people who actually knew what this meant.

Noonak crawled quickly into the igloo to greet Anok, my salty old grandmother. Did we have salt then? I can't remember. But we lived so close to the sea, which is full of salt, that some clever fellow must have thought of it. We definitely didn't have any pepper. When I first got to Los Angeles, and I did go to Los Angeles, and in fact am still there now,

---

of bagels and lox at him. When the producer refused to apologize on the spot, Noona bit off his fingers. This occasioned a much-publicized lawsuit, Kramer vs. Noona, in which the irate producer tried to collect both damages and the purchase of a burial plot at Forest Lawn in which to inter his fingers, according to Orthodox Jewish custom. Noona won the case on the grounds that you don't need fingers to produce, only a telephone.

I had my first experience with pepper. Now I know pepper. Los Angeles has the good pepper and the largest grinders, which I take to be a good sign. In fact, I have my own maxim: "You can always judge a waiter by the size of his grinder."[6]

Anok greeted Noonak excitedly, to the great dismay of Koonan. "You think you can disappear for six months and come back with your fancy clothes and impress everybody?" he said. "Well, I'm not impressed."

"And neither is the Old Salmon," added my Uncle Ano, who never talked about anything but the Old Salmon.

"Why don't you take your Old Salmon and stuff it?" Noonak heatedly responded to my Uncle Ano, but even my grandmother could see that this insult was meant for Koonan.

"I'm an artist, not a taxidermist," answered Koonan indignantly.

"You call these chicken scratchings on a piece of whalebone art? No one will ever buy this junk. Wake up and smell the coffee, Koonan," said my brother Noonak, using another one of those expressions that nobody understood.

"Well, at least I'm not exploiting my people by building shoddy, low-income igloos. And what about those iceboxes you've been peddling around town? Everyone knows Eskimos don't need iceboxes."

"Except the droves of people who've been lining up to buy them," countered Noonak.

"You're a disgrace to your tribe," said Koonan. "You make me sick."

"And you make the Old Salmon sick, too," Uncle Ano interjected, right on schedule.

"The Old Salmon is sick," said Noonak. "Sick and old. And he smells bad, too, just like Uncle Ano."

"You're so crazy about those little metal discs, you'd probably sell your own grandmother," Koonan retorted.

This upset my grandmother, and she threw them both out of the igloo, saying, "This igloo isn't big enough for the two of you."[7]

Outside the igloo it was so cold that my brother Koonan had to catch two rabbits and slit them open and wear them on his hands as mittens

---

[6]This fairly lame maxim may provide a clue as to why Noona was not more successful as a writer. She was, however, known in Hollywood for her cocktail party chatter.

[7]Reference to size of space not being big enough for two adversaries. Variations on this phrase appear in the folklore of Blackfoot, Cree, Cherokee, and basically all cultures, including that of Hollywood screenwriters.

so he wouldn't get frostbite. It was so cold that my brother Noonak's sled shrank down to an embarrassing size.[8]

"More seltzer, hon?" inquired the waitress, across 6,000 miles and what seemed like as many years. There I was, back in Hollywood in the place across from Nate 'n' Al's.

I didn't want more seltzer; I only wanted to sink back into my reverie, so I did. The years fell away, and I was back in my childhood. It was the time of the month when we asked the Old Salmon questions.

All of the tribespeople gathered around the ice hole, or as my people call it, "The Swallowing Place"; why they call it that, I haven't the foggiest, as my brother Noonak said, or still would say today, although I haven't seen him for fifteen years. Anyway, it was an expression that always made me want to swallow. I guess it made other people feel that way, too, as the men were swallowing large quantities of a drink they called "sea lion whiskers,"[9] because "first it tickled, and then it roared."

People waited patiently enough for several hours, but still the salmon had not appeared. "He'll be here when he gets here," said Uncle Ano, much to the annoyance of those people who had foolishly made back-to-back appointments with a seal two ice holes down.

Suddenly, the Old Salmon leaped up through the ice hole. But instead of diving back into the water, this time it landed standing upright on its tail on the ice, poised like a ballerina in second position. Uncle Ano rushed up, embraced the Old Salmon, and together they waltzed across the ice in an elaborate pas de deux. The crowd parted to make room for them, seals applauded, and penguins scurried about with trays, serving champagne. Uncle Ano and the Old Salmon concluded their dance with a flourish, bowed graciously, and accepted a tribute of roses from a passing walrus. The Old Salmon executed a perfect grand jeté[10] back into its hole.

[8]The writer may be taking poetic license here. However, it is true that metal contracts in cold weather, which is why aluminum luggage was never popular among Eskimos, not even Eskimo photographers.

[9]A drink made from fermented yellow snow. This is believed to be the origin of the term "pissed" to describe someone who is drunk. The Indians of the Pacific Coast who shared this recipe followed the barbaric practice of drinking it out of human skulls, thus giving rise to the expression "pissed out of your skull."

[10]While penning "The Ballad of the Canned Salmon," Noona was also writing "for money" "The Maria Tallchief Story," a never-to-be-produced screenplay about the famous Indian ballerina which did not earn her any money. Of course, neither did "The Ballad of the Canned Salmon," until now, but sadly she's not here to collect it.

Everyone wondered what this meant. Many who had spent a great deal of time preparing their questions and thought they had good ones were disappointed. Others left immediately to keep their appointments with the seal.

Those who remained, however, realized that Uncle Ano and the Old Salmon had traced a message on the ice. It looked a lot like the Eskimo word for "beware." Beneath that was a second message: "P.S. I wish I had ice skates." It was signed, "The Old Salmon." Accompanying that was yet a third message: "Me, too. Uncle Ano."

"Gee, Uncle Ano, what does it mean?" I asked.

"There is always something to beware of," said Uncle Ano mysteriously.

"But couldn't you put us in the ballpark?" replied my brother Noonak, using another one of the unintelligible expressions for which he was famous.

"Suddenly the Old Salmon leaped up through the ice hole. But instead of diving b
ballerina in second position. Uncle Ano rushed up, embraced the Old Salmon,
make room for them, seals applauded, and penguins scurried about with trays, ser

"That's what he's talking about," Uncle Ano exclaimed, pointing to Noonak. "What the hell is a ballpark? You and your foreign expressions.[11] And what about those gol-darn, newfangled contraptions you bamboozled these good folks into shelling out their hard-earned clams[12] for?[13] Do you know that this morning a small child suffocated while playing in one of your iceboxes?"

"It's not my fault if they didn't read the instruction booklet," responded Noonak. "A refrigerator is not a toy. Never let a child play in it. Who do you think you are, dancing with a fish and then telling me how to run my life?"

[11]Noona took liberties with Eskimo speech patterns here. Eskimos have no word for "foreign," having not known that there were other people besides them when they invented their language.

[12]They often did pay in clams, which were easier to carry than dead fish or a whale.

[13]During this time, Noona was writing "for money" a screenplay, "Town and Country Cheese," a

he water, this time it landed standing upright on its tail on the ice, poised like a
her they waltzed across the ice in an elaborate pas de deux. The crowd parted to
pagne . . ."

This incensed Koonan, who knocked Noonak[14] flat on his back with the piece of whalebone he had been carving. Holding the whalebone to Noonak's throat, Koonan told him to apologize. But rather than apologizing, Noonak, who after all was my brother and still is, bit off Koonan's nose and spit it out on the ground. From that day forward, the brothers became enemies and never again crawled into the same igloo if they could help it.

Years later, though, they did crawl into my igloo—on the same night, but not at the same time. As if it weren't difficult enough to deal with both of them in one night, it was especially inconvenient because that night I was demonstrating the Eskimo tradition of Northern hospitality by sleeping with a friend of a friend of my grandmother's who had come by to borrow a cup of blubber. Luckily, however, it was winter, and the night was six months long.

I miss those long nights here in Hollywood, where there isn't even any winter. And I miss our traditions. Here, when people sleep with you, politeness has nothing to do with it. And they seldom even say thank you. If you sleep with someone else's husband, they seem to get angry. White people are funny.

—Now I think it is time to tell you the story of Big Stupid. Like all my stories, it is an Eskimo story. In the vast white reaches of the Arctic live many spirits, some good but most of them evil and scary. In our region, which was known as Nokono,[15] dwelt the meanest and largest of monsters, Big Stupid. Or so the legends say. Big Stupid was as ferocious and as mean as a killer whale in heat. Fortunately for my people, Big Stupid was also very stupid. If you encountered Big Stupid, it was easy to escape, provided that you didn't die of fright the moment you saw him. All Eskimo children were taught the simple tricks which allowed them to slip through Big Stupid's clutches. For instance, if Big Stupid was tracking you, all you needed to do was walk backwards for a while, and he would follow the direction in which your tracks pointed. Or if he suddenly came upon you, you could simply point behind him and say

ex:—
myth

ITH
THI TH
A
HIT
OR A
MITH ?

bitter, Budd Schulbergesque indictment of corrupt business practices in Vermont country stores, which was never produced and did not earn her dollar one, as her agent Swifty Leibowitz was fond of reminding her.

[14]Say "knocking Noonak" three times fast, and then try not to laugh.

[15]This translates as "Don't lick the ice or it will stick to your tongue."

excitedly, "Look, an elk!" and then run away while he wasn't looking. The people of my tribe found Big Stupid so easy to distract that he did not cause much of a problem. However, strangers, who knew only how big but not how stupid Big Stupid was, were often found mauled by the monster.

Big Stupid loved salmon even more than he loved elk and was always trying to catch the Old Salmon. Uncle Ano saved the Old Salmon several times by telling Big Stupid his mother was looking for him. Big Stupid, who was a very well-mannered monster, never failed to come whenever his mother called him, and thus the Old Salmon was easily able to escape.

Early one morning, however, when Uncle Ano was sleeping off the effects of too much "sea lion whiskers" the night before, Big Stupid did something really stupid. Trying to catch the Old Salmon, he fell in the ice hole and was swallowed up. Everyone thought the monster was dead, but when Uncle Ano and the Old Salmon traced the ominous message "Beware" on the ice, a good many people, who didn't believe that Big Stupid was gone for good, thought it might have something to do with his return.

The following Really Cold Time was really cold, colder than any Really Cold Time we've ever really known. It was so cold that the refrigerator was the warmest place in the igloo. Many children, not heeding their mother's advice, crawled into them to keep warm and had to be rescued by the fire department.

The constant opening and closing of the refrigerator doors meant that the refrigerators needed frequent repairs. Since the Eskimos still did not have any little metal discs, let alone an easier way to refer to them,[16] they were forced to pay Noonak in blubber for the repairs.

Thus, Noonak was able to gain control of the blubber supply of the entire tribe. This economic disaster for the tribe made them powerless in the hands of the now very wealthy Noonak, who became known as "Noonak the Blubber Baron."

While Noonak feasted on such delicacies as poached blubber, blubber Wellington, and blubber quiche, our people were starving. Without

[16]Such as "money."

"... In our region, which was known as Nokono, dwelt the meanest and largest of monsters, Big Stupid. Or so the legends say . . . All Eskimo children were taught the simple tricks which allowed them to slip through Big Stupid's clutches. For instance . . . if he suddenly came upon you, you could simply point behind him and say excitedly, 'Look, an elk!' and then run away while he wasn't looking."

their minimum daily blubber requirement,[17] they were too weak to refuse to do Noonak's bidding. In exchange for a tiny ration of blubber, he forced the older members of the tribe to pull his sled for his refrigerator deliveries, so his dogs could take it easy.

Meanwhile, Koonan kept on carving. By the end of the really cold Really Cold Time I was telling you about, my brother Noonak had single-handedly carved every available piece of bone and soapstone in the tundra. He had recently taken to carving ice and, in order to support my grandmother, since she would not accept anything from Noonak, had done several ice sculptures for parties. He would have gotten more requests, except that he didn't know how to carve swans, having never seen one.

It seemed as if my people would never emerge from this dark cloud which had fallen on our heads. Just when things seemed as if they couldn't possibly get any worse, the white people arrived.

One morning when everyone climbed outside their igloos to search for breakfast, they were surprised to find a giant yellow monster with big glassy eyes, strange, round feet, and an enormous mouth lined with metal teeth. The monster was greedily chewing up the earth at an incredible rate. It was roaring and belching smoke. Big Stupid had returned, it seemed, from the Swallowing Place, only this time bigger, more ferocious, and more stupid than ever. This Big Stupid was so stupid, he let the white man ride on his back. My people renamed him Giant Stupid Stupid.

Soon there were more Giant Stupid Stupids and many white men riding on them. Uncle Ano claimed that the white men were building a giant igloo to house the monsters. But Noonak knew better.[18] He said that the white men were building a supermarket, where those who had enough little metal discs could buy garlic-flavored potato chips, cat food, garden hoses, and anything else they needed. I hoped he was right because I wanted to buy a garden hose so I could write my name in the snow.[19]

Meanwhile, Grandmother Anok said that no good would come of this. She said that the old ways were ending, and the new ways were not the good ways, and anyway, there was no way she was going to go the white

[17] An average male Eskimo needs twenty pounds of blubber per day.

[18] Try saying that three times fast.

[19] Noona did not have a penis and obviously wanted one.

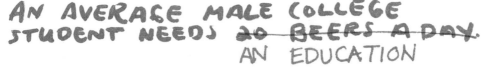

AN AVERAGE MALE COLLEGE STUDENT NEEDS ~~20 BEERS A DAY~~ AN EDUCATION

man's way, so there was only one way for her to go: her way.[20] She gave away all her possessions, which took about three or four minutes, rubbed noses with everybody except Noonak, and then wandered out onto the ice floes to die.

Finally the monster igloo was ready. The white man hung lots of little flags outside and opened the doors. Much to everybody's surprise, my brother Noonak turned out to be right. It was a supermarket. I went there to look at garden hoses but couldn't buy one because I had no little metal discs. Then a friendly white person told me about something called credit. I thought it was the most wonderful thing since sliced eel, and still do, and probably always will, even though Swifty says otherwise, and he should know because he has a lot of money. I took the garden hose home and wrote a novella[21] in the snow with it.

Soon all of the tribespeople knew about credit. They began to charge large quantities of Ho Ho's, Ring Dings, and Ding Dongs, which didn't quite substitute for their minimum daily blubber requirement but gave them a fantastic sugar buzz.

Contrary to my brother Noonak's expectations, the arrival of the white man did not prove advantageous to him. My people had credit now and no longer needed his blubber to fill their refrigerators. His once-strong grip on the community was slipping. No longer "The Blubber Baron," he became known as "The Blubber Flubber."[22]

One day during a shrimp riot (sixty-nine cents a pound) at the supermarket, who should show up but Grandmother Anok. After two weeks on the ice floes trying to return to her ancestors, she had come to the conclusion that her ancestors weren't ready for her yet.[23]

I immediately ran to fetch my brother Koonan. When he saw Grand-

[20]The Chairman of the Board, after all, was not the first to do things "his way." Jilly Rizzo recently admitted in a private phone call with the editors that Frank Sinatra greatly admires Noona's work.

[21]Honk if you know the difference between a novella and a short story.

[22]An executive at Walt Disney Productions recently admitted in a private phone call with one of the editors that Walt Disney greatly admired Noona's work. In fact, he was considering optioning her unproduced screenplay "The Littlest Eskimo" when he died. Ironically enough, Mr. Disney had himself frozen.

[23]A William Morris agent recently admitted in a private phone call with one of the editors that both Thomas Berger, author of *Little Big Man,* and Dustin Hoffman, Oscar-winning actor and star of the hit movie based on Berger's book, are great admirers of Noona's work.

mother Anok standing there in aisle three, he was overjoyed. He grabbed a lamb shank from the freezer case and frenziedly began carving a welcome-home sculpture of her. Coincidentally, my grandmother did look something like a frozen lamb shank, especially after being out on the ice floes for two weeks. As Koonan was taking my grandmother and the lamb shank through the check-out counter, one of the white men began examining his carving.

"Did this lamb shank come this way?" he asked.

"I carved it," said Koonan proudly.

"Amazing," said the white man. "Could you carve more?"

"Yes, but I have many bones already carved at home," said Koonan.

The white man went with Koonan to his igloo and offered to buy his entire collection, as well as to commission more work.

"Jeez," the white man said, "this stuff will sell like hotcakes back in the good old U.S. of A.," and he gave Koonan so many little metal discs that he was forced to trade them for paper rectangles. Koonan was now the most prosperous man among my tribespeople. He was generous to all and even gave Noonak some of the paper rectangles, with the provision that he would no longer exploit his people, a job that had now been taken over by the white man.

Everyone was happy except for my Uncle Ano, who discovered that the Old Salmon had mysteriously disappeared. The solution to this mystery unfortunately proved to be all too simple: the white man had opened a canning factory just upstream, and the Old Salmon would give yes-or-no answers no more. However, the Old Salmon soon resurfaced on the shelves of the supermarket. My uncle bought up most of the cans. The few that he missed were purchased by other people, who, upon eating their contents, succumbed to a mild attack of botulism.

"It serves them right," said my Uncle Ano. "I guess the Old Salmon had the last laugh."

And that's the end of my story. It's a story with a message, a moral, a postscript, call it what you will, and that is why I keep telling it so relentlessly. In thirteen short words, it is easier to sell art in a supermarket than in an igloo. And that's why I came to Hollywood.

For Further Study

1. Noona was impoverished and unsuccessful until she was discovered by the young, aspiring agent, Swifty Leibowitz. Do you think that poverty is a prerequisite for being discovered? Explain logically why it makes good business sense to give someone 10 percent of everything you have when 10 percent of your phone calls are to remind that person to make phone calls to people who owe you money so they can collect their 10 percent. Wouldn't it make you nervous to have an agent named "Swifty"?

2. What Southern writers influenced Noona? Does this mean that Noona made frequent references to: a) homosexuality; b) incest; c) interracial dating; d) insanity; e) the weather; f) violence; or g) fried chicken; or did she simply drink a lot of bourbon? For extra credit, what prevents Norman Mailer from being a Southern writer, even though he writes about these things all the time? (See Chapter 15, *Norman Gene.*)

3. How did the weather where Noona lived differ from the weather where William Faulkner lived? How did it affect their style, clothing, housing, and means of transportation? If Noona had written about Yoknapatawpha County would she have won the Pulitzer Prize? Would Faulkner still have won the Pulitzer Prize if he had had air conditioning? Speculate.

4. In Noona's writing, she elegantly slides from one time to another, gracefully swims from place to place, and, yes, we dare to say it, she frugs her way through the psychic turmoil of the fast-moving, modern, push-button world of America today. For extra credit, try stylistically doing the pony through your own past.

5. Can you name any other depressed, alcoholic women novelists or screenwriters? Were any of them asked to do a Blackglama ad? Why didn't they ask Noona? How much worse than Lillian Hellman could she have looked?

6. Referring to your thesaurus, compile a list of all the words Eskimos have no words for; i.e., there are 200 words for "ice," but not one for "antifreeze." No fair asking your Eskimo friends. If you happen to be an Eskimo, move on to the next question. Better yet, move on to the next chapter.

7. Ascribing human characteristics to animals is known as anthropomorphism. Explain how Noona employs this as a literary device in "Ballad." Give other examples of anthropomorphism. We'll give you one to start you off—*Cats.* Have you seen *Cats* yet? Take it from us, don't bother. It's just a bunch of actors who apparently never saw a

real cat in their lives wearing costumes that look like they were made by the whisk-broom department of Lighthouse for the Blind crawling around the stage yowling. And at $45.00 a ticket, who are they kidding—you could have more fun at the ASPCA, and they take Master-Card, too. Sheesh! T. S. Eliot must be spinning like a top.

8. Rivalry between brothers has been a theme in literature since Cain killed Abel. John Steinbeck used it in *East of Eden;* Sam Shepard used it in *True West.* Would Noona's work have been more successful if she had

called it, say, *North by North Pole?*

9. What was there about Eskimo sex practices that attracted Swifty Leibowitz to Noona? Do you think Noona's depiction of sex was influenced at all by the fact that in her culture Eskimo women sometimes had to wait years for some lost member of Admiral Byrd's party to wander into their igloo and freshen up the gene pool?

10. What is the moral of Noona's story? How many words does it have? Does this seem unlucky to you?

Amid the family poplar grove, teen diarist Anaïs Zit daydreams in her favorite spot, pondering such perpetual twizzlers as life, death, and why you always mount a horse on the left, even though you're worried that you might be investigated by the House Un-American Activities Committee for doing it.

Anaïs Zit
1941–1975

THIS young authoress was truly a child of her times, the inhumanly repressive fifties.[1] As a sensitive adolescent, her blossoming sexuality was thwarted, slapped around, and forced to take a long walk off a short pier by such confusing social phenomena as the McCarthy hearings, Allen Ginsberg, and the "Ed Sullivan Show."

In an era when the Mickey Mouse Club brought about the popularity of names like Cubby and Karen, this gifted prose virtuoso was saddled with the name "Anaïs." The kindest of the nicknames which followed her from schoolhouse to schoolhouse was unfortunately an epithet that derived from the lowliest portion of the human anatomy.[2] She was no luckier in surname: "Zit," an Ellis Island derivation of Zitowsky, which, in her case, was all too often linked with the word "face."

While her classmates rocked around the clock to Bill Haley and the Comets, Anaïs stayed off the guys' blue suede shoes[3] by retreating to the seclusion of the stable, where she would spend hours writing in her diary.

Her parents misinterpreted her creative fervor as a morbid pastime. Caught up in the frenzy of psychiatric treatment that possessed many ordinary people in the fifties, they dragged her to every psychiatrist in the tri-state area, of which there were only two (both named Glickman). After several sessions with the first Dr. Glickman, she was pronounced cured.

Subsequently, her mother, finding Volume VIII of her journal under some blankets in the tack room, marched her off to the second Dr.

[1]Not since the thirties and forties had there been a decade this inhumanly repressive, particularly to youth.

[2]That's "anus" to you, asshole.

[3]Not meant literally to refer to footwear; reference to early chart-topping tune by Carl Perkins.

Glickman, who seized her diaries and then contacted his publisher. The publisher immediately recognized the incredible depth of feeling and honest evocation of girlhood in these naïve pages and brought out a special airport edition.

Publication was a traumatic experience for Anaïs, especially when one wag at her high school got hold of a copy of the book and scrawled "Hank, Hank, oh Hank" all over her locker. Anaïs stopped going to school but continued to write even more feverishly than before, filling looseleaf notebook after notebook with her candid revelations and even more explicit drawings.

During this fertile period, she completed two unpublished novels, which enjoyed a widespread underground circulation amongst other young girls who collected horse figurines, *Bonjour Misty* and *Aimez-Vous Oats?* So enduring is their literary reputation that the second Dr. Glickman is still anxious to obtain the airport rights, particularly the rights to O'Hare Airport, where one plane lands every thirty seconds, thus providing hundreds, if not thousands, of potential book buyers.

After Hank's death, however, Anaïs became more and more reclusive, refusing to come out of Hank's stall until someone offered her a carrot. Her parents moved away, and she might have disappeared from public view forever had she not been spotted in 1974 by an itinerant cover talent scout for *Ms.* magazine.

Today, the work of Anaïs Zit is considered representative of the "stream of consciousness" school of twentieth century writing. In her case, the stream flows inexorably into the ocean of feminine sensibility, whose emotional tides, as we all know, are governed by the moon.[4] The ebb and flow of her phrases seem to lull the reader into a dreamlike state which often lasts for days, during which the reader is unable to leave the house or even brush her hair.

The 2,000 volumes of her diary, of which Volume XIII is excerpted here, provide a provocative insight into the female heart. As Anaïs meanders along the path between simile and metaphor, she unwittingly illuminates the feelings of nearly all women, except for a few freaks and phonies, and some inner-city ghetto dwellers who think a horse is just a zebra without stripes. As we read this profoundly moving document, we cannot help but read. Thank you, Anaïs, Anaïs.

---

[4]At least until menopause. After that, we're not sure what governs the feminine sensibility, but some women over fifty have been known to burst into tears at an increase in the price of pet food.

The Diary of Anaïs Zit: Volume XIII

I SKIM the mists of consciousness; my eyes fly open suddenly, the room comes into focus. I find myself awake. I am not always awake, but I am now. Lying here being awake makes me wonder what it feels like lying here being asleep. Not much different, I suppose, except that in one instance I am awake and in the other I am asleep. Some people, mainly my mother, have warned me that I am sleeping my life away,[1] but I need to sleep. Sleeping replenishes me. I must sleep. I will sleep.

Soon. But not now. Now I gaze upwards, searching for what always appears to be there. Indeed, it is there—my ceiling. A random thought strikes me. I wonder what would happen if my room were turned upside down (like my life is sometimes) and my ceiling became my floor. What would happen to the light fixture? I ask myself. And then I answer myself, because there is no one else there. Unless a hole were cut for it, who could deny that it would make a big bump in the rug? Even though I am not familiar with interior decorating, I understand it.

I feel bored, then titillated. I feel my nightgown stretched taut over my prepubescent body. A crack in the ceiling brings to mind Hank's classic Grecian profile. I find myself touching myself. My petals open. I feel better, then worse.

My gaze takes me abruptly to the reassuring sight of Hank's shoes, which I have hung on the wall for good luck.

Today I brought Hank a treat. An apple, the fruit with which Eve tempted Adam. If only Hank and I could live in our own garden of Eden.

---

[1] Most people do, in fact, sleep their lives away. After years of study, scientists have concluded that the average person spends one-third of his/her life in bed. Those with Magic Motion beds spend two-thirds. And if you had one, you'd be asleep right now.

Here there is always June. And Hank's work. I keep telling myself I must understand this. After all, where would I be without my secret writing?

Nonetheless, today I feel that Hank senses my innermost thoughts. He, too, would like to escape with me to another world. But today our world is this apple. Carefully, I take the first bite. Hank needs no further invitation. His lips part to reveal his large, even, white teeth. Hungrily, he snatches the forbidden fruit from my palm and eagerly consumes it. We are joined in a union of sensual pleasure.

I fear his eyes.[2] They are so large, impossibly large. Enormous eyes, exaggerated eyes, impossible eyes. Impossibly clear, transparent. Impossibly transparent. Clearly impossible. And yet they are possible, because there they are, one on each side of his head.

Then June came, all in red, in a stunning riding outfit which I had never seen before. How I admire and dislike her all at once. Even though she has the most boyfriends of any girl in her class, she won't leave Hank alone. Hank was startled by her new outfit. I sense that red frightens him.[3] June is so insensitive. Yet I envy her self-absorption. She'll never know how often she comes between Hank and his work.

Now she offers Hank some sugar. He gobbles up her superficial treat like a child eating candy. I wish June would stop bringing Hank sugar. It's bad for his teeth. On the other hand, how can I deny Hank these simple pleasures? After all, he doesn't smoke or drink.

I love to watch Hank work. His concentration is complete and total. How admirably he plows ahead, determined to cover as much ground as possible every day. I think I like him best in harness. I wish I were as singleminded about my writing as Hank is about his work. Maybe if I wore blinders.

[2]Fear of eyes is a not-uncommon phobia, known as "eyephobia." Eyephobics are easy to spot, because they will never look you in the eye and often wear dark glasses at night, although they are frequently confused with shy people and rock stars.

[3]Fear of red is an equally common phobia, known as "redphobia."

I saw Hank nuzzle June today. She stroked his neck with great tenderness. She has him eating out of her hand. I cannot trust Hank. He is too generous with his affections, but then some feel that is the charm of the rake. Sometimes I wish Hank were a Clydesdale.

Wrote three letters to Hank today. Didn't mail any. People would think I was mad. I am mad. Mad like the poet.[4] Oh, Hank, what a child I am, and yet how ancient! I have no use for the petty transactions of daily life. Give me the eternal verities anytime. June, on the other hand, is as shallow as a fish pond. But I do not envy her propensity for trivia, only her pink angora sweater, which doesn't look so good on her anyway. Not with her coloring. When I told Hank my theories about June, he only snorted.

I go to see Dr. Glickman. His room reminds me of Hank's. Both are dark and warm. I want to sit astride the arm of the couch, but the doctor would prefer I lie down. We talk about my studies and my parents. I only want to discuss Hank. But Dr. Glickman forces me into the past.

Dr. Glickman: Can you recall any particularly happy moments in your childhood?

Me: When I was very little, Daddy would take off his belt and . . .

Dr. Glickman: And beat you?

Me: No, that was Mommy. He would use his belt to tie a pillow to his back. Then he would get down on all fours and take me for a ride. It was the only time we were close.

(My petals opened as I related this story to Dr. Glickman and are opening, even now, as I set it down in my journal.)

---

[4]In her controversial essay, "Those Crazy Authors" (Tenure Press, 1962), Dr. Cynthia Corrasable Bond stipulates that Zit is referring here to Ezra Pound. Other Zit experts maintain that the teenage diarist is referring to all poets except Ogden Nash, who was definitely not mad, just slightly silly.

WHOOOAAA!!! WILBUR!!!

SEPTE ER 23

2 good
2 be
4 gotten !

Photograph courtesy of Dr. Glickman (the second one).

In the adolescent musings of teen diarist Anaïs Zit, we find an occasional drawing which gives us a startling glimpse into her tortured psyche. The drawings themselves are not without merit and indicate that Anaïs was a fan of both Aubrey Beardsley and *Turf* Magazine.

Hank is so taciturn. He will never say what he feels, but I know he feels deeply. His placid exterior conceals a torrent of emotion. Considering the few conversations we have we are amazingly in tune. Hank is always there for me.

I go to see the other Dr. Glickman. His room reminds me of Hank's and of the first Dr. Glickman's. I want to talk about Hank. He wants to talk about the first Dr. Glickman. We settle on the past.

Dr. Glickman: Can you think of something in your childhood that made you particularly unhappy?

Me: Yes, when Daddy said I was too heavy to play the pillow game any more.

I'm struck by a frightening thought. Did June ever play the pillow game? Probably not.

If my mother were to see this diary, she would ridicule me. She thinks I should channel my efforts into more productive outlets, like algebra homework. But can I trust anyone who married my father? I will not give up my writing. I feel that my feelings cannot be felt unless they are committed to paper so I can feel them again later.

Today for the first time Hank and I go as far as Pine Bluff. The sun comes out from behind a cloud. Sweat glistens on Hank's forehead, and his hair tosses in the wind. He looks over his shoulder at me with the sidelong glance which never fails to stir me.

Then I confess that I have omitted my panties, and Hank shudders in delight, as if to say "Whoa, Wilbur."

He is so sensitive to my every need that all I have to do is tighten the muscles in my thighs and he varies his movements accordingly. A scream of ecstasy rises in my throat, and I dig my heels into Hank's sides. It is all Hank needs to take me to another plateau.

My breath is coming in short pants, like a Boy Scout. Hank moves rhythmically, faster and faster. The wind on my cheeks cools the hot flush of my desire. I burn, I freeze, I burn. Faster, faster, faster we climb until we reach the peak. My petals open. One thought keeps running through my mind: Clip-clop, clip-clop, clip-clop, clip-clop, clip-clop, clip-clop, clippety-clop. Clop.

So there, June.

You are my only friend, dear diary. Through you, I seem to feel that I exist, both asleep and awake. With you I have shared the things that are most important to me: riding, riding equipment, pictures of riding, riding outfits, riding crops, riding trails, oats, horses with blazes and whiskers on kittens, bright copper kettles and warm woolen mittens, brown paper packages tied up with string. These are a few of my favorite things.[5]

I seem to have run out of paper. Tomorrow I start Volume XIV of this lifelong adventure in thought. For now, dear diary, Abyssinia.

[5]Oddly enough, these are also a few of the singing Trapp family's favorite things, despite the fact that they grew up in Switzerland, where most people's favorite things are chocolate, cheese, cuckoo clocks, and chocolate-covered cheese-flavored cuckoo clocks that come in little bags that you can buy at the duty-free shop in the Geneva airport.

For Further Study

1. Compare and contrast the Mc-Carthy hearings and the "Ed Sullivan Show."

2. Did Allen Ginsberg like Cubby better than Karen? Extrapolate.

3. Who is Hank? How is Hank hung? What was the significance of this in the life of teenage girls of the 1950s? Will this ever change?

4. What resulted from Anaïs Zit's psychotherapy, and how did it affect her writing? Do you think June ever played the pillow game? Did you play the pillow game?

5. Do you think society has benefited from the writing of Anaïs Zit, or would we have gained more if she had gone on to become an algebra whiz, as her mother desired? Which occupation pays more?

6. What are a few of Anaïs Zit's favorite things?

7. Besides Hank, who was Anaïs Zit's best friend? Wouldn't you like to have a best friend like that? You could, you know. Oh? You don't want one? Too much work for you? Don't want to put too much energy into a relationship because you've been burned so many times before? Don't you think this is a relationship where only you can do the burning?

8. What was Anaïs Zit talking about when she referred to her "petals"? Was she an innocent, average, prepubescent American, or was she just another tart like Lolita?

9. Did Dr. Glickman violate professional ethics by publishing the diaries of Anaïs Zit, or was he simply helping her fulfill an unexpressed desire? Is a psychiatrist supposed to fulfill your unexpressed desires for you, or should you express them yourself? What if you are a paranoid schizophrenic who can't express yourself? Wouldn't you secretly want someone to express your desires for you? Or would you rather wallow in your despair, sharing private demons with only a piece of paper? If that's the case, then you're a sick individual and should seek professional help immediately.

10. If June is "as shallow as a fish pond," describe your mental picture of this particular fish pond. Now go jump in it.

"Going my way?" Beat writer Camille Cassidy Cassady seems to be asking. Not that it mattered. Although she often posed for photographs hitchhiking, she never really accepted a ride. Oddly enough, this was one Beatnik who always got carsick!

Camille
Cassidy Cassady
1933–1968

WHEN *On the Rag* first came out in 1958, reviewers hardly knew what to make of it. Partly because they were preoccupied with the emergence of 3-D movies and what effect they would have on the publishing industry,[1] but mainly because they were disgusted by the character, the subject matter, and the title, they refused to imbue *On the Rag* with literary credence. One critic, in fact, dismissed it as a hysterical chronicle of the unchecked emotional outpourings of psychologically unstable women. "It's no wonder their men always stayed out on the road," self-appointed guardian of English literature Elliott D. Whiteout wrote in *Dissentary*. "I wouldn't come home either to this disagreeable gaggle of unleashed zasus."

This controversy took on larger proportions when the *New York Times* reviewed the book on the front page of the Sunday book review, describing it as "further evidence that the Beat Generation[2] exists."

Camille Cassidy Cassady was born Camille Cassidy in 1933 in Pittsburgh, Pennsylvania, and for some strange reason always took great

---

[1] 3-D movies had absolutely no effect on the publishing industry, except that a few book editors who went to them when they should have been reading manuscripts got headaches.

[2] The term "beat" has long been the subject of heated debate. Some believe it means beaten down or tired, as in "Man, am I beat." Others maintain it derives from the well-known street expression "Put an egg in your shoe and beat it." In the riveting yet overexposed video of Michael Jackson's chart-topping tune, "Beat It" appears to mean "Get out of here," "Get over it," and "I did it my way," to refer to yet another chart-topping tune. Still others feel it has something to do with masturbation. Jack Kerouac himself explained that it was just another way of saying "holy" and came from the word "beatific," or blessed, as in the oft-quoted Biblical phrase "Bless them, Father, for they know not what they write." (*Lavoris*, II, 4.) Arguments about the precise interpretation of this troublesome expression continue to rage at literary cocktail parties all up and down the eastern seaboard, and more than one tenured professor has been seriously injured in the ongoing lexicological melee, leading to the theory that the term comes from "beaten up." If you want to know our opinion, it beats us.

delight in quizzing new acquaintances on the subject of "What three rivers converge at Pittsburgh?"[3] Her pubescent years were filled with the torment of unusually acute menstrual cramps, thus enabling her to miss years of gym class, during which time she hung out in the school washroom, reading, smoking cigarettes, and starting fires in the wastebasket. It was here that she first displayed her antisocial behavior and cultivated an interest in such figures as Kafka, Spengler, and Maynard G. Krebs.

Whoops!

At New York University, she was attracted to the bohemian world of coffeehouses, where she also spent most of her time in the washroom. She first met beat poet Allen Ginsberg in the ladies' room of the Kettle of Fish, when he asked her if her stall had any paper. They became fast friends. Ginsberg commemorated her in his celebrated beat anthem, "Howl," as the person who handed him a beer after he jumped off the Brooklyn Bridge.

The young, vivacious speedfreak Camille soon became a popular character on the "Beat Scene," especially because, unlike many of Allen's friends, she had her own apartment. She was famous for her "subway chili" in which one lucky guest would receive a subway token in his or her serving of chili.

To know Allen was to know Neal Cassady, an exuberant drifter who personified the unfettered American spirit of the open range and the open fly. To know Neal and Allen was to know Jack. Allen, who at the time was wrestling with his homosexuality and more often than not getting pinned to the mat, had a crush on Neal and Jack. Nevertheless, avant-garde thinkers that they all were, they dealt with their emotions in a mature fashion: by getting dead drunk and falling down a lot. Sometimes they fell on each other. Other times they fell on Camille.

Neal was thrilled by the coincidence of his and Camille's last names, which differed by only one letter. "Cassidy Cassady," he would chant over and over. "Ah! Hmm! Wow!" He thought the sound of the two names had a jazz beat, like scat singing. Because of this fascination, Camille had no difficulty convincing Neal to marry her.

Immediately after the ceremony, to celebrate their honeymoon, Neal took a bus to California to visit an old girlfriend.[4] Camille took a train

[3]For you geography buffs, the rivers are the Ohio, the Allegheny, and the Monongahela.

[4]According to Camille, "They were just friends. Nothing heavy."

to Long Island to visit Jack.[5] Jack's mother took a broom to Camille. Allen wrote a poem[6] about the whole thing, altering the principal characters slightly by making Camille into a Mexican madonna, Jack into a volcano, and Jack's mother into Kali, the many-armed Hindu goddess of destruction.

This stormy beginning to the Cassadys' married life was typical of their ongoing relationship, as revealed in both their works. However, Camille's railroad flat remained the eye of the hurricane, a place of refuge for all the "sad gone lost lonely chicks" whose men were invariably on the road. Despite the pain that these prolonged absences evidently caused Camille Cassady, the student of literature can only be grateful, because as a result of this enforced separation from the man (or men) in her life, Camille had plenty of time to write. Of course, she could never work out a really good schedule and spent more time washing out her leotards than she did writing, but if any men other than Allen Ginsberg had been around all the time, she would have written even less.

The final break between Camille and the beats came when she revealed in an interview that Jack Kerouac not only was a bad driver, he didn't even have a license. Jack cried, Neal refused to speak to her, and Allen told her she had "done a Bad Thing." The trio then took off for Mexico, but only made it as far as St. Louis, Missouri. When Camille refused to wire them bus fare, the circle of rebellious visionaries was broken, never to be mended again.

Shortly afterwards, Camille Cassady was going downstairs to answer a phone call in the drugstore below her apartment when she slipped on loose carpeting and broke her neck. Her last words are said to have been, "I'm dying. Don't accept the charges." Unfortunately, it was too late: the druggist already had. Thus, by an ironic twist of fate, the literary world was the poorer, and the phone company the richer, for Camille Cassady's death. Not since no one had saved Zelda Fitzgerald the waltz had there been such a tragic loss to the world of letters.

Camille Cassady's prose style was a veritable bouillabaisse of words, a ratatouille of adjectives, a cassoulet of conjunctions, all simmering on the hot plate[7] of her imagination. During the years when women were

[5]Nothing heavy there either.

[6]*Sitting Shiva*, City Lights, 1951.

[7]Or iron, as the case may be, cf. the text.

all-too-often minor characters in the literary drama, she made it accept-able for female writers to describe in detail all the dreary domestic squabbles of their daily lives. Her legacy lives on in the work of others.[8] Yet hers was the first authentic whiny voice of womanhood, enslaved by the moon.

[8]Viz., Nora Ephron.

Rare photos of beat writer Camille Cassady at work. She often used marijuana for inspiration, claiming that it helped her find her way out of metaphors and into similes.

On the Rag
Part Five

THE DUKE[1] had just finished taking the A train uptown on the record player, and I was drifting off into a familiar tea-induced haze when I heard a violent pounding on the door. Someone was calling my name, "Camille, Camille!" I figured Maggie forgot her keys again. It was the third night in a row, but I knew she had been to a crazy rent party[2] and probably had copped some bennies.[3] So I decided to get up and let her in.

"Wow, man, I'm glad you're up," Maggie said. "I just took twelve uppers. I thought maybe it would bring on my period.[4] I'm three weeks late."

"Oh no. Not again," I said. "Got any bennies left?"

"Nah. I popped them all. Do I look like I'm pregnant?"

"How could you take them all? Don't you even have a cigarette?" That slut had been crashing at my pad rent-free for six months, and she couldn't even save me one Benzedrine. This pad was the best pad I've ever had, and I've had some good pads, thousands[5] of them as a matter of fact. There was a table, some pretty spackled linoleum on the floor and on the counter, a lamp with a busted shade, a mattress on the floor, and a cracked mirror on the wall; it was delightful. The three of us lived

---

[1] For those readers who are laboring under the misapprehension that this refers to the Duke of Earl, it doesn't.

[2] Party where guests pay an entry fee in order to cover the host's rent. Nobody throws rent parties these days; we can't imagine why, since it sounds like such a good idea. In fact, we're planning to try it next month.

[3] Slang for Benzedrine, a drug favored by beats, truck drivers, housewives, and air traffic controllers. Its side effects include sleeplessness; euphoria; a feeling of being the best at everything you do, whether it's writing, driving, controlling air traffic, or picking lint-balls off your sweater; and a tendency to write in long run-on sentences.

[4] The ceaseless quest for "the period" ("the curse," "the monthlies," "my friend") is a recurring theme that flows intermittently through all of feminine literature (and feminine hygiene). In *On the Rag* it is as vivid a symbolic device as Ahab's quest for the elusive white whale in Melville's *Moby Dick*.

[5] Camille Cassidy did not mean that she had literally lived in thousands of "pads"; this is an instance of the hyperbole common to "beat" writers, of which you will find literally thousands of examples throughout the rest of Cassady's work.

there quite comfortably, although we had trouble with our washing schedule. It was a wonderful pad and we knew it; nobody had ever seen a pad like it. But I couldn't stay angry at Maggie for long, with her mad Modigliani mane and her Picasso smile. She was the epitome of crazy knocked-up American[6] womanhood, and I knew that no matter how much she bugged me, I would never kick her out.

Just then Maggie dragged the record needle across my Ellington, and I screeched louder than the machine. It was a nightmare to be in such a small apartment with Maggie when she was in this state. I knew the routine. Now she would start washing the dishes, dusting, sweeping, and rearranging the few sad sticks of furniture. She would have cleaned her way clear across America if she could have.

Sure enough, Maggie began washing the dishes. The clattering of the pots and pans woke Marylou, who stumbled out wearing only a T-shirt, panties, and crazy pincurls. "Man, these cramps are killing me," she said. "It's a drag being a chick."

"Tell me about it," said Maggie from the sink. "You got cramps you don't want. I want cramps that I don't have. Ain't life a bitch?"

I knew what she meant. I was five days late myself. Together we yearned for that first rush of hot blood from the velvet portals of the soft source, the beckoning furrows in which the seed of life is sown, only to be rejected every twenty-eight[7] days if you're lucky or not Catholic. There we were, three children of the earth, wide awake in the sweet American night, begging the mysterious moon to perform its sorcery and take us for a ride on the red cotton pony, except for Marylou, who was ready to dismount.

Bang! Blam! Bang![8] More banging at the door. There was a phone call for me in the drugstore downstairs. The old guy who ran the place had to come all the way up the stairs yelling, and puffing like hell from

[6]Cassady and her group of fellow rebellious visionaries, despite their rebellion against American society, were constantly tipping the Hatlo hat to their American roots. There are literally thousands of references to "American" and "America" in *On the Rag*. This makes sense, because Camille Cassady was, after all, an American living in America and had never been to Europe. Nor did she ever go, although she did get wildly excited about leaving to join Jack Kerouac and William Burroughs in Tangiers once, but they returned to the States before she could find someone to sublet her "pad."

[7]Although Camille Cassady was vague about dates, times, birthdays, and everything else involving numbers, tending to refer to anything over three as "innumerable" (see Footnote 4), she always remembered the exact number of days in her monthly cycle.

[8]An example of onomatopoeia, a favored device of "beat" writers, who liked to make clicking noises with their mouths while they wrote. This probably accounts for Miriam Makeba.

his asthma. He always threatened he wouldn't do it again, but he always did, probably because Maggie was banging him, *bang! blam! bang!*[9] That always brought on an asthma attack, too. I felt sorry for the guy in his sad[10] old ratty sweater. No matter what he did, life always took his breath away.

I ran down. The call was collect from Paris, Illinois. It was Neal again. He was off on one of his crazy road trips, meeting mad[10] people and having a wild time. He really dug the road because it took him to the America that he had to know, with its beat cowboys, grape-eating hobos, dusty Mexes, holy derelicts, sullen Okies, gay sailors, sad Negroes, happy Negroes, all the crazy types who live in this land of the free. They thought Neal was a real gone cat, and they were right. He was gone most of the time.

But here was his voice again, coming to me across the plains. "Hey, babe, is your heart still beating for me?" He was trying to sweet-talk me, but I knew he wanted something.

"Neal, do you realize what time it is?" I asked him.

"Aw, honey, you weren't sleeping, were you? You haven't slept since I've known you."

"But I might have been sleeping, and if I had been, you would've woken me up."

"Listen, doll, I just called 'cause I missed your sweet face."

Neal could be really romantic sometimes, and I kicked myself for having blown up at him.

"I need to ask you a favor," he said. "Remember that guy I was telling you about who took me and Jack to the whorehouse in Paris?"

"Paris, France?"

"Paris, Illinois. Where I am right now. Remember that one-legged guy? What was his name? I need to find him right now."

"Even if I remembered, what the hell makes you think I'd tell you?"

"Hold on, honeycakes. It's not for me," he said in his calmest voice. "It's for Jack. It's absolutely essential that I get Jack a girl. You know how sad he gets. If he gets any sadder, he'll bugger me." He laughed his maniacal laugh, like the laugh of a radio maniac.

---

[9]Fucking doesn't sound anything like this.

[10]"Sad" and "mad" were Camille Cassady's favorite adjectives, partly because they characterized the wild mood swings common to the "beat" experience, but mainly because they were easy to type.

These candid snapshots show Camille and her friends enjoying themselves in a typical "beat" pad. LEFT: Irene Schwartz, the model for "Maggie"; Camille; and Joan Krupsak, on whom "Marylou" was based. Camille has obviously been working hard.

RIGHT: The same trio has been joined by "Bongo Pete" Yankovich, uncle of "Weird Al" Yankovich. They are shown here enjoying pizza, a mainstay of the beat diet.

I was swayed by the power of his logic. Life was like a bottle of beer to Neal, and it was meant to be shared. I said the one-legged guy's name was either Panzo or Pancho,[11] and his number was either 555-4511 or 555-6731. Neal was ecstatically grateful.

"Is everything straight between us in the deepest and most wonderful depths of our souls, dear darling?"

We hadn't had anything straight between us for months, but I let it go. With Neal, you had to let most things go or he'd be gone. Of course, he was gone most of the time anyway.

[11] Professor Melvin Wopat, Chairman of the English Department at Oberlin College and noted homosexual, was the first to give Camille Cassady's work any literary credence whatsoever, and even then he referred to *On the Rag* as a "flimsy tissue of childish exaggerations." According to Wopat in his landmark essay "Of Men, the Moon and Madness in the Work of Camille Cassidy Cassady" (Tenure Press, 1978), the use of the name "Panzo or Pancho," i.e., "Pansy" indicates that Camille knew all along about Neal and Jack. Of course Wopat *would* say that, the old faggot!

He said goodbye with promises of faithfulness forever and a request for clean underwear, socks, and some salami[12] sandwiches to be sent to his next stop on the road.

Walking up the sad stairs to the pad, I felt lonely. I was lost in the beat and evil days that come to young women in their twenties whose periods are late and whose men are never home.

I couldn't help but wonder about Neal and Jack. They spent so much time together on the road, and when they weren't together on the road, they spent all their time talking about the experiences they had together on the road. And when they weren't talking, they were wrestling.

Jack once told me about a recurring fantasy. When he was a kid and rode in cars, he used to imagine that he held a big scythe in his hand and cut down all the trees and posts and even sliced every hill that zoomed past the window. And according to Jack, Neal had the same fantasy, only his scythe was bigger, and I believe there was some mention of "throbbing poles."[13] Somehow this summed up "IT"[14] for them and made them hot and excited. Their friend Allen once told me that they had an unusual love for each other, and he was pretty unusual himself. Come to think of it, maybe they were all a bunch of queers.

Upstairs, I found Maggie still washing dishes. The dishes were endless, like the road. She had worked her way through the dishes in the sink and had started in on the clean ones—it was a holy rite, a pure act of joyous reverence.

That evening the pad was a sinister place. When you turned on the light, even the roaches were too sad to move. It was mysterious, and I felt awful and sad as I smashed them. I couldn't breathe. I felt as though I had to get out, but I was paralyzed. It was the saddest pad I'd ever known, and I'd known thousands of them.

Marylou was hunched over the crazy table, working feverishly on her Chianti-bottle candle holder. For weeks now she had carefully melted crayons and let the wax drip down the sides of the bottle, creating layer after layer of wax drippings as colorful and as varied as the teeming streets of the American continent. Nobody could drip wax like Marylou;

[12]Back off, Wopat!

[13]Take it down a thousand, Wopat, you have a filthy mind!

[14]"IT" summed up everything for them. According to the "beats," everyone has their own version of "IT"; in other words, Papa may have, Mama may have, but God bless the child that's got his own.

she was the most fantastic wax dripper in the world. She could empty a wine bottle, slam it down, jam a candle into it, light it, grab the crayon box, open it, slip a crayon out before you could say "Burnt Ochre," rip the paper off the crayon, melt it down *plop-plop, drippety-drop-drip,* directing that melted wax like the mad artist that she was, grab another crayon, strip, melt, drop; working like that for eight to sixteen hours at a stretch in her crazy pincurls and torn t-shirt and beat furry slippers, and all the while Billie Holiday's sweet sad smooth harmonies were urging her on. She was hoping that the guy who owned the spaghetti joint down the street would buy her candle holders some day, when she finished them, and so was I, because there were fifty of them in the closet.

"Was that Neal or Jack on the phone?" Marylou asked.

I told her about the phone call, and asked her what she thought about Neal and Jack and their crazy madness. She told me that she'd thought there was something funny about them ever since the night the three of them took off their clothes and drove around naked until they ran out of gas.

"Jack couldn't keep his eyes off Neal's enormous dangle,"[15] Marylou said. "And I had the feeling he wanted to do more than just look."

"Do you think they ever did?" I asked.

"Oh, don't worry about it," Maggie said from the sink. "They're just maniacs. Nothing they say or do means anything."

Maggie had a beat way of putting things into perspective.

"I hope I'm not pregnant," Maggie went on. "But if I am, I hope it's a girl so she won't go on the road and run around knocking girls up."

I dug what she was saying, but I thought that if I was pregnant this time, I'd rather have a boy because they didn't have the sad, pleasure-destroying worry about getting knocked up.

There was a ruckus in the hall. Asthmatic Al from downstairs was shouting something about another phone call, as best as we could make out between the wheezes, and swearing that this was absolutely the last time. Maggie, hopped-up as she was, jumped at the chance to run up and down the stairs.

Marylou grabbed some more crayons and asked me to find some music that matched the colors she was now melting: the crazy yellows, the angry reds, the gone greens, the sad blues. I flipped on some Dizzy

---

[15]Common "beat" term for penis.

Gillespie because frankly all those colors on the candle were making me dizzy. Oh how I wished I were a Negro, or an Indian, or even a paraplegic,[16] anything but what I was, a "white woman" disillusioned and possibly pregnant. I longed to exchange worlds with the happy, true-hearted, smiling paraplegics of America, rich as they were with the mysterious wisdom of their simple chairbound existence.

While I was longing, Maggie bopped into the room, back from the phone call. This time it was Jack that had called, wanting to remind the chicks to put mustard on the sandwiches we were supposed to be sending, not mayonnaise. Last time they had to give the sandwiches away to some Negro pimps in a wretched bus station, just because they had mayonnaise on them.

After her late-night amphetamine snack, Maggie's motor was revved up and racing faster than Jack or Neal could possibly be driving. "Oh, man, man, man, these dumb dumb dumb men, they'll never change, how completely and how unbelievably dumb. They're such babies, I don't know how they ever get anywhere on their own. They remind me of my father. Sometimes I think they're responsible for everything that's wrong with the world. All they ever think about is kicks—and mustard." She quivered and shook and sweated with the excitement of her holy rage. I dug her righteous fury.

"Forget about it," said Marylou. "I'm *hungry,* I'm *starving, let's eat right now.*" Marylou was getting a potbelly from eating voracious meals out of boredom. I would have thought she was pregnant, but she complained too much about her cramps.

"I'll heat up the iron," I said. Our gas had been off for weeks, so we had worked out a system of heating up cans by turning the iron upside down on a coat hanger in the wastebasket. Maggie started rummaging through the cupboard, looking for something to heat up. Marylou went back to her candle holder.

"Are you sure you don't have any smokes?" I asked Maggie. She paid absolutely no attention to me. I found a butt in an ashtray and lit it up, even though it was covered with wax. The mention of food set my stomach gurgling. Through the open window the smells of the street floated in on the night air: the frying sausage from the Italian joint

I SURE COULD
GO FOR A PIZZA
RIGHT NOW.

[16]Camille Cassady harbored a childhood crush on Franklin Delano Roosevelt, secretly fantasizing that he was her real father, despite the fact that he was paralyzed from the waist down. Her fantasy, which she confessed in a letter to Allen Ginsberg, could possibly be true because her mother was in Washington once during his term of office. In any case, even though she did not herself know any paraplegics, she retained a lifelong admiration for them.

across the street, the fried rice from the Chinaman, and the refried beans from the chili shack on the corner—my ah-dream of American nightfood.

By this time Maggie had all the canned goods out on the counter and was poring over them. "Wow. Cling peach halves packed in their own syrup, brought here all the way from Tacoma, Washington, on boxcars over thousands of miles of roadbed, pulled by locomotives puffing clickety-clack, hurtling clackety-boom, whoo-whoo, past Walla Walla, Pocatello, Topeka, and Chagrin Falls.[17] And this creamed corn from Iowa, breadbasket of our nation, picked by sweating farmers and their sons in their holy, holey straw hats, creamed in the factories of Des Moines by milk-fed lovelies with honey-colored hair glistening on their forearms, packed by muscular, aching day laborers anxious for a smoke, shipped by rail, across amber waves of grain, across purple mountains' majesty to dusty warehouses where raggedy Negroes load them on trucks, vroom, vroom all the way to Mr. Hinkel's grocery store right here on this crazy street."[18]

"There is no Mr. Hinkel's on this crazy street," I told her. "That was at our last pad, and it was around the corner."

"Yes, yass, yes," she said, paying absolutely no attention to me. "Dig this," she said, holding up another can. "Whole, peeled tomatoes from California. Sac-ra-mento. Are you digging what that means, man? Are you, are you? These tomatoes are sac-red, man, the holiest of holies, they hold only truth in their perfect roundness, and they're red, a pure red, as red as ketchup. If I could just tell you all the thoughts I have about these tomatoes—that's what I'm trying to tell you, but not now, we have no time, and we all know time. Someday I have to tell you everything that's ever happened to me in my life . . ."

She patted her head and rubbed her stomach, all the while shaking her head jerkily up and down and sideways, nervously jiggling her leg at a hundred miles an hour, looking up and saying, "Umm, umm, yass, um." I suddenly realized that Maggie was the Idiot, the Imbecile, the

[17]Birthplace of the late Doug Kenney, brilliant humorist and cofounder of the *National Lampoon*. Oddly enough, Kenney died as a result of an accidental fall from a cliff in Hawaii, much to his chagrin.

[18]Unlike the classic wanderer heroes of American literature, such as Natty Bumppo, Ishmael, Huck Finn, and the Hardy Boys, Camille Cassady as the heroine of her own work never went anywhere except downstairs to the telephone. However, as a writer she was able to evoke an astonishingly vivid picture of the diversity of American life, which she had never seen but only heard about over the phone.

Saint, the one true beat among us. She was the HOLY GOOFUS![19] Suddenly she collapsed and went to sleep. It occurred to me that if Maggie had a kid, it would probably become the hip President of the United States.[20] Marylou and I heated up the tomatoes and ate them by candlelight. I was tired of life and it was a sad night.

It made me angry and sad that chicks everywhere in this sad universe, and for all I knew, on other planets, too, were controlled by the

[19]The foolish person who is nonetheless holy or saintly is a character that has been celebrated through the ages. The first recorded reference to "the holy fool" can be found in the Lascaux cave paintings, where one drawing depicts someone upside down on the back of a cow, dancing without any clothes on even though it was the Ice Age. A modern-day example of the "Holy Goofus" is Steve Martin.

LEFT: Some critics of *On the Rag* have claimed that you can't cook anything over an iron, but in fact this method of food preparation was not uncommon, as this photo of Camille Cassady attests: A classic example of art imitating life.
BELOW: On the other hand, sometimes life imitates art. After reading *On the Rag*, Marylou got the idea to sell drip candles in order to pick up some spare cappuccino money. This later had tragic consequences when she accidentally set fire to the Bank of America building in the 1960's, triggering yet another wave of imitations.

ebb and flow of life-juices in their mystic wombs. It occurred to me that if all the women who thought they were pregnant were laid end to end, they'd still be pregnant. I guess the world will never find peace until men fall at their women's feet and ask for their forgiveness. Neal had fallen at my feet many times, but he always passed out before he could ask for anything.

Maggie woke up as suddenly as she had collapsed. "It's all right, it's just kicks," she said. "You only live once. You might as well have a good time while you can."[21]

"You call this kicks?" Marylou asked. "Here we are, cooped up in this lousy pad, cooking dinner on an iron, wearing the same black turtle-neck sweater day after day, the same frayed huaraches, scrounging for butts, dripping this stupid wax, not knowing when or if the guys will come back, or how long they'll stay here before they're off on the road again. If we only had a car like they have, think what we could do."

"What do? Where go? What for?" asked Maggie.

"To the store to buy milk?" asked Marylou.

"You just don't get IT, do you?" Maggie exploded.

"Get what?" Marylou said.

"IT! IT! I tell you."

Suddenly I felt a warm gush between my legs. "I got IT," I yelled. And I did get it, only five days late, after millions of senseless nightmare visions. I realized that life was just a tedious race that no one wins. All the sweet nauseas were for naught. Nobody, nobody knows what's going to happen to anybody. Except for us women, with our intricate natural clockwork, which leads us to expect every month the comforting yet inconvenient visitation of a friend. My friend had arrived. Well, lack-a-mommy, I was on the rag again.

[20]Not if the kid turned out to be a Holy Goofus. In 1972, the American people forced Democratic Presidential candidate George McGovern to dump his Vice-Presidential running mate, Thomas Eagleton, on the grounds that he had received electroshock therapy, thus proving that they didn't want a buzz-bunny even a heartbeat away from the Presidency. We are still waiting for a hip President of the United States. Some people thought it was John F. Kennedy, but they were wrong. Talk to Daniel Ellsberg.

[21]This paragraph sums up the core of the "beat" philosophy, later adopted by a well-known beer manufacturer, which advised consumers to "grab for the gusto."

For Further Study

1. Define the term "beat." How has it evolved from Camille Cassidy Cassady to Michael Jackson Jackson? Is there an echo in the room? Compare and contrast Michael Jackson and Diana Ross. Who is better looking?

2. What was it about coffeehouses that made people stay up all night? Was Mrs. Olsen the original beatnik? What about Anna Maria Alberghetti? What role did Marcus Welby, M.D., play in the demise of the so-called "beat" scene?

3. In your view, is being "on the rag" merely a minor physical discomfort, a metaphor for the human condition, or a fucking drag anyway you look at it? Make a flow chart indicating which characters were on the rag and which weren't.

4. Do you ever feel the urge to hit the road, Jack, and not come back no more, no more? If Kerouac's first name had been different, would he have stayed home? If Camille's first name had been Jacqueline, would she have gone on the road herself?

5. Why did Camille identify with people in wheelchairs? Was it because they couldn't go anywhere, either?

6. On stiff construction paper, prepare a graph indicating the approximate size of Neal's "enormous dangle." Don't be afraid to use as many sheets as necessary.

7. Who is the "Holy Goofus"? Would you have bought or would you now buy a "Holy Goofus" muppet/doll/stuffed animal/video game/lunchbox/sexual aid? If not, do you know someone who would? If so, send $2.00 to "Holy Goofus Catalogue," Drawer H, Port Authority Terminal, New York City, New York. Enclose S.A.S.E.

8. What's the difference between mustard and mayonnaise? Compare and contrast using rye bread and an assortment of luncheon meats. For extra credit, repeat, substituting Miracle Whip and Pepperidge Farm sprouted wheat.

9. Is there a difference between "mad" and "crazy"? What do you think? Making up these stupid questions is driving us a) mad or b) crazy. Which one are you?

10. What is "it"? Who gets "it"? Did you get "it"? That's it.

Photo courtesy of UPI and the Abraham Lincoln Archive, Smithsonian Institution.

Marilyn Monroe was a fervent admirer of Abraham Lincoln, a man who rose to prominence from humble beginnings not unlike her own. When she first met Arthur Miller, he reminded her of Lincoln, perhaps due to the size of his nose, which she took as a promise of his greatness in other areas. Inevitably, she was disappointed, as was Mary Todd Lincoln. Perhaps the two of them are comparing notes in the big powder room in the sky.

Marilyn Monroe
1926–1962

NO QUESTION but that Marilyn Monroe is the most famous of all our authoresses; yet few are aware that she was an authoress at all. She was born Norma Jean Baker on June 1, 1926, in Los Angeles, California. A bank loan application which she filled out in later life gives her mother as Gladys Monroe Baker and her father as "a whole slew of people." After her mother was committed to a mental institution in her early childhood, Norma Jean was raised in an orphanage.

It was in the midst of that Dickensian environment that she began her literary career, seeking solace for her lonely, drab existence in the written word. Only allowed one sheet of paper a year, the resourceful and prolific little Norma Jean cadged stale slices of bread from her fellow orphans in order to record her inner thoughts, using grape jelly diluted with water as ink.[1]

She spent her adolescence in a succession of foster homes, continuing to turn to her writing whenever she felt abandoned and alone, which was all the time. In her early teens, she was momentarily distracted from the pursuit of literary excellence when she put on a sweater for the first time.[2] A few weeks later, she married Jim Dougherty, who kept her on a short leash attached to the stove. Their marriage dissolved when Dougherty was shipped overseas, and she managed to chew through the leash.

In 1946, Norma Jean bleached her hair, bought a sweater one size smaller, and signed with Twentieth-Century Fox as a contract player

---

[1]Unfortunately, since the orphans were also allowed only one meal a week, nothing remains of her early writings, save for a few crusts.

[2]It was a red sweater. In fact, several eyewitnesses attest to the fact that it was actually a cardigan worn backwards.

under the name Marilyn Monroe. She appeared in roles even smaller than her sweater in a number of films, including "Love Happy," with Groucho Marx, "All About Eve," with George Sanders, and "Asphalt Jungle," with a lot of sidewalk.

Shortly before the release of "Clash by Night," news of her nude calendar pose was leaked to the press, supposedly by studio flacks. The photo succeeded in convincing all and sundry that Marilyn was indeed a natural blonde. "Thank God for peroxide, Dear Diary," she confided to her diary, Dear Diary.

Her fame skyrocketed when she began dating baseball great "Joltin' Joe" DiMaggio, also known as the Yankee Clipper, whom she married in 1954. During this period, she made some of her best-known films, including "Gentlemen Prefer Blondes," "How to Marry a Millionaire," in which she perfected her famous breathy, wiggly style of acting, approximating the behavior of someone who has either just swallowed a medium-sized flying insect or had something nasty dropped down their back or both.

By 1956, DiMaggio was battin' zero with Marilyn, who divorced him, broke with Twentieth Century-Fox, and moved to New York, where for the first time in her adult life she dated men without tans. Some of them were even without subway tokens.[3] She began studying with Lee Strasberg at the Actors' Studio, where she made friends with Marlon Brando, James Dean, and Montgomery Clift.[4]

But her heavy date was a scrawny, balding, bespectacled Jewish guy from Brooklyn.[5] Arthur Miller and Marilyn were the Woody Allen and Diane Keaton of their time. Marilyn even started wearing glasses in imitation of Arthur, though she balked at neckties because she couldn't get them to lie flat.[6]

Meanwhile, Marilyn formed her own production company in partnership with Milton H. Greene, a fashion photographer. She made "Bus Stop," directed by Josh Logan, and talked about playing Grushenka in a film version of *The Brothers Karamazov,* an idea that appealed to her because she'd always wanted to have brothers.

[3]This never fazed Marilyn, who never had any trouble hailing a taxi, even at rush hour, probably as a result of her love of full billowy skirts and dislike of restricting undergarments.

[4]Marilyn never slept with Montgomery Clift, and could never figure out why.

[5]Points off for everyone who said "Neil Simon."

[6]Fortunately for the fashion world, this did not appear to be a problem for Diane Keaton.

After her marriage to Arthur Miller, Marilyn entered her most prolific period. Being married to a famous writer seemed to give Marilyn the stimulus she needed to pursue her own writing career, even if in secret. Arthur gave her one of his old typewriters, and she would bang away happily for hours, humming to herself, determined not to stop writing until she could tell by the silence emanating from Arthur's nearby study that he had given up any further attempt to work that day. She never showed anyone anything she had written, but she would call up friends and ask them how to spell the hard words, like "Dostoevsky."[7]

However, the newlyweds' writing idyll was interrupted by the demands of Marilyn's other career. The Millers left for England to make "The Prince and the Showgirl," with Laurence Olivier. Shooting was long and tedious because Marilyn couldn't remember her lines and was three or four months late to work every day. No one except Arthur knew it was because she'd been up all night writing. He wouldn't tell because he was several months late on a publisher's deadline himself[8] and felt it would make him look like an idiot[9] if it got out that the "dumb blonde" was writing more than he was.

Marilyn eventually returned to Hollywood, where she filmed "Let's Make Love," with Yves Montand (they did), and "Some Like It Hot," with Tony Curtis and Jack Lemmon (they didn't). While she was away, Arthur and his teenage secretary managed to complete the screen adaptation of "The Misfits," and the Millers went on location to Reno, Nevada, to make the film, directed by John Huston, with Clark Gable, Montgomery Clift, and Eli Wallach.[10]

Marilyn, driven by the true writer's instinct, naturally brought along her typewriter and continued to work, despite the scorching heat. She had become such a workaholic she resolved not to have sex unless she had completed her self-assigned task of 10,000 words a day. This was

[7]She couldn't ask Arthur, because he would just tell her to look it up. One Christmas he even went so far as to buy her a dictionary, but she never got the hang of it and merely used it to wedge her closet door open.

[8]Tell us about it, Arthur, we've all been there!

[9]He was right. It did.

[10]Rumor has it that Clark, Monty, and Marilyn all tempted fate by lighting their cigarettes on one match, and when they realized it and asked Eli Wallach to break the jinx by being the fourth, he refused. Another version has it that he agreed, but before he could do anything, the match went out. In yet another version, Marilyn dropped the match.

Drawing courtesy of Rosa Caliente.

Self-portrait of Marilyn Monroe discovered behind the chiffalrobe by her cleaning lady, Rosa Caliente, while she was looking for a diamond solitaire that Marilyn had thrown at Joe DiMaggio in a fit of rage when he told her that her ass looked like "two cats in a bag fighting." Oddly enough, singer-songwriter Paul Simon also made the same mysterious mental hookup between Joe DiMaggio's name and the phrase "Ku Ku kajew," only he spelled it differently.

especially difficult on days when she had to spend eight to ten hours in front of the camera.

Meanwhile, Arthur was having problems because, having given Marilyn the portable, he was stuck with the electric typewriter, and there were frequent blackouts due to the hotel's overloaded air-conditioning system.

A crew member[11] recalls, "There would be Marilyn, typing away in her old bathrobe with a kerchief tied round her head, no glamour at all, just an ordinary writing jill, happy as a clam—and there would be the

[11] Even if we hadn't made him up out of whole cloth anyway, this crew member would be dead now as a result of using the match that was spurned by Eli Wallach (and later getting altogether too friendly with Karen Silkwood), making his story, which of course is entirely apocryphal anyway, impossible to verify. Arthur Miller's lawyers please take note.

great Arthur Miller, all hot and bothered, running around lugging this enormous IBM machine, looking for a working outlet to plug it into."

Why couldn't Marilyn have let Arthur use "her" typewriter? "She used to plead with him to take it, just so he could keep from falling behind on the script rewrites. When you're on location for a picture, you're all in it together, and nobody knew that better than Marilyn. But, oh, no! That wouldn't satisfy the great man. He had to have his IBM Selectric. Anything else would have been a comedown. His ego wouldn't let him, even though it was best for everybody, for him, for Marilyn, for the picture. It was making her crazy."

Indeed, Marilyn was admitted to the Payne-Whitney Mental Clinic for a brief stay in the winter of 1960. Marilyn and Arthur Miller were granted a Mexican divorce on January 20, 1961, the day of John F. Kennedy's inauguration.[12] As a result of the eerie timing, Marilyn never managed to forgive Arthur for making her miss the chance to see Carl Sandburg, one of her heroes, on TV.

After that, Marilyn split her time between the Coasts. She reportedly had a brief affair with Frank Sinatra and resumed seeing Joe DiMaggio. Of course, nothing could induce her to abandon her writing, which became more and more important to her, especially as she got older and her upper arms began to sag just a touch. She got up the courage to show some of her work to DiMaggio, who said he liked it, even though he had trouble with some of the big words.[13] "She was writing a play about her life with Arthur," he revealed years later. "It was going to be called *Before the Fall*."

Unfortunately, once again, her movie career came between Marilyn and the first love of her life, the written word. She returned to Los Angeles to begin shooting "Something's Got to Give." After completing the famous nude swimming scenes, Marilyn caught a chill,[14] and filming came to a halt. Following complex negotiations involving a lot of yelling, the film was scheduled to resume in the fall, after her co-star, Dean Martin, had fulfilled his nightclub engagements.

Then, on August 5, 1962, Marilyn Monroe was found dead in the bedroom of her Brentwood home. Her death, which remains shrouded in mystery, has been attributed to various causes, including a drug overdose, an FBI plot, and terminal cellulite. Whatever the reason, Mar-

[12]Weird, huh?

[13]This was before he made the Mr. Coffee deal and became much more hyped-up.

[14]No doubt from standing around without wet clothes on.

ilyn's secret literary output, by this time totalling millions of words and hundreds and thousands of pages—if you can call cocktail napkins, used Kleenex, and old Tampax wrappers pages—might have died with her if it were not for the killer instincts of former L.A. coroner-to-the-stars Thomas Noguchi, who salvaged the manuscript and hung on to it until the price was right. We have to thank both him and noted necro-journalist Lawrence Schiller, who bought it from him, for having the foresight to preserve it for posterity.

Schiller packaged a book-length section of the original manuscript, including the chapter excerpted here, together with never-before-published candid photos of Norman Mailer and others, and sold it to unsuccessful Presidential candidate, born-again Christian, and T&A mogul Larry Flynt. The book, which is to appear this fall, will be edited by Albert Goldman.

The film of the book, from a concept by Allan Carr, is being produced by Allan Carr, scripted by Harvey Fierstein, and directed by Bob Fosse. It will star Kurt Russell as Norman Mailer, Jacqueline Bisset as Jacqueline Kennedy, Blair Brown as the young Jacqueline Kennedy, and Martin Sheen as all the other Kennedys, including Rose. The part of Marilyn herself will be played by Mariel Hemingway, who is having herself surgically made over for the role.[15] The world anxiously awaits the results.

In the meantime, we are lucky to have an indelible picture of Marilyn's world "in her own write." The verve and vivacity of her prose style more than compensate for her slim grasp of grammar, tense, and syntax. In fact, so adept is she at evoking the seething snakepit where the powerful and famous of Hollywood and Washington meet and mingle that one almost feels one has been there before and will be again.[16]

---

[15]Modifications include enlarging her tush, her bust (again), and her lips; removing all trace of muscle tone from her upper arms and thighs; and reducing her height by several inches. However, says Mariel, she's not just doing it to get the part, she's always wanted to be shorter and have bigger lips.

[16]This feeling, known as déjà vu, was popularized by nasal-voiced, scraggly bearded Canadian rock star Neil Young in the sixties. But why he would be able to popularize anything, or why anyone would even consider sleeping with him in the desert tonight or any other night, beats us.

→ Is memoir a valid form of lit? Comp. Eudora Welty! Ed McMahon, Lana Wood

Norman Gene

IT GOT all hot and hazy in Hollywood that May, like it went right to summer without even making a whistle-stop at spring, like spring forgot to whistle or something, which I can tell you it might have done if I'd been passing by since I remember that guy in the gas station one time who recognized me and just stood there with his mouth hanging open wider than the door to the ladies' room which I'd forgotten to lock, sort of accidentally-on-purpose. He was a skinny guy with straw for hair and the name "Dave"[1] written on his shirt—he looked like every mother's son with a nickel in his pocket and a taste for a fifty-cent ice cream cone on his tongue. Just like those guys in Korea[2] who gave me such hot looks I had to peel off my parka before I melted, even though it was about forty degrees below whatever it is that degrees are below of.

Anyway, those funny purple trees were blooming that always remind me of the part in "The Wizard of Oz"[3] where they have "a horse of a different color," you could say these were trees of a different color, and they just made everything seem more unreal than it normally does, if there is such a thing as normally out there, like the fake maraschino cherry on top of a fake plaster ice cream sundae. So I knew I had to get out of there and go to New York City,[4] never mind that I was supposed to be shooting "Something's Got to Give" at the time. I had to have a

[1]"Dave" Baker, forty-three, now the manager of a 7-Eleven in Indio, California, is proud to report that he can still fit into the same shirt that he was wearing when he caught Marilyn off guard in the ladies' room that day. However, the last time he tried it on, he noticed the collar was frayed. Isn't research wonderful?

[2]Pfc. Isaac Shapiro of Brooklyn, New York; Pfc. Michael O'Roarke of Scranton, Pennsylvania; Pfc. Roosevelt Washington of Detroit, Michigan; Pfc. Glenn Bush of Xenia, Ohio; and Pfc. Stanley Krupsky of Chicago, Illinois, known to the rest of their outfit as "Ikey, Mickey, and company." After the war, they started a store called "Five Guys from a Whole Mess of Different Places" but it failed because the name wouldn't fit on their shopping bags. However, the enterprising Stanley Krupsky is now flourishing as the owner of a Christopher Street boutique that panders to the endless craze for "Marilyn" memorabilia, including some items from his "personal" collection that, strangely enough, nobody seems to want.

[3]Supposedly a great and terrible wizard, but actually the man behind the curtain.

[4]Major naked eastern seaboard metropolis where there are eight million stories. This is one of them.

change of scenery as they say, and not one that could be made by stagehands, otherwise I knew I was the something that was going to give.

I should say right here that I did have one other little small reason for hopping on a jet and skipping to New York and that happened to be the President of the United States, John Fitzgerald Kennedy,[5] whom I was a hop, skip, and a jump away from being in love with. He had promised to take me out on his boat, the Honey Fitz, and you can well imagine that the name alone caused a tingling in my little honeypot. Honey fits indeed! And perhaps he would.

Although to tell the truth, at that point I wasn't really sure whether, given the choice between John and Bobby,[6] I wouldn't really prefer the younger brother to try on for size. Bobby had more of the shark in him, I felt like those white white teeth would close on you and shake you and never let you go, and you wouldn't want them to because when he finally did there would be nothing left of your most secret self. And besides, he didn't have to wear a back brace. Then there was Teddy,[7] who promised more danger, and perhaps more honey, than the other two. He wanted to take me swimming, and believe me, I was ready for a dip.

So you might say I was looking forward to a little Irish smorgasbord that warm Friday morning when I lit out for New York. But first, I had to make a short stopover in Madison Square Garden in front of about twenty thousand people. It was Peter Lawford's[8] idea, one of about two he'd ever had in his life, the other being to marry Pat Kennedy Lawford.[9] I think around then he was getting another one, which was to divorce her, and he was awful friendly and all, but something about his hair seemed sort of suspect to me and I just couldn't get interested.

Still, it was pretty nice of him to ask me to sing in front of everyone like that, just as though I was a real person and not some Hollywood sex symbol, two bazooms under glass, lift the lid and cut everybody a slice,

[5]Our first Catholic president. Famed for asking people not to ask what their country could do for them, but what they could do for their country.

[6]Robert Francis Kennedy. He was the one with all the kids.

[7]Chappaquiddick.

[8]Supposedly the "nice" member of the famed Hollywood Rat Pack.

[9]The one who was married to Peter Lawford.

which I don't mind telling you is how some of my fellow Thespians made me feel, like for instance Peter's old pal Miss National Velvet with her famous velvet violet eyes who could show her cleavage with the best of them but got treated like Hollywood royalty just 'cause she'd started out on her knees sooner than I had.[10] Still and all, I do not wish to appear ungrateful. It was a big honor to sing for the President. It was a command performance. I liked the sound of that, command performance. It made me feel like Pablo Casals.[11]

So anyway that bright Friday instead of going over to Fox[12] where everybody was waiting for me, Marilyn, that troublesome and expensive piece of female horseflesh, to be gotten in front of the camera, I made up my mind I was going to fly out of there. I kept missing planes right left and center and everybody in Madison Square Garden[13] was waiting for me, too, but at least they were waiting for Somebody. To them I was Norma Jean the Movie Queen, which is what I looked like to myself and everybody else when I finally did show up, in champagne chiffon and sequins to knock their eyes out.

People who complain about "the late Marilyn Monroe," which is how I wound up being introduced there at the Garden and everybody did laugh, even the ghosts of famous fighters who had gotten punch-drunk in past bouts I think were up there laughing in the rafters, well, those people should realize that it takes time to go from Slob to Star. Time and concentration and not a little magic to make myself into what so many people want me to be, a sex goddess they say in *Life*[14] magazine.

[10]Marilyn is referring here to Elizabeth Taylor, fat actress, whose bumper sticker, according to Joan Rivers, reads, "Honk if you have groceries." If Marilyn were alive today, she'd be thrilled to see what Liz currently weighs in at, since she harbored a grudge against the star—witness her cattiness here. As far as we know, Elizabeth Taylor has never been on her knees to anyone in her life, and we can't imagine why Marilyn would say such a thing. Shame on her!

[11]Famed cellist who gained even greater fame as President Kennedy's favorite musician. Long before JFK took office, he had hopes of honoring all artists named Pablo by asking them to perform at the White House, but, unfortunately, Pablo Picasso and Pablo Neruda were unavailable during the first 1,000 days of his administration. They were scheduled for day 1093 and 1187, respectively, but alas, fate intervened, and President Lyndon B. Johnson didn't want to have anything to do with anybody named Pablo because it reminded him of a shifty ranch hand he once had to fire. And people ask why we yearn for the days of Camelot!

[12]Twentieth Century-Fox, a movie studio. Now owned by Coca-Cola, as are all major studios.

[13]Madison Square Garden is neither square nor a garden. In fact, it isn't even located on Madison Square. This is typical of the verbal and geographical mishmash with which New Yorkers delight in confusing out-of-towners.

[14]Life is a magazine. How much? Too much. That's life. What's life? Life is a magazine.

I SURE COULD GO FOR A SLICE AND A COKE RIGHT NOW.

You don't just become a sex goddess overnight, like it was a cockroach[15] or something.

"Happy Birthday, dear President," I sang in my best breathiest champagne-colored shimmy of a voice. Someone said afterward that my voice sounded nude, but it wasn't, it was half-naked, like a bare back with a silk scarf thrown over it. Whatever it was, they seemed to like it.

The President said he could retire from show business, I mean politics, now that I'd sung "Happy Birthday" to him, and I was half ready to retire with him. It made me think of that old poster they had for Goodyear tires with the little boy with his sleeper flap falling down where he was rolling this tire and yawning, "Time to Re-Tire." It seemed real cozy and comfortable to me.

Then I thought about how Joe D.[16] had wanted me to quit making movies and learn to cook something besides peas and carrots and how there was another lady in the White House[17] that was always going to come first, that was why they called her the First Lady,[18] and I got this cold shiver down around where my backbone started, and it wasn't just the low-cut dress.

So then that shiver turned to iron, just a little sliver of iron, a shiver turned to a sliver you might say, and I made up my mind that whatever happened later that night I was going to make all those Kennedys and Kennedy in-laws sit up and take notice. Let them get a whiff of my perfume, and I didn't mean Chanel No. 5.[19]

---

[15]Reference to "Metamorphosis," the short story by Franz Kafka in which the hero, Gregor Samsa, wakes up to find he has become a giant cockroach. Clearly, Marilyn was no dumb bunny, if she was familiar with the works of Kafka. In fact, she once commented to Lee Strasberg that she identified with Kafka's hero because she felt trapped inside the body of a blonde bombshell. Lee empathized immediately, replying that he often felt trapped inside the body of an aging Jewish man. (In 1983, God let him out.)

[16]Joe "Say It Ain't So" DiMaggio, famous baseball player, once known as the "Yankee Clipper," today known as Mr. Coffee.

[17]Large white building located at 1600 Pennsylvania Avenue, Washington, D.C. Once the home of great leaders, now occupied by a geriatric movie star.

[18]Jacqueline Bouvier Kennedy. Although Jackie doesn't seem like the kind of person who would come first, she always did, which made things considerably easier for Jack, who was a busy man.

[19]The perfume in which Marilyn preferred to sleep. She was once audited by the IRS, who found it hard to believe that her perfume bills totalled $30,000 a week (today's equivalent would be $300,000, or four billion francs at current rates of exchange). However, after the auditor spent an evening at her house examining her records and, not incidentally, sniffing her sheets, the claim was allowed.

Of course Frank[20] was there, and he wanted everyone to go to Jilly's[21] with him. "Come on, let's go to Jilly's," he kept saying. He was meeting his agent there, or something. I dunno, maybe it's on account of he was so skinny as a young man, but Frank always wants a lot of people around him, I think it keeps him warm, just like a fur coat.

But it seemed like Jack was all for leaving the Garden and going directly to the hotel, where I knew you-know-who was waiting with Caroline and John-John,[22] probably still wearing her leopardskin pill-box hat, unless someone had remembered to tell her to take it off.

However, this was one night where I resolved to stay no more than a heartbeat away from the Presidency, if I could help it. I persuaded the President to lose his Secret Service escort and come downtown with me to the Village[23] to this place I know—it's no more than a bar, really, and I knew no one would bother him there 'cause they would never expect to see a President there in the first place, so who could believe it was really him.

Joe's,[24] for that was the name of it, was a family-type place to which I had been introduced by Joe D., and then again by Mr. Miller,[25] whose idea of fancy was always to go someplace simple where you could run into members of what he called the proletariat, though after a while all you ran into there were other writers who I guess were looking for the proletariat, too. It seemed to be a hard thing to find, for some reason.

The guys who ran Joe's were okay, too, although I don't think any of them was named Joe. With each introduction they acted like it was the first time they had ever met me. And they didn't even raise an eyebrow one time when I showed up there with Frank. They just played Tony

[20]Frank Sinatra, no stranger in the night to Marilyn.

[21]Popular midtown eatery owned by famous Sinatra sidekick, Jilly Rizzo. We have nothing bad to say about these people. They are outstanding human beings who, both individually and as a group, have made a significant contribution to American society.

[22]Children of JFK, who have suffered enough without our taking any cheap shots. See, every once in a while, even we lapse into good taste.

[23]Greenwich Village. Longtime mecca for artists, writers, and real estate agents.

[24]Obviously, none of Marilyn's mothers ever told her the old adage, "Never say 'dese,' 'dem,' or 'dose,' and never eat at a place called Joe's."

[25]Arthur Miller, Marilyn's third husband. Well-known playwright, novelist, and short-story writer whose works have entertained millions with their devastating depictions of death, depression, and a lot of other words beginning with "d" that we're too depressed to think of right now.

Bennett[26] on the jukebox, that was their little way of telling me that Joe D. wouldn't approve.

We ordered manicotti, a real proletarian dish. Jack was just digging into it like he hadn't tasted a thing except fancy French food for weeks, when someone came by and bumped against our table, spilling red sauce on the President's shirtfront. The kind of thing you have Secret Service men around just to keep from happening.

Of course the waiters dashed in immediately with club soda and condolences, but the curly-haired gentleman who did the spilling lingered so long over his apologies that finally we had to let him sit down and buy us a drink, indeed I had the tiniest suspicion that he had walked by wanting to start a conversation but was too shy to do so.

So we got to talking and this fellow got to guessing who it was that the two of us reminded him of. When he said Rita Hayworth[27] I almost spilled a little red sauce myself but then I realized he was just being cute and he called the next one right on the nail as John F. Kennedy. Well, before we would say yes, we had to know who he was, and when he said "Norman Mailer,"[28] we thought he was just carrying on with the game, he didn't look tall enough to be a famous writer, not like Arthur, and besides, his ears stuck out.

So we called one of the guys who wasn't named Joe over and asked who it was that was buying us drinks. "Well, he is whoever he wants to be, but he's got a bar bill here as long as your arm under the name of Norman Mailer." So Norman just sat there smiling, like he had swallowed a whole bowlful of cream. I knew about him from Arthur, who, while he didn't exactly approve of him—he always said "Norman" with his face sort of pinched up, like he was tasting sour grapes—at least thought Norman Sour Grapes Mailer had some kind of a talent for something, even if it was only publicity.

Now that we knew he was somebody famous, and he knew we were somebody famous, we had to go on talking to each other. It's some kind of pact that famous people have, I guess. It's like "Miss Norma Jean

[26]Miracle singer who left his heart in San Francisco and yet continues to travel, performing in front of literally thousands of people a year, to the amazement of medical science.

[27]Glamorous redheaded actress of the forties, best known for her portrayal of Gilda in the movie of the same name and her marriage to the Aga Khan. Today, Rita cannot remember any of this, due to her losing battle with Alzheimer's Disease, which goes to show the futility of human existence. What's it all about, Alfie?

[28]The guy this story's about, bozo.

Baker, hello, how are you, nice to see you, goodbye," but "Miss Marilyn Monroe," well that means we have to have a conversation, especially if you are somebody famous, too. It's sort of like a club to keep people who aren't anybody out. Of course there was nothing Jack and I wanted more than to be alone and playing footsie under the table, but now we had to talk to Norman.

"I've read your books. I read *The Deer Park* . . . and the others," Jack said.

"That's what you said the first time I met you, Mr. President," Norman said, convinced by now that his guess had been right. "Don't you remember?"

I could see Jack was thrown. He hates to be caught out on things like that. "Oh, yes, it was in the White House, once, wasn't it?"

"Twice. In Hyannisport,[29] before the election," Norman said. "My

[29] Massachusetts seaside town made famous by the Kennedy clan and frequented by people who can't pronounce their final r's.

Walt Whitman was one of Marilyn's favorite authors. In fact, she hoped one day to meet him, not realizing that he had a lot in common with Montgomery Clift.

wife Adele[30] came the second time. Your wife was very gracious to her," this with a malicious nod at me.

"Was she the one you stabbed, or was that the other one?" I inquired, oh-so-sweetly. You must know by now that there is an imp in me that's always happy to pop out.

"I try to stab pretty ladies with another implement these days," Norman said back, wickedly. It seemed that there was an imp in him, too.

Quick as a wink, Jack came back with, "Would that implement be your pen? I seem to recall that you had some rather, ah, biting things to say about Jacqueline in an article for, ah, *Esquire*, was it? Of course I only buy *Esquire* for the pictures."[31] For he, too, must have had an imp of a leprechaun back in his ancestry somewhere.

"I may have been a little hasty there, Mr. President," said Norman, adopting a most Presidential manner himself. "I couldn't understand why the lady in question didn't wish to spend an intellectual evening with me discussing the Marquis de Sade.[32] But then I suppose she's something of a homebody," once again with just a little glance in my direction.

Now, according to the rules of the Famous People's Club, we could have stopped right there. Everybody had scored a point or two. It was time to kiss cheeks and be on our way. But Jack still hadn't finished his manicotti.

Anyway, here was Mr. Norman Mailer, famous author, with his famous fake Southern accent, talking to the President just as though it was a press conference in the Oval Office[33]—only he was the one that was holding it. "Mr. President—" he said.

"Jack," Jack said.

"Jack, then," said he, easing into it as though it were a mouthful of

[30] Adele Morales Mailer, wife No. 2. Norman's other wives were: No. 1 Beatrice Silverman, No. 3 Lady Jean Campbell, No. 4 Beverly Bentley, No. 5 Carol Stevens, No. 6 Norris Church. He's just a guy who can't say no.

[31] Although Mailer's article on the First Lady didn't appear in *Esquire* until July 1962, this conversation supposedly took place in May of that year. Evidently JFK had received a complimentary advance copy of the issue, which indicates that when he said "I only buy *Esquire* for the pictures," since he didn't actually have to *buy* it, he was indulging in an example of the famous JFK wit.

[32] French marquis who gave his name to the practice of sadism, such as the kind of things Vicki Morgan reportedly did to Alfred Bloomingdale and certain close personal friends of Ronald Reagan.

[33] Office that's just a little thinner than a round office.

fine old bourbon. "I fear it would be highly ungracious of you, Jack, if you failed to acknowledge the not inconsiderable debt you owe to your humble servant, one Norman Kingsley Mailer."

"And just what, ah, debt is thay-at?" asked Jack, becoming more Boston than I'd ever heard him before. They were dueling, accent-to-accent, I guess you could say.

"Merely that one might venture to say—" Norman had all of a sudden switched to British. "One might indeed conjecture that were it not for a certain article in a certain *Esquire* magazine, the luck of the draw might well have fallen differently in the last Presidential contest. In other words, not to put too fine a point on it—" here he was back to pure Brooklyn—"I won the election for ya."

There was a kind of a little hush in the restaurant and I could tell that the guys who weren't named Joe were listening just to see what would happen next. Myself, I got another cold chill down my spine, just like when somebody accidentally-on-purpose dropped a spoonful of ice cream down my dress at a party, only because I happened to be showing a little extra cleavage, back as well as front. And that shiver joined with the other one, the one that had formed earlier and turned to iron, and somewhere between the ice and the iron was the knowledge of exactly how Jack felt at the moment.

It was the way I felt whenever I read this or that article that would say whoever-it-was created Marilyn Monroe, whether it was Joe Schenck or Johnny Hyde or Lee Strasberg or even Milton H. Greene.[34] For the plain and simple fact was, nobody invented me but me. Marilyn created Marilyn. Sometimes when I would look in the mirror without any makeup on and see this pasty-skinned person staring back at me, like a ball of dough with two raisin eyes and an almond for a nose, I would cheer myself up by saying, "Norma Jean," for that is what I called my most secret self, "Norma Jean, Marilyn can't come out and play. She isn't here today. She'll be back tomorrow or the next day." And she always did come back, or at least she had up 'til now, although not always precisely in sync with whenever the director of whatever movie I happened to be working on at the time wanted her to. She could be stubborn about such things.

I knew as sure as I knew anything that Jack had invented himself the same way I had, only his invention happened to get elected President of

---

[34]Studio head, publicist, acting teacher, and photographer, respectively. Marilyn knew a lot of people.

the United States. So he couldn't exactly afford those secret moments at the mirror. "Mr. President, it's the Cuban missile crisis." "Sorry, the President isn't here right now, it's just me, Jack. Call back later." He had to live it all the time. He couldn't let anyone see in that place behind his eyes. And here was Mr. Mailer coming along trying to take all the credit, just because of some words he'd put down on paper.

Jack was real calm, though. "I always wondered how I managed to win that one," he said.

I could hear the guys who weren't named Joe let out their breath.

"Sometimes I'm not so sure you did me a favor," Jack added, with a laugh.

"The favor, sir, was the one you did the country." Now Norman had honey on his tongue. "But to talk politics in the company of such a beautiful lady would be tantamount to an insult." I wasn't sure what "tantamount" meant or if it was anything like Paramount,[35] but I caught the "beautiful lady" part, just the way I was meant to.

"Yours is an arcane and unusual loveliness, my dear." The honey was dripping on me now. "You have the beauty of an unmade bed."

"Well, that certainly is an arcane and unusual compliment, Mr. Mailer," I said. "You might even say it was recherché." I wasn't going to let him win any word games, oh no, not me who'd been married to one of the greatest living dramatists of our time.

"Oh, you witches, you witches," Norman began. "You silver-haired daughters of the moon—" I could tell he was just winding up, but before he could get a chance to let go with his pitch, as Joe D. might have said, we were interrupted by the arrival of Jack's baby brother Bobby.

Bobby was in quite an uproar about something and we all, even the guys not named Joe, soon got to find out what it was. "Jack, what do you think you're doing here?" he wanted to know. Only he said "hyeah." Even more Boston than Jack had been when Norman got his dander up. "Excuse me, Miss Monroe—" he was a well-brought up boy, they all were, Mama Rose[36] had for sure seen to that. "Excuse me, but you just can't go disappearing like that. Anything could happen."

"Now, Bobby," Jack said, all sweet reasonableness. "What could happen to me?"

---

[35] Fooled ya. This one's owned by 7-Up.

[36] Wife of Joe Kennedy, Sr., and matriarch of the Kennedy clan. Some are already considering her for sainthood.

"You might fall under the spell of a beautiful blonde witch," Norman added mischievously.

"Yes, that would indeed be tragic," Jack said, as though he was seriously considering it. "But after all, I am only human."

"Oh, I sincerely hope so," said I.

We had all had a few by that time and were in that stage of tipsiness where everything must be carefully weighed and debated, pro or con, stay or go.

But Bobby was in no mood to be argued with. "You're not human, you're the goddamned President," he shouted. "And you're coming back to the hotel with me right now."

Well, I guess Norman decided to jump in, and before anyone could stop him he was down on all fours inviting Bobby to butt heads with him.

"Who is this geek?" Bobby asked.

Well, of course that enraged Norman and he began butting Bobby anyway, even though Bobby was still standing up, and there was this "crack" as Norman's head came in contact with Bobby's kneecap I guess it was, and all of a sudden Norman was bleeding. Later someone said that Bobby had sapped him and I suppose maybe he did. I know for sure Norman had a really hard head, it must have taken a tough kneecap to make a dent in it.[37]

By this time our little party was the center of attention down at Joe's, and the guys who weren't named Joe came in and surrounded Bobby and the President, by that time he wasn't just Jack any more, and they hustled them out of there so fast it was like a magic trick. Now you see them, now you don't, like it was levitation or something.

I remember President Jack looking over his shoulder at me sort of surprised, like he'd wanted to say goodbye or hello or even call me later, hang up if Jackie answers, and then he was gone and there I was with Famous Author Norman Mailer down on the floor on all fours, well on three fours actually, 'cause one hand was up holding his head where there was blood on it.

It was the blood that got to me. I don't know if you know this about me yet but I am very sympathetic, I believe it comes from being an orphan. Us orphans are somehow so used to crying about our own

---

[37]Later on, actor Rip Torn did try to make another dent in Norman's head with a hammer, during the filming of the movie "Maidstone," but met with little success, although he himself almost lost an ear when Norman sank his teeth into it. That's show business.

misfortunes that we always seem to have enough tears left over for somebody else, they're ready and waiting to spill whenever we hear about a drowned kitten or a sick puppy. Well, Norman didn't look like a kitten or a puppy down there on the floor, but he did look oh-so-unhappy, like a little boy at a birthday party who thought he was going to get cake and ice cream, too, and then spills it on his lap and is told he can't have any more because he didn't behave. Here he had been living it up with President Kennedy (the cake) and me (the ice cream) and then bang! the balloon burst and the party was over. What could I, the orphan girl, do under such sorrowful circumstances but act in character? All my Method training came to the fore. I made contact with the ice cream, and I melted.

The one thing that didn't melt was that sliver of iron that had come into my backbone earlier in the evening, the one that said, "Marilyn, tonight you are going to make some kind of history." It didn't matter if it was underground history, the kind nobody would ever know about, history was what I was after. First I got Norman to get off the floor and sit down in a chair like a person before the owners came and did their disappearing magic trick on us, only with us there wasn't a limo waiting so we'd be disappeared right out on the street, at least Norman would and I would too if I stuck with him, which is what I was intending to do.

Then I told the waiter to bring me some ice and I put it in a napkin and held it to Norman's head until the bleeding stopped. And I got us each a brandy which experience had taught me was very essential on these kind of occasions, and I told Norman that since he seemed to have kind of effectively changed the course of my evening, I'd go anywhere with him that he wanted to, we could go back to my suite at the Sherry[38] if he liked.

And I don't know but that his mind might have been wandering after the blow because he kept calling me Cherry, maybe he got it mixed up with Sherry, and then he said we should go to Las Vegas[39] together. "We must escape the dark night of the soul, you and I," he kept saying. Vegas in my opinion is not the best place to go to escape any dark nights, since in a way it is all one long dark night, only lit up of course.

[38]The Sherry-Netherland, fashionable midtown hostelry, where one of the editors once spotted Pia Zadora in an elevator.

[39]Viva!

♀ WE WANNA BE A VERB!!

CALLING ALL WOMEN . . .

JUST BECAUSE WE'VE MADE ALOT OF PROGRESS IN ERASING SEXISM FROM THE FACE OF THE EARTH, IT DOESN'T MEAN OUR JOB IS FINISHED. HAVE YOU EVER THOUGHT ABOUT THE FACT THAT THE WORD "MAN" IS A VERB, AND THE WORD "WOMAN" ISN'T? DON'T LAUGH! THINK ABOUT IT!

WHEN A WOMAN IS IN CHARGE OF A SPACE MISSION, WILL THEY STILL SAY THAT SHE'S "MANNING" THE SHIP? OR WHAT IF A WOMAN STEERS HER WAY TO A GOLD MEDAL DURING THE WINTER OLYMPICS LUGE COMPETITION? WHAT WILL OUR EARS BE ASSAULTED WITH THEN -- THAT SHE "MANNED" THE WINNING BOBSLED?

HAVEN'T YOU HAD IT UP TO HERE WITH THIS KIND OF STUFF? SHOULDN'T "WOMAN" BE A VERB, TOO? ISN'T ALL THIS JUST ANOTHER WAY MEN SUBVERT AND CONTROL OUR SELF-IMAGE? IF YOU AGREE, PLEASE JOIN US AT AN URGENT MEETING THIS FRIDAY AT 4:00 P.M. AT TRISH HALL IN ROOM 403. (IF THE ROOM IS LOCKED LIKE LAST WEEK, WE'LL MEET OUT ON THE QUAD.)

WE'LL BE DISCUSSING THE VERBIFICATION OF WOMEN AND FORMULATING A NEW DEFINITION WHICH WILL THEN BE PROPOSED TO MAJOR DICTIONARIES AND WILLIAM SAFIRE.

JOIN US!
DON'T LET MEN MAN OUR LANGUAGE!

WOMEN FOR A BETTER VOCABULARY ON CAMPUS.
IA STEINEM DORMITORY FOR MEN & WOMEN
ROOM 1003, EAST WING

Well, then Norman wanted me to arm-wrestle him right there in the restaurant, "just like Papa,"[40] he said. I took that as a bad sign. Experience has taught me that with most people who have had too much to drink, first they start talking about their parents, then they cry, and then they pass out. I figured I had better get this man home, wherever that was.

I had admittedly had just a few encounters of this nature before when times were hard and I had to think about whether the free hors d'oeuvres that they served during the happy hour in my local bar would be enough to get me through the night or whether I would have to find someone who could escort me to their home so I could rifle their refrigerator. My favorites were the ones who had those Oriental houseboys, who would come out bowing and smiling, never raising an eyebrow at whatever state of nudity they found me in—"Missy like some bleakfast before I call taxi, yes, please?" And chop-chop, there would be breakfast, one fried egg for each cute bazoom they'd caught a glimpse of through those discreetly narrowed eyes.

However, the number of individuals with houseboys of any persuasion other than sneak thief making up the not-so-exclusive clientele of the Beach-a-Tiki Bar on Melrose was slim, to say the least. Most of the time I had to make do with peanut butter and celery. Once I was so hungry, I ate a lemon.

Norman, on the other hand, looked to me like the kind of substantial individual who would keep plenty of food on hand for emergency late-night snacks and might even turn out to have a little leftover Mama's[41] homemade chicken soup in the fridge. That little roll of fat around his middle wasn't nourished by self-esteem alone, you can be sure. But that wasn't the immediate problem. The problem was, where was his refrigerator and how was I going to get him to it?

Then I remembered Arthur, and how when I was first secretly keeping company with him we used to go for these long walks through Brooklyn[42] admiring old buildings and talking philosophy until Arthur could work up enough courage to put his tongue in my mouth. And on

[40]Ernest "Papa" Hemingway. An example of Marilyn's sly sense of humor, in that she certainly knew who Papa Hemingway was, even though here she is pretending not to. What a laff riot that girl was!

[41]Mama Mailer, not Mama Hemingway.

[42]Second biggest little city in the world.

one of these walks he pointed out Norman Mailer's house. I remembered because he deep-kissed[43] me right in front of it, I guess hoping that Norman would come to the window and look out.

So I said to Norman, "Let's go to Brooklyn," and I must have hit the jackpot because he got all excited and began singing "Cherry, Cherry baby, won't you come out tonight" to the tune of that song by the Four Seasons. I got one of the not-Joes to call us a taxi—and somehow I got Norman into it, so there we were, off on our way to Brooklyn.

I was having a good time with my head stuck way out the window like a collie dog, enjoying the ride, while Norman just sat back mumbling about "seizing the existential moment." I figured at any moment he would start seizing, if you know what I mean, and I was in a mood where I certainly wasn't going to object to a squeeze or two in the back seat of a taxi. I felt like a sexy person was let loose in me who maybe wasn't me but she wasn't all that much of a stranger either. I felt this way especially when we went over the Brooklyn Bridge. Bridges always do that to me, maybe because they aren't really anywhere in particular, they're just going from one place to the other.

Then on the Brooklyn side I saw this big clock tower put up by the Jehovah's Witnesses. "Repent," it said, and that was enough to dampen my mood and dry up any dampness I might be feeling, if you know what I mean. Jehovah's Witnesses make me nervous, the way they're always saying "Good News!" like without that you'd be bound to expect that the news would be bad. One of my foster mothers used to be a Jehovah's Witness and I guess I don't like to think about the little Norma Jean Baker she used to be witnessing.

Next, Norman began to talk about his wife and that really got me shook. He said she was a witch, "spawned by the Luce-monster through the Time machine." He wanted to know if I thought it was a coincidence that "Luce" and "Lucifer" both began with the same letters. I had a hard time following what he was talking about, but it seemed that the wife he was married to then, Lady Jean Campbell,[44] was some kind of

---

[43]Not to be confused with deep-sixed, which is what many people thought had happened to Marilyn's writings, until they recently resurfaced.

[44]Wife number three.

British aristocrat who supposedly played footsie with Henry Luce,[45] who was somebody I remember Arthur wasn't too crazy about, probably because he thought Art was some kind of a Communist.

At any rate, Norman had worked up this theory where Henry Luce had used some kind of time machine (*Time* magazine; *Time* machine, get it?) to go back and impregnate Lady Jean's mother, who was married to Lord Beaverbrook,[46] who was some kind of high muck-a-muck in publishing over in England. So Lady Jean had basically been fooling around with her own father. And now she was pregnant and Norman was deathly afraid that Henry Luce might have struck again. Of course you must realize that I'm trying to put this all together from the way I remember it and I'm not sure I've got all my facts exactly straight, but anyway, nutsy as it sounds, it was something like that.[47]

Norman was saying, "The witch must be punished," and I was shivering, thinking how loony he was, and meanwhile we were getting closer and closer to that street in Brooklyn Heights where as far as I knew Norman and the witch in question had set up housekeeping together. Then a funny thing began to happen in my brain, certainly to one of my two selves, for I've always felt I had at least two, which was: I began to want Norman to get even crazier. I began thinking, "True, she must be punished," only I wasn't sure who I was thinking about, Lady Jean or Norma Jean. They got all mixed up in my mind. I began thinking of this person, this aristocratic nose-in-the-air lady with a blue-blood baby in her womb when I had had so many little squirts that never became any more than just that because I had to have some doctor cut them out of

[45] Husband of Claire Booth Luce, another blonde and contemporary of Anita Loos, brunette author of "Gentlemen Prefer Blondes." Henry was one gentleman who was an exception to this rule, as he seemed to prefer Lady Jean, who was a brunette.

[46] Only Canadian member of the British peerage. He was under the illusion that his title derived from the Canadian national animal, the beaver, whereas actually it was a reference to the type of photo he ran on the front pages of his newspapers; specifically those of Mandy Rice-Davies and Christine Keeler.

[47] Either Marilyn got this totally screwed up or, if her recollection is correct, Norman was indulging in the kind of crackpot theorizing that has contributed so much to his literary reputation. Other theories of his include the idea that JFK's assassination was caused in part by Norman's "fornicating with a witch on the afternoon of the deed," and that Marilyn's spirit gave "a witch's turn to the wheel at Chappaquiddick." He also believes that plastic causes cancer. He may be right about that one, but Henry Luce's astral body zooming around impregnating people? Sheesh! Tell us another, Normie.

me. And some part of me began to want her to die, and yes, I have to say it, for that baby to die, too, just like the baby that Norma Jean Baker Dougherty DiMaggio Miller was going to have with Mr. Arthur Miller did. And for nobody to witness it but Jehovah.[48] So it came as no surprise when Norman said we were going to kill his wife.

I wanted to know how. Norman said not with a knife, because "so long as you use a knife, there's some love left." I didn't like to think that love was something that could just be used up, like leftovers when you're hoping nobody took the chicken wing you were saving for a bedtime snack and you look in the refrigerator and whoops, it's gone. "And so the poor doggie had none," that part in the poem about Old Mother Hubbard[49] always makes me tear up. Plus you can tell I was getting pretty hungry by this time, not having had a chance to finish my manicotti and all.

But I guess Norman thought about love that way because he said there was nothing left, the cupboard was bare, so to speak. "So the dread deed must be done, and done quickly," he said. He said something like whenever he got to feeling good about himself he wanted to murder someone else. "The perception of greatness in myself has always been followed by the desire to murder the nearest unworthy." I think it went something like that. I would have hated to have to choose between him and Bluebeard[50] as a husband.

Anyway he said he was going to do it and I would watch and it would be like a magical bond between us that would go on forever and ever.

---

[48]God of the Old Testament, also known as Jahweh, spelled by Orthodox Jews as "J-hw-h," on the paranoid premise that vowels are dangerous. This vowel-fearing sect even goes so far as to remove these killer ciphers from alphabet soup, or as they call it, "-lph-b-t s--p."

[49]Nursery rhyme character who kept bones in her cupboard, which sounds pretty unsanitary to us. The roaches must have had a field day. No wonder the cupboard was bare. Incidentally, if you really want to get rid of those interesting little creatures, who have been around since prehistoric times and probably will survive well into the post-nuclear age, long after Reagan and his irresponsible foreign policy have blown us all to smithereens, we recommend boric acid. Forget Black Flag or even those sprays with all the Spanish instructions on them, *las cucarachas* eat those things up. They're like air freshener to them by this time, kind of a roach version of Glade. Boric acid. They get it on their tiny little feet, lick it off, it goes into their itsy little tum-tums and hardens there, and they fall dead from the sheer effort of dragging all that weight around. Plus, it's safe for plants and animals. Trust us. Of course, if you're really lonely, you might want to keep them and train them as pets.

[50]Legendary wife-killer who married almost as many women as Norman has.

"Provided we stick together, nobody can prove a thing," he said. "We can say we were in bed."

Some people may think of me as a dumb blonde but I'm not that dumb. Tell that to the judge—"And where was Mr. Mailer on the night of the crime?" "In bed with Marilyn Monroe." The jury would wet their pants over that one.

But you must remember that only one of my selves knew that Norman was serious. The other one figured that sure, Norman might be a major league bozo, but published authors don't just go around killing people on the spur of the moment.[51] I didn't know Norman had what you might call two partners in crime: Bennie and Mary Jane.[52] They had both been whispering in his ear all evening, urging him to do the deed; and I, why I wasn't exactly restraining him by sitting in the taxi holding his hand while he went on muttering about it. He said that there was a hole at the center of his personality, and that only by committing a murder could he fill it. He said murder was "the ultimate existential act by which a man affirms his own being."

"Sort of like 'You're dead and I'm not'?" I asked him.

He said it was something like that, only more complicated. I had a feeling with him everything was complicated. He certainly made getting into the house real complicated, once we got there. It was his house so he could have just opened the front door with his key, but no, that would have made things too easy for the long arm of the law, we had to climb in the kitchen window and Norman very nearly got stuck. I was just wondering whether to run away and leave him there, half in and half out, when he wriggled through and came round to the kitchen door to let me in.

Laying his finger aside of his nose, he reminded me of Father Christmas[53] in some kind of old children's book illustration; and I felt just as

---

[51]Published author and jailbird Jack Henry Abbott put the lie to this assumption when, after his release from jail on Norman Mailer's recommendation, he stabbed a waiter to death for no good reason.

[52]Benzedrine and Marijuana, the fun couple of the fifties.

[53]It is a little known fact that Norman Mailer, in his years as a starving young writer, once got a job playing Santa at Klein's department store, but unfortunately children cried when they sat on his lap, and consequently he was let go.

benevolent. So, Marilyn, you have become the Angel of Death,[54] one self said to the other, and it wasn't any different in feeling than any other character anyone might have asked me to become, I could make contact with that, just like Lee told me to. I followed Norman into the house.

Norman, moving with unusual grace for a man under the influence, tiptoed to the dining-room table and selected a banana from the bowl of fruit that had been nicely arranged there. I was ready to go see if there was any Skippy[55] left in the refrigerator—peanut-butter-and-banana sandwiches have always been one of my weaknesses—but Norman announced that he had plans for this particular piece of fruit. A man, a plan, a banana, he said, which sounds like it ought to spell something backwards but doesn't.[56]

"Exhibit A," he said. "Ladies and gentlemen, I give you the murder weapon." Well, I could give you an adjective that immediately sprang to my mind to describe Norman's mental condition as he waved that banana around—you guessed it, bananas.

I still felt like we were Peter Pan and the Lost Boys[57] going after Captain Hook.[58] I didn't know when the cartoon would end and the feature begin. Norman took me by the hand and led me into a bedroom where a considerable mound disturbed the bedcovers. I never felt more calm as if, ha ha, I was on "This Is Your Life"[59] and they were talking

[54]The Grim Reaper. Also known as "Major Wipe-Out," "Woody Allen's Gin Rummy Partner," or "Mr. First Strike Capability," depending on whether you are a surfer, a comedian, or a national security adviser.

[55]Brand of peanut butter favored by actresses noted for their chest measurements, such as Marilyn Monroe and Annette Funicello.

[56]Marilyn was probably thinking of the phrase "A man, a plan, a canal, Panama," which can be spelled the same way backwards as forwards, if that's the kind of thing you like to spend your time doing. It's called a palindrome, and no, it's not in the glossary.

[57]A troupe of boys who refuse to grow up, preferring to remain in Never-Never Land, or Christopher Street (including Pfc. Stanley Krupsky). (See Footnote 2)

[58]The bad guy. Now working as an undercover cop for the Sixth Precinct, posing as an amputee in order to get into S & M fetish clubs.

[59]Mercifully defunct TV show where guests were forced to reunite with people they had been trying to avoid for years.

about me. I was waiting for the moment in the cartoon when Roadrunner[60] goes splat and Wiley Coyote[61] pops up from behind a cactus. There is a brief pause, and then Roadrunner is on his way again. I felt as though in that brief pause, my real life would begin.

Norman stopped at the edge of the bed and began peeling the banana and eating it. He didn't offer me any. When he was finished he carefully arranged the banana peel on the little throw rug by the edge of the bed. Apparently his idea was that his wife and arch-enemy the British witch would wake up, get out of bed, slip on the banana peel, hit her head on the edge of the bedside table, and suffer a fatal concussion, just like on that "Twilight Zone"[62] episode where the woman's husband pulls the rug out from under her. Sounds crazy but it just might have worked.

But of course Norman, Mr. Complicated himself, couldn't leave it at that. He had to make sure she woke up right then, so he could watch. One of my selves was prepared to stop him. God knows we had gone far enough. The other one was composing statements to the press: "Ironically enough, Miss Monroe . . ."

"Fug you!"[63] he shouted to the mound, and switched on the lights. The mound moved. Lady Jean Campbell sat up in bed, shrieking.

There were a lot of dirty words in what she shrieked for a member of the British aristocracy but I couldn't help admiring the extent of her vocabulary, it might even have exceeded Darryl F. Zanuck's[64] and he was a man who could shriek obscenities with the best of them. I wished I had a pad and paper, I would have written some of them down.

Lady Jean jumped out of bed and rushed at Norman. I remember she

[60]Beep-beep.

[61]Resilient but not very wily coyote who never did catch the Roadrunner; cartoon character based on unsuccessful presidential candidate Harold Stassen.

[62]Television show created by Rod Serling, who has since made it his address. And you can be sure that somewhere in the world, someone is about to enter it, right now.

[63]Norman Mailer is apparently the only person, besides the writer Tuli Kupferberg and the rock group Foghat, who thinks "fuck" is a three-letter word. Fug off, Norm!

[64]Head of Twentieth Century-Fox, who screwed a lot of people he did business with, giving rise to the widespread belief that his middle initial stands for "Fug."

was wearing a Lanz nightgown[65] with a high collar and I was truly concerned in case it choked her, she was getting so red in the face. But the wonderful flow of British obscenities never stopped.

"You abysmal fucking cretin," was one of them. Norman appeared somewhat taken aback. He made a move for the door, and sure enough, slipped on his own booby trap. I had never seen anyone slip on a banana peel before, except in the movies. But then I guess real life[66] is getting more like the movies every day.

Lady Jean did not relinquish her advantage. She was on Norman in a second, like a tigress defending her young, which I guess in a sense she was. Catching Norman in a stranglehold, she pounded his head against the floor repeatedly until his face was almost as red as hers. I was full of admiration. As a matter of fact, I wanted her on my side. She was one female you wouldn't want to mess with.

"Bloody idiot," she muttered to herself. She was a strapping woman who looked to me like she could have held all the keys to a medieval castle. "Shall we pour the boiling oil now, milady?" "Not yet. Wait till they're all inside the gates."

Norman curled up on the floor like a hedgehog, at least I'd never seen a hedgehog but the way they looked on those cute Christmas cards that people who live in Connecticut[67] or someplace send out, dressed up in human clothes and blowing trumpets. "Beat me, whip me, make me write bad checks," he said.

I was relieved to see he hadn't lost his sense of humor.

Lady Jean ignored him completely. "Would you like a cup of tea?" she said to me.

So it was that an evening which started out with Marilyn singing "Happy Birthday" to the President ended up with Norma Jean sitting in a kitchen talking to this tough Englishwoman who knew where all the pressure points were on the human body. My life turns out that way a lot.

Want to know the really funny part? The funny part is that Norman

---

[65] Brand of long flannel nightgown favored by preppies, Englishwomen, and other people who aren't interested in sex.

[66] A movie by Albert Brooks.

[67] Favored locale of *New Yorker* cartoons featuring the kind of people who wear Lanz nightgowns.

was so juiced that evening that afterwards he couldn't remember a thing. He couldn't even remember having met me. That's the funny part.

Although somehow I get a feeling that someday, never mind the fact that he can't remember it, he just might try to make money off of his association with me. I don't know why I feel that way, except that I guess my experiences have taught me that people are like that.

Aren't they?

Mr. & Mrs. Hyman Blichstein
of
La Jolla, California
invite you to share their joy
at the wedding of their daughter
Caryn Pamela
to
Mr. Mel Gibson
of
Sydney, Australia
Temple Beth-El   at precisely 3 p.m.

For Further Study

1. If you had your druthers, would you rather be a) a famous movie star; b) a famous playwright; c) a famous novelist; d) a famous baseball player; e) a famous President of the United States; f) a noted necro-journalist; or g) Allan Carr? Diagram the pitfalls inherent in your chosen profession. On second thought, wouldn't you be happier as Jimmy Stewart in "It's a Wonderful Life?"

2. What do you think of the way Marilyn dressed? Have you ever worn a cardigan sweater backwards or gone out without any underwear on? If so, what if you were hit by a bus and had to be rushed to the hospital? What would your mother say?

3. Explain the concept of "déjà vu" and give its derivation. How many times have you heard people use that expression? Every time you hear it, don't you have the strange feeling that you might have heard it before?

4. In your opinion, is *Norman Gene* literature or just gossip? Define literature in twenty-five words or less. Is your definition literature? If not, why not? Could gossip be literature? Could literature be gossip? Which is more interesting? For extra credit, write a short story revealing something intimate about a) your neighbor; b) your professor; c) your dry cleaner; d) your President; or e) Allan Carr. Which of these revelations has the most chance of being published?

5. Do you think Marilyn really knew John F. Kennedy, or was she using poetic license? What is a poetic license, and where do you apply for one? Do you think poetic licenses should be revoked for drunken writing? Have you ever heard of Dylan Thomas? Whatsha matter wi' you, you tryin' to shpoil th' party or somethin'?

6. What was "Camelot," and why was it a term applied to the Kennedy Presidency? Was it because JFK drank, swore, and womanized as much as Richard Burton? Or was there some other reason? Compare and contrast President Kennedy's favorite musical artist, Pablo Casals, with the performer favored by our current President, Wayne Newton. If you think this last sentence means that Wayne Newton is

President, you're wasting your time in this course and should go directly to Vegas.

7. Have you ever eaten at a place called Joe's? What was wrong with it? Don't tell me you found hair in your food? If so, lady, you probably put it there. I don't know what you're trying to pull here, but we have a name for people like you—ex-customers. If you don't like it you can leave, and don't think you can get out without paying your check, either.

8. Is it true that when she was First Lady Jacqueline Kennedy had her sister buy her dresses in Paris and then cut out the labels so everyone would think she was wearing American-made clothes? Do you think this was fair, or was she duping the American people? Do you care? Do you think it's fair that she should have all that money and still look as good as she does for her age in spite of all she's been through? Or has she suffered enough? Take a straw poll of your fellow students and send it to *The Star,* or any other publication owned by Rupert Murdoch, under our byline and

we'll split the mazoola with you. We should at least get a kill fee, oops, sorry, Jackie.

9. Did Norman mean to kill his wife? Why? Do you suspect many male writers fantasize about killing their wives? Could it be that they secretly believe the sword really is mightier than the pen and wish they could switch? What kind of fantasies do women writers have? In your opinion are they more likely to involve knives, swords, pens, or Bloomingdale's charge cards?

10. How did Marilyn Monroe die? Make up a conspiracy theory of your own, using at least four of the following elements: a) a missing hypodermic syringe; b) a mysterious phone call; c) a CIA plot; d) an FBI plot; e) Howard Hunt; f) Jean Seberg's black baby; g) the grassy knoll; h) Beatles' song lyrics; j) Communists; k) anti-Communists; lmnop) we could go on; but you get the basic idea. Isn't this fun? Wouldn't you like to do it for a living? Talk to us after class, and we'll give you a letter of introduction to housewife/conspiracy theorist Mae Brussell.

Photo courtesy of Mozambique Press.

"Soul Mama #1" of the avant-garde black theatre, playwright Ja'net Crook is at work on a dictionary of ghetto slang with the hope that white critics, and even black ones from the suburbs, would like her plays better if they could understand them. Go for it, Ja'net!

Ja'net Crook
1952–

THIS dynamic young black woman writer is perhaps the most misunderstood modern talent of all the women represented in this collection, partly because of her insistence on spelling the word "be" with one letter. Born under a bad sign in Peoria, Illinois, she did not graduate from the nearby University of Illinois, Illinois Normal College, Illinois Wesleyan, Western, Sarah Lawrence, Bryn Mawr, or Mount Holyoke, although she spent a few weeks in the neighborhood of each of these institutions of higher learning, "looking for an apartment" so she could "get her shit together."

Following this brief visit to the groves of academe, she did not work for the *New York Times*, the *Boston Globe*, the *Sacramento Bee*, or the *Louisville Post-Dispatch*. Nor has her work appeared in the *Antioch Review*, *Harper's*, *Harper's Weekly*, or *Harper's Bazaar*. This singular career placed her among the ranks of many other writers whose work has never appeared in these publications either.

Ja'net's creativity came to full flower in her resume. "I've never seen anything like it," said Boo Radley, the editor who gave her her first job at a prestigious Washington daily.[1] "This chick made up more credits than you could shake a stick at. I never would have believed anyone would have the balls to do that."

[1] Not the *Washington Post*.

After six months of interviewing people who went to school with wives of congressmen, her first front-page breakthrough came when she wrote a dramatic account of the heroin addiction of an unnamed friend of the wife of a black congressman.

Recognizing a nose for bad news, Radley immediately switched her to the Depressing Desk[2] of the inner-city beat, considered a plum by many envious reporters, who couldn't say anything because she was a double minority. Ja'net electrified both her editor and her readers with a series of grim exposés of the seamy side of heroin addiction in nursing homes. However, her true inventive masterpiece dealt with the heroin addiction of an eight-year-old boy in a lower income housing project, for which she won the Pulitzer Prize.[3]

Shortly afterwards, the Pulitzer committee revoked the award on the grounds that she had made everything up. Her alleged fabrications were uncovered by an ambitious investigative reporter who compared photos of Ja'net before and after publication of the article and discovered that in the "after" photo her nose had become long and pointy.

After returning the Pulitzer, Ja'net left journalism for good. She never looked back, and now she's an artist. She's got everything she needs: paper, pencils, a loft space with track lighting, a dozen folding chairs, and as many actors willing to sign Equity waivers. Her creative impulses, once held in check by the narrow repressive strictures of journalism, where it's the facts that count, just the facts, ma'am, nothing but the facts, now find free rein in the theater.

As a middle-class black, she describes ghetto life with a poignancy and relevance that indicate an amazing insight and depth of feeling in one who has never experienced it. With the generous support of the Mobil Corporation, several of her dramas have been videotaped for public television. She is currently hoping to receive a grant from the Rockefeller Foundation, or any other foundation whose money derives from the unchecked drilling of petroleum, which will allow her to com-

---

[2]As opposed to the Uplifting Desk, where reporters cover stories about poor people who adopt stray dogs, who then save their masters during potentially fatal gas leaks.

[3]This prestigious award, which is given out annually, is named after the same family who was involved in the juicy Palm Beach divorce scandal of the early eighties in which Peter Pulitzer accused his wife of sleeping with men, women, animals, and trumpets. Ironically enough, another controlled substance, cocaine, was said to account for these strange proceedings.

plete the work-in-progress, "For Pulitzer Prize Winners Who Have Considered Fiction When Facts Are Not Enuf," an excerpt from which follows here.

It is perhaps most appropriate to end this introduction with the words of the playwright herself, when interviewed by Bill Moyers on his television show, "People of Historical Import I Can't Stand Not Having Met So This Show Is a Good Way for Me to Meet Them." When Mr. Moyers asked Ja'net, "Where do you get your ideas, anyway?" she said, "To paraphrase Bakunin, or was it George Bernard Shaw? Art is theft.[4] Good artists are the ones who don't get caught. And as long as I stick to art, I'm safe."

[4]We thought property was theft, but I guess we were wrong. Or does that mean that property is art?

For Pulitzer Prize Winners

Who Have Considered Fiction

When Facts Are Not Enuf

The stage is bare, except for a Barcalounger, a toy chest, and a kiddie lamp with Bozo the Clown as its base. Bozo has been painted black. "Paint It Black" by the Rolling Stones is heard. Jimmee enters, carrying arithmetic flash cards. He is an 8-yr.-old in running shoes and a striped Izod T-shirt. He drapes his thin frame over the chair and flips through flash cards.

jimmee
dam! i thot 4 + 4 waz 7 no wonder i got ripped off on my last oz. of s--t[1] i best study up if i wants 2 deal smack profeshunally when i grow out of dese expensive running shoes & into some fine fine superfine leather boots all the way from sunny Spain dam! i bin missin 2 many o' them math classes lately gotta hustle my butt back 2 skool but i b truly wasted jack

Jimmee starts to nod out. "Me and Mrs. Jones" by Billy Paul is heard.

jimmee
this h b the meanest i dun since i waz 5 goin' on 5 1/2

Jimmee nods out to music. A fat woman wearing a white uniform and blond wig totters across the room with a needle jabbed in her arm.

---

[1] Official journalism school spelling of "shit."

fat woman
i feel fine
wooooo - eeeee!
i feel fine

> *Music fades out. Jimmee wakes up and heads for toy chest. He picks up a green "Star Wars" force-field toy and begins flashing the light on and off.*

jimmee
sugar![2]
i b so bored & alienated & oppressed
i sho 'nuf don't no whut 2 do wit my bad self
hot dam! mebbe i don't need 2 study up on no math
i just go out & boost me a fancy ass calculator
then i b sharp

> *The bongos and flutes of alienation are heard. A young, heavy-set, dark-complected perpetrator with a medium afro enters.*

ron
allow me 2 introduce myself
i'm a man of wealth & fame

jimmee
hey my man ron

ron
u been chippin' at my stash again boy?

jimmee
no man i waz in math class all day
from 9 2 1
honest injun

[2]Official Vassar College spelling of "shit."

ron
u b 8 yrs old jimmee almost a man
time for u 2 bring in 2 this firm whut u
been takin' out
u been coastin' man the free ride b over
& another thing pretty soon man
u gotta learn how 2 do this fo' use'f

> *Ron goes to shoot Jimmee up. A lady in red, a
> lady in brown, and a lady in yellow dance in.*

all 3 ladys
mama's little baby likes turkish turkish
mama's little baby likes turkish horse

lady in red
he grabs jimmees left arm
just above the l-bo

lady in brown
his massive hand tightly encircles
jimmees small limb

lady in yellow
the needle slides into the boys soft skin
like a needle sliding into soft skin

lady in red
liquid ebbs out of the syringe
replaced by bright red blood which is
then reinjected into the child[3]

ron
damn if the little dude's lungs
didn't almost collapse

---

[3]If you find this disgusting, bear in mind that it appeared verbatim in a front-page article in the *Washington Post*.

Photos from production courtesy of Tiffany Shabazz.

Scene from a backer's audition for "For Pulitzer Prize Winners . . ." staged at Ja'net Crook's Noho loftspace. Here, little Jimmee, played by Gary Coleman's brother Harry, the one who *did* grow up, studies flash cards to hone the skill that will help him fulfill his entrepreneurial dreams and buy "an octagonal bathtub wif simulated brass fixtures."

Ron exits. The ladies do a short dance, then freeze. The area of the stage on which they are standing slowly rises as they sing "Stairway to Heaven." They disappear into the darkness above the stage.

A lady in plaid dances down the stairs. She is Jimmee's mother, Ndreea.

ndreea
i not b crazee bout seein my little boy fired up
but like i always sez
que sera sera
whatever will b will b
the future ain't ours 2 see
que sera sera

In the middle of a deep nod, Jimmee falls out of his chair. His flash cards are flung across the stage.

ndreea
when u b black
good at math
well dressed
and livin in a comfortably furnished home
in southeast washington
you bound 2 b gettin into -hit[4] 1 day
or nother
it's a matter of survivin
when jimmee b old enuf
2 deeside fo hissef what
2 do bout his jones
den he can jes go deeside fo
hissef
in the meantime i jes don't
pay it no nevermind.

Jimmee rises from his stupor and begins to pick up his flash cards. Ndreea gives him a tender pat on the head.

ndreea
drugs bin good 2 black folk
bring in lotsa extra $$
hep us stay up all nite
& rite bad playz . . .

jimmee
hey mama
can i rap wif u for 60 seconds
i bin contemplatin mah futur
as a profeshunal drug dealer
n i got some big plans

[4]Official stupid way of spelling shit.

In this scene, Ron, played by Abdul Kareem Coffey, gives Jimmee some fatherly advice. Mr. Coffey later went on to guest-star in an episode of "C.H.I.P.s" in which he played an innocent bystander who was mistakenly killed by a choke hold.

way i see it
by the time i'm bout 11
i shud b a respectd resident
of the drug community
pullin in maybe 4 bills a week

> *Jimmee shuffles through flash cards, pulling out one that says "4 + 4," and holds it up to show his mother.*

jimmee
now bitch do dese numbers
mean anything 2 you?

ndreea
lissen jimmee
you know the only numbers i knows
is the kind i run

jimmee
mama i b talkin bout how much $
we b pullin in every month
and i'm talkin in the thousands mama
u know what i wud do wit
dat kind of money?
i'd b gettin me a 10 speed bike
maybe a new basketball
a big ole German Shepherd guard dog
n save the rest so i can buy you n ron
an octagonal bathtub wif simulated brass fixtures

ndreea
son after i was raped
everybody told me to have an aborshun
but i didnt have no money
then when you were born
i was so poor
i couldn't even afford a name
so my sister said
"girl you give this boy a name"
n i sed i dont give 2 fucks
u name him
so she named u after her favorite song
"jimmee crack corn"
but son you b one aborshun
i b glad i didn't have
cause you b one speshul little person

jimmee
dont worry mom
things b cool from now on

*Jimmee picks up his "Star Wars" force beam toy
and begins to play with it. Sitting on his chair,
he nods out again. Lights dim. Spotlight on descending platform with 3 ladies in same position
as before. They dance to center stage.*

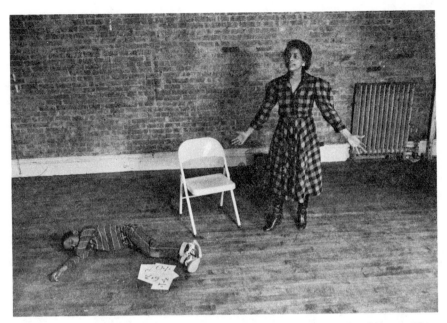

Here Ndreea, played by Thulani Shabazz, delivers an emotional soliloquy. This was Thulani's first and last role as an actress. Ja'net Crook cast her in the part, even though she was an amateur with no previous theater training or experience, hoping to convince Thulani's father, self-made bean pie baron Frank Shabazz, to invest in the production.

lady in yellow
death

lady in red
has

lady in brown
never

lady in yellow
visited

lady in red
this

lady in brown
house

all ladys 2gether
ding-dong

> *Ndreea opens door. Standing there is a figure draped in a black hooded garment, holding a scythe. This is Death.*

death
is jimmee home?

> *Lights dim.*
> *There is the poignant, lonely sound of a single, alienated bongo roll.*

M E _ _ I B S O N

For Further Study

1. From what university did Ja'net Crook not graduate? Name at least five of the newspapers for which she did not work. Extra credit for publications not mentioned in the introduction.

2. Are there easier ways of becoming a dramatist than by making up stories and passing them off as journalism, winning a Pulitzer Prize and then being totally humiliated for it, not to mention breaking your parents' heart? If not, is it worth it? Expand.

3. If Jimmee didn't exist, would it have been necessary for Ja'net to invent him? Expand and contract.

4. What do you think of the way Ja'net Crook spells? Would your sixth-grade teacher have made you stay after school if you spelled like that? Didn't it make you want to put tacks on her chair? Doesn't it still cheese you off when someone writes "sp." in the margin of your essay? Maybe this whole "correct spelling" thing is just one big fascist conspiracy designed to keep you in your place and sell dictionaries. We would have written this book a whole lot faster if we didn't have to keep looking everything up. Why can't we just all spell aftegeylup weretynom ja isssznt?

5. As a field assignment, go to a black area near you and attempt to score heroin from an eight-year-old. If there are no black areas near you, try Mexicans or college graduates. Write about your experience. Try not to exaggerate or overdose.

6. Can bongos and flutes be used to express other states of being besides alienation? What about anger, happiness, or needing to go to the bathroom? Discuss.

7. Describe Ndreea's attitude toward her situation in life. Would you call her an existentialist, or just plain stupid? What kind of welfare mother would dress her son in Lacoste shirts? Why should she get a free ride at the taxpayers' expense? And what about those sunspots? Is the weather crazy these days, or what? I ask you.

8. What is the significance of the lady in red, the lady in brown, the lady in yellow? Do these colors go together? Would you wear them together? If so, what kind of mother do you have?

9. What important social statement is Ja'net Crook trying to make in this play? What does it say about the human condition specifically and about black eight-year-old heroin addicts in general? Who's she kidding? What's her problem anyway? What kind of mother did she have?

10. Explain the significance of "Death" in this play.

Photo courtesy of the Sino American Take-Out Window.

In this picture, Jiang Qing (Mrs. Mao Zedong) flashes the widescreen smile that won her coveted roles in such films as "Blood on Wolf Mountain," "Twenty Centers," and "Old Bachelor Wang." Long after she had given up acting and turned to writing, the fledgling actress was approached by producer Dino De Laurentiis to play the Jane Wyman part in a remake of "Bedtime for Bonzo" opposite Clint Eastwood, but after prolonged negotiations, the role went to Sondra Locke instead.

Jiang Qing
1914–?

THERE is, perhaps, no woman in modern times quite so qualified to write a marriage manual as Jiang Qing, the former movie actress and sometime model who bagged the father of the People's Republic of China, Chairman Mao Zedong. The story of how she did so against insuperable odds and hardships is one that should be read by every young woman who hopes one day to get married and manipulate one billion people.

Jiang Qing was born of cranky and uncreative parents in March of 1914. There is no record of her birthdate in the histories because she always refused to tell it, saying rather humbly that she didn't want "the masses to go to the trouble of making another party." She left home at an early age because she had so many brothers and sisters, she would joke in later years, "It was like living in a crowded city already," and headed for Shanghai to break into show business. There, fate was kind to her, and after appearing as Nora in Ibsen's *A Doll's House,* and in David Mamet's *Means Nothing But Sounds Like Real People Talking,* she was offered several film roles and soon became a movie star.

She first got wind of Mao Zedong at a publicity party for her most successful film, "Boulevard of Broken Feet," in 1933.[1] It was at that event that she overheard her agent and manager, both Kuomintang supporters, discussing how a Communist victory would drastically lower their rates of commission and mentioning the name "Mao Zedong" as the renegade they would both hold responsible. Previous to this time, Jiang Qing, who had taken the stage name, Lan P'ing, which means "Removes Her Shirt Only When Relevant" in translation, was a

[1]Although Jiang Qing's agent and manager were Kuomintang supporters, "Boulevard of Broken Feet" was a Communist-backed production, a thinly veiled diatribe against footbinding while on the casting couch. She did, in fact, appear without her shirt, but it was, in fact, relevant.

political neophyte. But the thought of no longer having to pay 30 percent of her wages to two whiny-voiced back-stabbers who cared more for Ming vases than her career so raised her political consciousness that she determined to seek out this Mao Zedong and join with his Communists in the struggle for liberation.

Carrying a tube of Erace, an eyelash curler, a push-up bra, and a spray can of Nair, Jiang Qing rode into Yenan, the Communist stronghold, in July of 1937. Although Mao was married at the time to his third wife, the woman was, fortunately, holed up in a mental institution in the Soviet Union, the Long March having proved a bit of a strain on her, and so the field was clear. Within two months, Mao had obtained a quickie divorce, and he and Jiang Qing were an item.[2]

Revolution is never easy. But trying to snag a man during one is a Herculean task, and Jiang Qing's efforts in this direction are well documented. Born "Li," on screen, "Lan P'ing," she begged Mao to choose a new name for her that she might begin life anew and make revolution in his image. He dubbed her "Jiang Qing," which means "On Your Back, Comrade," and every time he called her that, she did as she was told. Their sex life was notorious.

When Mao refused to retreat from Yenan during the bombing in 1937, she remained by his side, the only woman left in the area. During the March to Peking, when the Communists marched 1,000 miles to recapture the city, she gave him her rain cape, a gift from a former hairdresser in Shanghai, the only piece of rain gear in the entire army, so that he might not get wet. Slogging through the constant downpour, she herself got T.B. When, though they were living in caves and under the most primitive conditions, Mao demanded that his shredded wheat be of optimum crispness, she rose at dawn and built special fires to realize his wishes. By the time the revolution was achieved and the People's Republic of China had become a reality, her health was broken, and Mao was bored to death with her submissiveness.

The whole of the 1950s she spent in and out of hospitals in the Soviet Union for lung, spleen, and liver ailments, the only pleasant moments being when she and Mao's third wife, Ho, got together and traded

[2]That Mao may have caught a screening of "Boulevard of Broken Feet" before Jiang Qing arrived in Yenan is highly possible. At that point the Communist leaders often watched movies of "corrupt and obscene" context in the Great Screening Room at Yenan in order to remind themselves what they were up against. They often watched these movies over and over again so as to be able to enumerate the injustices with pinpoint accuracy. It is said Mao saw "Han Su Yin Does Landlords" fifteen times before he felt confident to lecture on it.

"Mrs. Mao Retrospective,"
Asia House, Sat. 2 pm
(Bring popcorn)

"marching-with-Mao" anecdotes. Jiang Qing always recalled with fondness that "Ho told some very good stories in spite of her lobotomy."

When Jiang Qing returned to China in the early sixties, Mao was growing old, and she began to prepare the ground for the return to the stage she had dreamed of since the thirties. Secretly, she secured an acupuncture tummy-tuck so that when she demanded a return to simplicity she could look as good as possible. She formed the Gang of Four with three male hairdressers who had been part of her set in the thirties: Yao Wenyuan, Wang Hongwen, and Zhang Chunqiao. Together, they were a snobby clique with artistic pretensions, not unlike Andy Warhol's Factory, but possessed of the license to kill.[3]

The Red Guards, who were the young and mostly gay army elite, she had seduced to her side over the years with contraband Marlene Dietrich records and unexpurgated copies of Christopher Isherwood and W. H. Auden. They would have killed for her and did. With their aid, she set about ridding the country of everyone who had impeded her career in the 1930s. Her agent and manager were, of course, the first to be executed.

It was during this, her period of ascendancy, that she wrote *How to Catch a Chairman, How to Keep a Chairman, How to Get Rid of a Chairman,* which we know as *Mrs. Mao's Little Red Book.* By day, she wiped out intellectuals. By night, she wrote in longhand, reading the most barbed sections aloud to the now almost-senile Mao, and laughing uproariously at his humiliation. The text was printed in installments in *Dragon Women of China* magazine in 1968–69 and was so popular that she soon secured a lucrative movie deal. Due, however, to a rolling of the wrong studio heads by some overzealous Red Guards, the movie was never produced.

The style and tone of the work is remarkably like that of Zsa Zsa Gabor, interestingly enough also a woman from a Communist country. In fact, the translation printed here was indeed done by Zsa Zsa Gabor herself just after she divorced George Sanders. She came across the work while in pursuit of a new husband on the Inner Mongolia border in 1971. At the time, she was having an affair with a young Cossack in

---

[3]These three hairdressers were her party escorts in the Shanghai film world of the 1930s. They owned their own tuxedos, were known for their caustic remarks, and often took her shopping for evening gowns. They adored doing her makeup and hair, and she relied on them for protection in spite of the fact that, because of their constant presence, she was known in the clubs as a "fag hag."

his yurt in the Ural Mountains and happened to pick up the *Little Red Book* during a breather. At first, she was going to sue for plagiarism but decided to translate it instead.

In literary terms, Jiang Qing certainly stands equal to Daphne du Maurier in her brilliant evoking of the conundrum of submissiveness, and to Britt Ekland in her quest for revenge. She has been compared to the Brontës in her emphasis on the perfect fantasy man, although some critics find this comparison odious and see her more as an earthy Marie Antoinette, who may or may not have been literate but dictated once in a while when she was bored with cake.

In addition to her *Little Red Book,* Jiang Qing wrote and choreographed several modern Communistic ballets, most notably the famous "Riding the Red Cotton Pony," which stunningly and heroically details the struggles of women without sanitary towels on long marches during the revolution. Perhaps this is why she has been linked with Marie Antoinette, herself a crusader for sanitary protection.

By the mid 1970s, Jiang Qing finally achieved the goal she had set aside for twenty-five years in her struggle for Communism and reduced agents' commissions: an international fame for which, in fact, she paid no commissions at all.

Although posterity will thank her for writing her marriage manual, in political terms, it was an unwisely revealing thing to do. One month after the death of Chairman Mao on September 9, 1976, she and the other members of the Gang of Four were arrested and tried for treason. In the lengthy trial that followed, selections of the manual text were used as evidence against her.

In exile, Jiang Qing wrote an Addendum to the text which is printed here for the first time. She now lives under house arrest in an eastern province which is known for its cleanliness fetishism and a biannual festival in which wild dogs are clubbed to death.

—Emily Prager

Comp: Mrs. Mao
Eva Peron
Imelda Marcos
Nancy Reagan
MARGARET THATCHER
INDIRA GANDHI
HOPE COOKE

Mrs. Mao's Little Red Book

How to Catch a Chairman

WOMEN continually ask me to make policy on chairmen and love. First off I tell them: make up a poem clearly defining the obstacles you must leap and the goals you seek in your personal struggle for a united front. Here is the poem I wrote just after my arrival in Yenan in July 1937.

> Mao had three wives.
> The first, he abandoned.
> She was a peasant.
> The second was a martyr to his cause.
> The Kuomintang cut off her head.
> The third lost her mind on the Long March.
> Who could blame her?
> I will be the fourth.
> But you can bet on this:
> I will be the last.

—Jiang Qing
(Mrs. Mao Zedong)

Photo courtesy of the Chinese laundry on Bleecker and Charles Streets.

Jiang Qing was the cultural doyenne of the People's Republic of China while her husband was in power. Not only did she reorganize the ballet troupes, stage the ballets, paint the scenery, do the lighting, make the costumes, and clean the guns, but she photographed the ballets as well. In this scene from the popular ballet, "The Red Detachment of Women," the soldier girls are about to force the landlord's lackeys to lick their toe shoes, thus symbolizing victory over false capitalist values.

How Old Should a Chairman Be? 27

I HAVE never understood why a girl who marries a chairman who is older and powerful should be the object of criticism. These jealous reactionaries say the girl has bad values. To fall in love with a young chairman whose power lies only in the width of his shoulders and the thrust of his production force, that is bad values! The chairman who is more mature, who has a bit of a paunch and a lot of whining children by vindictive or dead ex-wives but who is leading a revolution, that is a real chairman! Remember: chairmen fall in love with their eyes, and women fall in love with their futures.

How to Attract a Chairman

THE best way to attract a chairman immediately is to have broad appeal to the masses and no intelligentsia and let both of them show.[1] If, however, you're a girl with a brain bigger than a golden lotus[2] and no time to pad your Mao suits, then how do you go about getting your chairman . . . or someone else's for that matter?

Say it with manual labor. Everyone knows that manual labor is a gift no chairman can resist. How many times I have done manual labor for my chairman! Chairman are like children about manual labor. I recall when we were in hiding in Nanniwan in 1939: I had T.B., we were living in a cave, but I went out every day and did manual labor (with only two days' reprieve when I had my menses, during which time I was expected to do laundry), and my chairman's peasant heart was in a constant state of uprising. When he saw my calloused hands, he couldn't get enough of me. Later on, I became his personal secretary and took charge of all secret correspondence, but it was manual labor that paved the way.

---

[1] It was this phrase in particular that caught Zsa Zsa Gabor's eye at her first reading of the text. Save for the Communist phraseology, it was suspiciously like a line from her own manual, *How to Catch a Man, How to Keep a Man, How to Get Rid of a Man* (Doubleday, 1970), which read: "The best way to attract a man immediately is to have a magnificent bosom and a half-size brain and let both of them show."

[2] "Golden Lotus" was the name men gave to the disgusting, shrivelled-up, rotten, ingrown bound foot of a grown woman. It was about six inches long and four inches wide at optimum "beauty." It was comparable in size and shape to a well-chewed cat toy.

The Long March of Engagements

ONCE you've found the chairman you adore, what happens next? It's very simple. *You* ask him to marry you. Yes, you do it. Look at it this way: after you are married, he will always claim that you asked him, anyway. Mao did. Just as, after years of his dictating those bloody quotations to me night after night and my writing them out in perfectly beautiful calligraphy till my knuckles swelled, he always claimed that he sat at his simple, rough-hewn desk and wrote them himself. You can't win. You may as well do it. But take heed: no engagements! An engagement is like going on a long march with bound feet: you're in a constantly dependent position, and you can't throw your weight about. Who needs it?

How to Keep a Chairman

KEEPING a chairman is the task of the keeper. Your chairman should be so busy keeping you in plastic shoes and cigarettes that he won't notice that it is really *you* who is keeping him. Chairmen have no political acumen when it comes to marriage. They tend to view it as a master–slave dialectic, which, frankly, makes it all the easier for you. You can, for example, under the guise of having your hair done, invite three male hairdressers with political aspirations whom you knew before you were married over for tea in the afternoons with no problem whatsoever. When your chairman comes home and asks what you did with your day, you smile mischievously and tell him you had your hair done and made plans to supplant him. Don't worry. He'll never believe you.

Fear of Flight

DON'T be surprised if your chairman gets upset when you start fixing yourself up. A chairman always objects when you do something drastic to yourself, like working openly with the people in the countryside on Land Reform or being the first woman to give a speech to the masses. You can't listen to a chairman, because, after all, you're the woman, you're the enchantress, and he's the one who's being enchanted, so what does he know? But you do run the risk of being sent to Moscow for ten years for a supposed medical cure. So, be warned.

On Common Cause

HAVING the same things in common often helps you to keep your chairman. In our case, of course, it was politics. I recall that during the March to Peking, when we were holed up at Wangjiawan in June of '47, there was a shortage of shelters. So the Central Committee decided to have their week-long meeting in our cave, as it was the biggest. Well, there were no other wives along, and even though I was a political instructor and had a perfect right to be there, I immediately grasped the political implications and gladly moved out and into a donkey shed.

By the end of the week, I had lost twenty pounds and a big lump had risen on my neck. When I moved back in with Mao, he immediately noticed there was something different about me. He looked me over and enlightened me to the fact that I had been sleeping on a heap of bedbugs. "Those were the aggressors who caused the swelling and weight loss," he said. Ordinarily, he would have taken his anger at dissension during the meetings out on me, but because of my political selflessness, he decided instead to wage an extermination campaign against the bedbugs. And together, we had a wonderful day executing the "aggressors," venting our political spleens and rejuvenating our marriage.

Destruction Must Precede Construction

EVEN if you follow all my policies, there may still come a time when you think if you have to hear your chairman's views on the Supreme Soviet once more, you'll take his 1000 flowers and stuff them down his pontificating throat. It is at this time that you must face

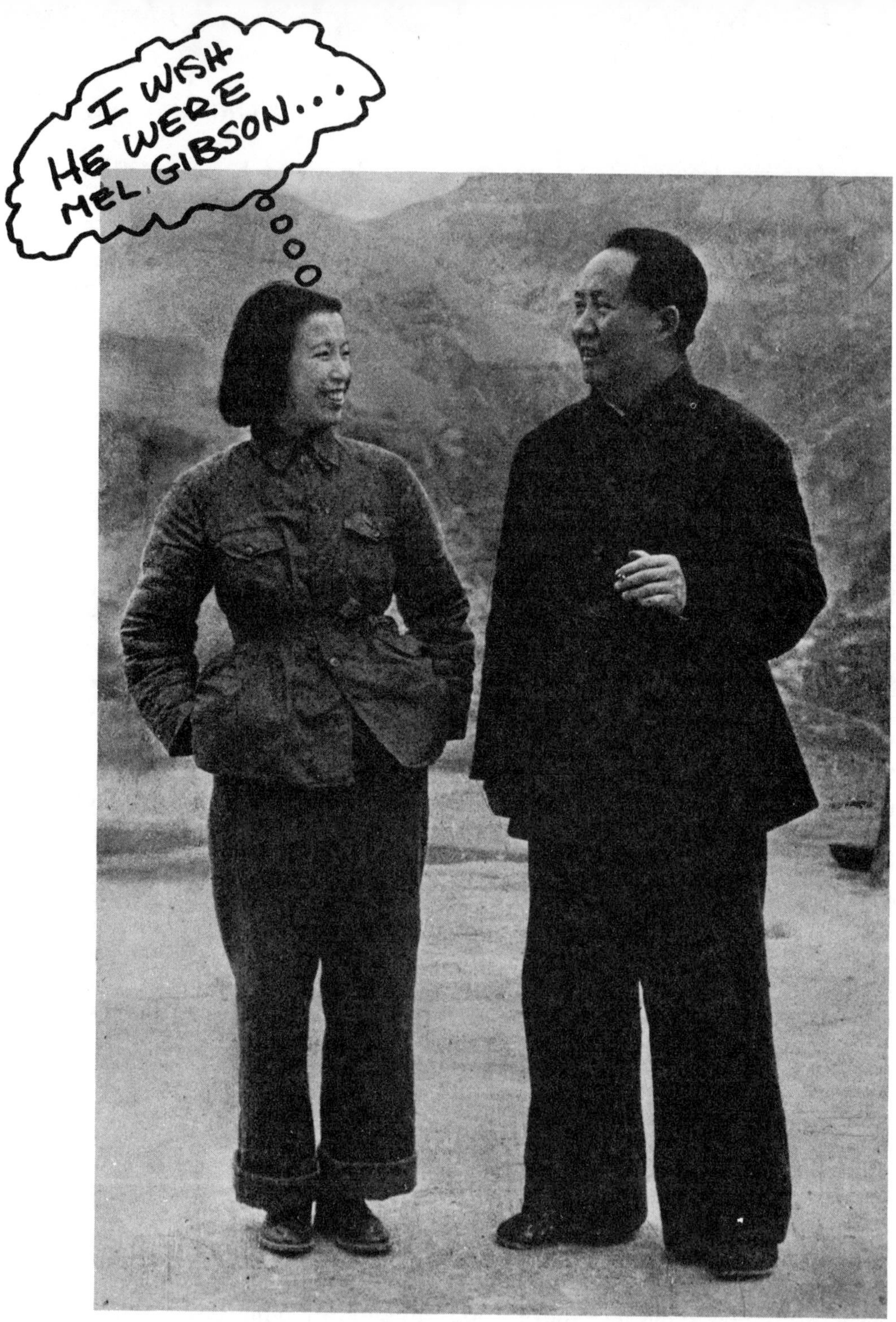
I WISH HE WERE MEL GIBSON...

the fact that you must begin to get rid of your chairman. Try not to be too discouraged over it. Try to think of it as I do; you're not losing a husband, you're gaining the People's Republic of China.

How to Get Rid of a Chairman

GETTING rid of a chairman is a cultural revolution in itself. If, however, you have taken my advice and married an older chairman, by this time he's probably dribbling food from the corners of his mouth and no longer in control of his own rectification. You, on the other hand, are still young and full of life and more than ready to assume your place as the life of the party. What you need is some younger friends to go to the ballet or theater with. Your own set or coterie. Your own gang.

Choosing your gang can be sticky because there is always the danger that your chairman can become jealous and publicly accuse you of factionalism or subvert your efforts to wrest control of the media. After all, he's home doddering in his camp bed while you're out having fun giving away copies of his quotations autographed by you. It's a difficult adjustment for any chairman. So, be gentle. Choose a small group to hang out with at first, people of little threat, like three male hairdressers he knows you've been having tea with for years. Later you can expand your sphere to include the masses. Go slow. You stood in the background for twenty years waiting for this moment. A few more months won't make any difference.

Addendum

When I wrote the previous volume, I was young and foolish. Although I still adhere to the tenets set down in *How to Catch a Chairman* and *How to Keep a Chairman,* I now realize that getting rid of a chairman is, as Mao once said, like lifting up a rock only to drop it on your own foot. A chairman is like a tattoo on your arm: even if you have it removed surgically, there will always be a scar there showing how stupid you were to get one in the first place.

—Jiang Qing
House Arrest
December 1983

Homecoming Dance FRI
Get earrings back from
ZBT House
~~Shave legs~~
~~Wash pantyhose~~
<u>PILLS</u> !!!
Bribe roomie to sleep at
Fran's.
Bribe Fran?

For Further Study

1. Given the fact that Jiang Qing reclaimed her career late in life and managed to keep the same chairman for the entire time it took to climb to a position of prominence, write an essay comparing her political style to that of Ruth Gordon. How does Garson Kanin compare with Chairman Mao? Give examples.

2. Before you read this, had you heard of Chairman Mao? Had you heard of the People's Republic of China? Did you care? Do you care now? Do you have any idea how much research went into the writing of this piece? How many parties went unattended? How many dates put off? Write a long letter apologizing to the author and relating your incredible arrogance and ignorance to that of Marco Polo when he set out from Italy in search of the silk route.

3. If Jiang Qing's chairman had been an actor and they had split up, might she have retained Marvin Mitchelson as her lawyer? What might her views be on palimony? Explain.

4. What do you think of Jiang Qing's methods? Would they have worked on an American man of similar stature to Mao? Would they have worked on Eisenhower? Vinegar Joe Stilwell? Mick Jagger?

5. Jiang Qing points out that chairmen might get upset if you fix yourself up. From the following three changes that might upset a Western man, pick one and tell why: a) getting a Mohawk; b) making an appointment for him to have his tubes tied; c) getting Johnny Ramone to make your telephone answering message.

6. How does the Zsa Zsa Gabor translation compare with the Jane Alpert translation? Discuss the relationship of Zsa Zsa and Porfirio Rubirosa versus that of Jane Alpert and Sam Melville. Why? Would Alpert have written her book if she had received diamonds from Melville, instead of anal sex? Why not?

7. Which of the following American designers have been most influenced by Chinese designers of Mao suits, cloth shoes, and the like: a) Betsey Johnson; b) Norma Kamali; c) Calvin Klein? Are any of these designers dying of A.I.D.S.? Are any Chinese designers? How do you know?

8. What did you do in the sixties? If you were not alive in the sixties, is there any point in your living now? Elaborate.

9. Which is more fun: a Communist Party or a Phalangist Party? Who serves better food? Give examples.

10. If Andy Warhol's Factory had been given a license to kill, who would be dead? Who would be alive? In your essay, be sure to mention Holly Woodlawn, Farah Diba, Steve Rubell, and Viva Superstar.

Annie Beattie is shown at home with her cat, Marmelade. This gifted young authoress numbers several felines, a dog, two parakeets, and a pet skunk named Crackers amongst the menagerie at her Vermont hideaway. "I often wish I could write books for animals," she says. "They're so much less depressing than people. For instance, Marmelade would never turn down an invitation to dinner just because she had a migraine."

Annie Beattie
1946–

ANNIE Beattie occupies the unique position of being one of the few writers in this book who we know for sure[1] is alive—not only that, we know her address.[2] She is only thirty-eight years old, yet she has already written two novels, three plays, and more short stories than Joyce Carol Oates combined, although the jury is still out on which one of the two has succeeded in depressing more readers per square inch of verbiage.

Born in Annandale-on-Hudson, New York, on May 12, 1946, she is the daughter of a college professor who specialized in "Death and the German Romantic Movement, 1822–33" and collected joke highball glasses as a hobby; and a housewife. The two had met and fallen in love in the thirties, when he went into the novelty shop where she worked looking for a fly in an ice cube. Not surprisingly, the dual influences of academia and comedy were to act as twin poles between which Annie's fragile talent has walked a tightrope throughout her meteorlike career.

Even as a child, Annie gave evidence of her unique perceptual powers. She would dress up her pet cats in dolls' clothing and spend long hours telling them depressing stories in which very little happened, while wearing a false nose.[3]

---

[1] The other two are Ja'net Crook and Mrs. Mao, although we're not sure about Mrs. Mao. Have you heard from her lately? Even a postcard?

[2] Vermont.

[3] This wasn't just any fake nose. The nose in question had sentimental value, since her mother had originally presented it to her father on the night of their wedding.

Others recognized Annie's potential, and having skipped high school, she graduated from Bard College at the age of sixteen with a degree in Tautology and went on to advanced studies in Pain at the University of New Mexico. It was there, at a grad student dissertation weekend and barbecue, that she first discovered her gift for standing up in front of people and making them feel depressed and sort of like calling their shrink sooner than they had planned to that week.

This revelation prompted her to abandon her studies and return to the eastern seaboard, where she began gigging around New York City and Cambridge, Massachusetts, in the kind of dank basement coffeehouses that always smelled like someone had just made an oil delivery next door. At first she accompanied herself on guitar and washboard,[4] but later she abandoned the musical portion of her program in favor of wispy anecdotes involving disjointed snatches of conversation she'd overheard in the street that day.

During this period, her two idols were Woody Allen and Jorge Luis Borges, whose photos she would tack up onstage on alternate nights,[5] just prior to starting her performance. Gradually, Annie gathered to herself a collection of like-minded individuals, dedicated to the principle that style outweighs substance, and a dog.[6] These formed the nucleus of her troupe, "Annie Beattie's Bread and Circuses Theatre Collective."

One of the original members, Sam Nickman, a former book salesperson at the Harvard Coop who is now a highly placed publishing executive, recalls those early days: "I remember living on yogurt, mostly. We used to steal milk from the coffeehouse kitchens—of course they weren't paying us anything so we didn't consider it stealing, really—and we'd always have this one thing of yogurt starter and we'd pass it around among us. So I remember it was always sort of, 'Whose turn is it to have the yogurt starter this week?' And then one time Annie dropped

---

[4]Occasionally, she played the spoons.

[5]When audience members saw the photo of Borges going up, they knew they were in for something really meaty.

[6]This versatile creature, known to the friends of the arts who petted him or threw him the occasional Milkbone as Fluffy, played all the animals and pets in sketches, although repeated requests for his performance of a pair of hamsters in "Snowbound" almost caused him to have a nervous breakdown and retire from show business to the kennel.

it, she dropped the starter, the whatchmacallit, acidophilus. She was quite a klutz, really."[7]

Klutz? Maybe. Prophetic genius of pointlessness? Probably. For what other talent has been able to sum up so aptly the quintessence of the "being there and not really caring much about it one way or the other" consciousness that has followed us out of the seventies and into the eighties?[8]

look up. nihilism

It is also oddly appropriate that Annie Beattie should first have flourished in comedy clubs, since the eighties might well be renamed the "Decade of Yuks for Bucks."[9] Borrowing a leaf from Second City,[10] Bread and Circuses evolved its repertoire by calling on suggestions from the audience and then spinning them into improvised storylines where nothing much happened except that the cat got hairballs or something like that.

Anyone who ever attended one of those memorable evenings will recall the surprising energy and verve with which the otherwise generally lethargic audience roused themselves to call out suggestions such as "braised endive," "pasta primavera," or "quilts." Invariably, with the consummate artistry and disregard for plot which became their trademark, Annie Beattie and her troupe would weave these disparate elements into the fragile-seeming yet strangely elastic warp and woof of performance art, or as Annie sometimes called it in interviews with the above-ground press, "Dramedy."

It is from the tape recording of just such an evening that "Whip 'n' Chill," the sketch presented here, was drawn. In the mid-seventies, Annie began to tape-record her works and sell the transcripts to *Manhattanite* magazine as short stories, thus virtually inventing a new means of creating literature.

Annie's greatest devotee was always the exuberant, handlebar-

---

[7]Reprinted from *Living on the Square,* by Sam Nickman (Knickerbocker Press, 1983). Used by permission of the author.

[8]We dare you to name one. We would, but we can't be bothered thinking about it right now.

[9]"Saturday Night Live," "Fridays," "The All-New Saturday Night Live," "SCTV," "Saturday Night Live" in syndication, "Not Necessarily the News," "Saturday Night Live" on videocassette, "Live from the Improv"—if that doesn't convince you, go count the number of Garfield books on this week's *New York Times* best-seller list.

[10]Who hasn't?

Annie Beattie, in a typically intense moment at the microphone, shares with the audience her feelings about split ends. Probably taken in 1973 when Annie was performing at the Cambridge comedy club, Chuckles.

moustached Sam Nickman. Once the young publishing tyro found his niche at Knickerbocker Press, Annie's future was assured. It was Sam who collected her "scraps," as she called them, and sold them to the reading public as her first brilliantly successful collection of short stories, *Sleeping in a Draft*. It was Sam who pioneered the whole *gerund* concept of packaging that made her next two collections, *Freezing to Death*[11] and *Running to Keep Warm,* so popular with the critics and the public[12] alike.

[11]Including the sketch which follows.

[12]Sam's secret weapon here was research, which showed that the average reader had trouble with authors' names and titles but was thrilled to be able to ask for "something with 'ing' in the name of it, I think," and be handed a short legible book that didn't cost an arm and a leg. He deviated from this publishing policy only once in Annie Beattie's case, with *Big Chilly Winterscape* (Knickerbocker Press, 1980), a novel about love, death, and remarriage in Vermont. It sold dismally.

And once again, it was Sam's insistence that if Annie kept on performing long enough she would have a long enough manuscript, which resulted in Annie's critically acclaimed first novel, *Shivering Slightly Now But Warming Up Okay I Think*[13] (Knickerbocker Press, 1979).

"It took a lot of blood, sweat, and spritzers,"[14] Annie has said. "We had to buy the audience spritzers to convince them to stay for the entire six-hour performance. But the management of Only When I Laugh [the club where they were booked] finally kicked in for the tab after I promised them a share of the royalties. God, I hope I never have to go through anything like that again. I don't know how most published authors do it. Who has the energy?"

Wisely, Annie divided the performance of her second novel into two nights, but perhaps for this reason, or possibly because of the title (see footnote 13), *Big Chilly Winterscape* did not do as well as her other books. In the future Annie plans to move on to screenplays, which she feels can be written "in half the time." Sam Nickman has already made plans for Lawrence Kasdan to direct her first script, tentatively titled "Tender Endearments." All we can say is, we're buying tickets.[15]

[13]Sam made her include two gerunds, "just to be on the safe side."

[14]Annie's initial title for the manuscript.

[15]Actually, we're not, we're having Sam put us on the guest list, but that doesn't mean you shouldn't.

Editors' Note: Annie Beattie has been plagued throughout her career by nomenclatural confusion, due to the existence of novelist Anne Beatty and humorist Anne Beatts, neither of whom she is. As an altogether different person, she would like to go on record here as saying she had nothing to do with the film version of *Chilly Scenes of Winter,* and does not know who wrote The Coneheads.

Freezing to Death

"Whip 'n' Chill"

OPEN ON INT. RESTROOM
We are in the pink-and-black-tiled art deco public restroom of a popular downtown restaurant. Two women, LIZ and ALISON, are repairing their makeup after dinner, even though neither of them wears very much makeup. Liz is a young woman with short dark hair, wearing a faded "Pep Girls"[1] t-shirt, a full skirt made out of some flowered material she bought at a yard sale when she was visiting her grandmother in Tennessee, sandals, and men's sweat sox. She lounges against the mirrors on the wall opposite Alison, who sits at the dressing table, thoughtfully brushing her thin shoulder-length blonde hair, in a tight black t-shirt dress with a hand-crocheted shawl over it that slips with every brushstroke.

> ALISON
> Oh, God, I can't go back up there. Justin keeps talking about *brunch.*

> LIZ
> (mildly)
> Can you blame him? His lover is a chef.

> ALISON
> What has that got to do with it?

> LIZ
> He works nights. So the only date they can have is brunch.

---

[1] The Pep Girls are a feminine version of Pep Boys Manny, Moe, and Jack, the well-known logo of a California automotive concern. The designer of the t-shirt was sued for copyright infringement, thus proving that people who sell automotive parts have no sense of humor.

ALISON
I thought his lover was a carpenter.

LIZ
(patiently)
That's my lover, Jason. Justin's friend.

ALISON
Sorry.
            (as she drops her hairbrush)
Do you have any Valium?

LIZ

I have a joint.

She picks up her Hello Kitty[2] pink plastic handbag, takes out a joint, lights it with a strike-anywhere match, and offers it to Alison.

ALISON
Uh-uh. If I get stoned I'll just call Hugo.

LIZ
(sucking on joint)
Your ex-husband?

ALISON
My dog. My ex-husband's keeping him for me, in Vermont.

LIZ
Does David know about him?

ALISON
Why should he care? He's still looking after Felicity.

[2]Hello Kitty is another famous logo, originating in Japan, that currently decorates a vast array of cheap plastic novelty items popular with extremely young children and the kind of trashy young modern who doesn't care that her underwear has a hole in it, even if she is hit by a bus.

LIZ

His ex-wife's dog?

ALISON

Cat.

LIZ

I still have all of Nick's plants.

ALISON

Do they have names?

LIZ

Just the coleuses. He never got around to nam-
ing the umbrella plant.

ALISON

Typical. Does Justin—I mean Jason—know?

LIZ

He ought to. He built shelves for them.[3]

ALISON

Very generous of him.

LIZ
(puffing on joint)
God, I wish I had a pizza.[4]

I you ain't just whistling dixie, whistling dixie, pixie.

[3]Statistics show that carpentry is the third most popular livelihood of those New Agers who actually have a livelihood; after number one, making stained glass; and number two, selling solar heating units. Results of a recent Yankelovich survey show that, when asked what they do for a living, this new breed of carpenter most frequently replies, "I just pound nails, man."

[4]Contrary to what you, the reader, may suspect, especially if you, the *nouvelle* reader, happen to be gushy *New York Times* food critic Mimi Sheraton, Liz is not referring to a pizza with *chèvre* and black olives, as goat cheese pizza tends to stick to the roof of one's mouth when stoned. Annie Beattie herself said in an interview with one of the editors that what she had in mind here was good old tomato-and-cheese pizza with everything but anchovies, which can often have the same effect as goat cheese. In fact, during this section of the performance, members of the audience were often moved to send out for pizza themselves, and that is invariably what they ordered, thus indicating the powerful interaction of Beattie's work with the *Zeitgeist* of our times.

                    ALISON
We could order one in.

                     LIZ
In here?

                    ALISON
Why not? There's a phone booth right outside.

                     LIZ
You're stoned.

                    ALISON
No, you're stoned.

They laugh.

                     LIZ
I remember last Halloween, when David got so
stoned he almost cut his thumb off carving the
pumpkin.

                    ALISON
That must have been Nick. David is my lover.

                     LIZ
He was my lover then.

                    ALISON
He didn't tell me.

                     LIZ
You didn't tell him about Hugo.

                    ALISON
Hugo has nothing to do with it. Hugo is
blameless.

LIZ
David might not agree. David might want to know where the bones are buried, so to speak.

ALISON
Well, I don't expect him to build Hugo a dog bed,[5] if that's what you mean.

LIZ
Leave Jason out of this.

BRADLEY enters. He is Liz's half-brother and Justin's ex-lover. He is wearing a faded Boston Red Sox cap and a white tuxedo jacket with the sleeves rolled up, over Oshkosh denim overalls and hiking boots, and holding a white wine spritzer.

BRADLEY
Girls! What have you been doing down here? Each other's toenails? Or are we talking *hard drugs*?

LIZ
Just one toke over the line, sweet Bradley, one toke over the line.

ALISON
Don't you know why they call them "hard drugs"? Because they're so hard to get.

BRADLEY
If Justin has one more spritzer in your absence, I refuse to be responsible for the consequences.

---

[5]Beattie's third reference to carpentry. Yankelovich demonstrates that 40 percent of the income of New Age carpenters derives from the manufacture of furniture for children and pets.

ALISON

You've carried Justin home and put him to bed
before, Bradley.

BRADLEY

Not anymore. Not this boy. Let his chef put him
to bed.

LIZ

Do I detect a note of bitterness?

BRADLEY

I'm just tired. I saw him through acid and TM
and yoga and est. I even moved to the country
and helped him throw pots.[6] Now I need a rest.

LIZ

Okay, okay, we'll take up the white man's burden.

*Before they can leave, CASSANDRA enters. She is David's daughter by
his first marriage. Fourteen years old, she is wearing a sky-blue Korean
baseball jacket with the name "Ted" embroidered over the left breast
pocket, a peach silk forties flowered nightgown, rubber thongs, and a
baseball cap identical to Bradley's. She is carrying Felicity, a large
orange tomcat.[7]*

CASSANDRA

Felicity's bored.

ALISON

Felicity's bored, Bradley's bored—

[6]This is not meant to imply that Bradley and Justin actually hurled pots at one another, or anyone
else. "Throwing pots" is a potter's term for making them on a potter's wheel out of potter's clay,
after which they are baked in a potter's kiln, a word which has already earned the "Animal House"
Award for Excellence in Joke Words, 1975–80.

[7]Naming pets without regard to gender is a whimsical gesture beloved of New Agers, probably
because of their confusion about their own sexual identity.

> BRADLEY
> (interrupting)

Not bored, just tired.

> ALISON
> (ignoring him)

Liz is bored, I'm bored, you're bored, for all we know *Justin* is bored. But that doesn't mean we have to go around *announcing* it to all and sundry, does it?

> CASSANDRA
> (to Liz)

Jeez! What's her problem?

> ALISON
> (to Cassandra)

I just want to know why you never bothered to mention to me that Liz had been seeing David.

> CASSANDRA

That was ages ago.

> ALISON

Last Halloween is not ages ago.

> BRADLEY
> (placating her)

Sweetie-pie, it's ancient history. Anyway, we all thought you knew. That weekend in East Hampton, when we had more zucchini than we knew what to do with, Justin said—

JUSTIN enters. He is black, gay, and wearing an Issey Miyake jumpsuit,[8] orange basketball sneakers, and a silver cuff on one ear.

[8]Jumpsuits are also beloved by New Agers, probably for the same reason.

JUSTIN

Justin said is that what you girls have been doing down here, gossiping about me? I knew my ears were burning for a reason.

CASSANDRA

Alison is upset because she didn't know Liz had been David's lover.

JUSTIN

Darling, who hasn't? Come on, children, let's all go upstairs and finish our white chocolate mousse.[9] If we stay here any longer, we'll run into the *brunch crowd.*

He exits. All follow, Cassandra last. As she leaves, Felicity jumps out of her arms and into the audience.

[9]Yum-yum! Sounds good to us. Moe, Larry! What are we waitin' for?

Illustration courtesy of Marmelade's personal collection.

Self-portrait of the authoress and Marmelade. Annie Beattie believes that "if one is truly a creative genius, one will naturally be proficient in all of the creative arts." She also plays the mouth harp.

For Further Study

1. What is the advantage to being alive if you're a writer? Name three dead writers, not including Anne Frank, who would benefit immensely from being alive today.

2. Pets play an important role in Annie Beattie's work. What do you think the fact that almost all her characters are pet-owners indicates about them? What does it indicate about the author? Is it true that only lonely people need pets? If Annie had performed with a goldfish instead of a dog would her work be different? For extra credit, give ten good names for a goldfish, not including Goldie.

3. Annie Beattie was doing graduate work in Pain when she decided to become a performer. What, if any, is the connection here? Are laughter and pain closely related, or are they just second cousins? God, that hurts.

4. What was the nature of Annie Beattie's relationship with Sam Nickman? Speculate wildly. Does everyone need a Sam Nickman in their life, or just girls? Do you think his theory of "gerund packaging" is valid? Suggest ten titles with gerunds in them that we could use for our next book. Please omit tedious variations on the infinitive "to be," as they have already been done to death by Sartre, Kosinski, and Kermit the Frog, the so-called troika of modern thought, who are known respectively for *Being and Nothingness*, *Being There*, and the chart-topping hit from Muppetville, "It's Not Easy Being Green."

5. Given that all Annie Beattie's work began with an improvisation based on suggestions from the audience, which of the following might have provided the inspiration for the short story you have just read: a) brunch; b) a chef; c) Valium; d) the Empire Diner; e) Odeon; f) coleus plants; g) spritzers; h) carving pumpkins; i) a green Frisbee; j) carpentry; k) extended families; l) the Boston Red Sox; m) Super Bowl Sunday; n) zucchini; o) a white balloon in a tree? For extra credit, write your own story, using the items she didn't use.

6. Do you like pasta primavera? Do you have a good recipe for it? If so, make it and invite us over. What time will it be ready? Should we bring white or red wine? You're not going to put snow pea pods in it, are you?

7. Many of Annie Beattie's characters wear clothes they purchased at thrift shops. What, in your opinion, does thrift-shop clothing symbolize? Did it ever occur to you that when your blouse dies for you, it could be reborn for someone else—provided you give it to the Salvation Army or some other accredited clothes redistribution organization of your choice? And if thrift-shop clothing does symbolize death and rebirth, does this mean that whenever someone in Annie Beattie's work is wearing it, he or she represents the Fisher King, i.e., Jesus Christ? Or is this just the kind of crackpot theory arrived at by graduate students in a desperate attempt to come up with something fresh to write a thesis on?

8. If David is Alison's lover and Liz's ex-lover, and Jason is Liz's current lover, and his friend, Justin, is the chef's boyfriend and Bradley's ex-lover, and Bradley is Liz's half-brother, and David is Cassandra's father, who is Nick?

9. Tom Wolfe characterized the seventies as the "Me Decade." Judging by Annie Beattie's work, would you say that the eighties are the "Not Me Decade?" DON'T ASK ME!

10. Annie Beattie's work is filled, not to say littered, with references to contemporary pop culture. Yet, often shortly after she mentions something in her work because it's "in," that trend will peak and whatever it is will become out again. If, for instance, Annie Beattie writes about quilts, does that mean that: a) quilts are in because she's writing about them; b) quilts are out and she's subtly letting us know by satirizing the kind of people who own them; c) quilts are in now but will be out in another few minutes because her mentioning them has made more people go out and buy them and nobody wants to be the kind of person who has something that everybody else has? In your opinion, is indulging in this kind of trend-spotting dangerous? Is it more or less dangerous than nuclear power? Is being opposed to nuclear power just a trend? If not, why don't you stop reading and get out there and do something about it? Okay, you can finish the Glossary first.

MONTEGO BAY HERE I COME !!!

Glossary

Arcane: Known or understood only by those having special, secret knowledge, so if you don't know how to use it, that's all we're telling you. It's a secret; what do you think we are, a bunch of blabbermouths?

Barcalounger: The thing that Dad's always in when he's watching T.V.

Bazooms: Fifties slang for hooters, knockers, melons, boobs, and bongos.

Bedbugs: Things you don't let bite you at night. If they do, take your shoe and beat them till they're black and blue.

Benevolent: If ya gotta have a dictator, you want this type.

Book Party: A gathering to celebrate the publication of a new book; not to be confused with the popular mid-western "book hop," in which people are admitted to a dance for free if they take off their shoes and bring a book.

Chart-Topping: That which tops the charts (chart being a term indigenous to the music industry, referring to the weekly ranking of commercially released songs). Who decides what tops the charts? People have pondered this question for years, but the most widely accepted theory is that once a week, middle-level executives from the record industry converge at the San Diego Zoo and play all current releases through a Dolby sound system to the monkeys in the monkey house. The rating system is complex and scientific. However, it can safely be said that a sure chart-topper has the monkey house rockin' and dancin'. During the anything-goes 1960s, the monkeys' reaction to a chart-topper inspired the popular dance craze "The Monkey," which was often performed on the T.V. music show "Shindig."

Cheesed Off: Active definition of "doing a slow burn"; not to be confused with "cheesed out," "cheesed up," or "cheesy."

Christopher Street: Located in Manhattan's bustling West Village, the meandering westbound thoroughfare which Ninth Street becomes at the Avenue of the Americas, colloquially known as Sixth Avenue. Immediately after that it crosses Gay Street, one of the oldest streets in the Village.

Cocoa Puff Tree: A tall tree, *Cocoa pufferus,* native to the tropics, bearing cocoa as bite-size puffs. Familiar in the Western Hemisphere as the popular breakfast cereal, "Cocoa Puffs." We're cuckoo for Cocoa Puffs.

Communist: A person who enjoys getting a pair of Levi's, new or used, for Christmas or any other time during the year. The Communist's second-most desired gift item is a bootlegged copy of the Beach Boys' chart-topping tune, "Help Me, Rhonda," which explains why former Secretary of the Interior James Watt refused to allow the Beach Boys to play at the Washington Monument on the Fourth of July.

Concordance: An alphabetical index of all words in a text, showing every contextual occurrence of a word. For instance, should an enterprising young person dare to compile a concordance of *Titters 101,* he or she would find that the words "dry cleaning" appear far too frequently, whereas the word "antidisestablishmentarianism" doesn't appear at all. (Except for this one time, right here, right now.)

Coterie: French term for "group sex," involving more people than a ménage à trois but not as many as the Olympic ski team.

Cuttle: A form of cuddling done with fish; variant of cuddle.

Dialectic: Something to do with contradictions and conflicts. See Karl Marx (*Das Kapital*) or the Marx Brothers ("A Night At The Opera").

Doggerel: Verse of a loose, irregular rhythm or of a trivial nature. Derivative of the Middle English term *dogge* (dog), because dogs were considered trivial animals at that time. Oddly enough, other animals have also inspired the rise of various literary forms. For instance, the Middle English term *catte* (cat), gave rise to the word catalectic, which designates a verse that lacks part of the last foot. It may sound as though there is no connection, but in the Middle Ages, it was customary to amputate a cat's hind foot as a poultice for boils.

Dry Cleaning: A process whereby stains are magically removed from clothing. First invented by Eve (Garden of Eden) when Adam's fig leaf got dirty.

Duck Blind: The way immigrants describe a duck that can't see. Also, a term for a certain kind of visual impairment in which the affected person, although still able to see rabbits, is unable to see ducks.

Eponymous: Giving one's name to something, as a city, country, era, or institution. For example, the lounge singer Johnny Toronto is the eponym of Toronto, and fun-loving Fred Roaring was the eponym for the "Roaring Twenties."

Existential: Type of philosophy (see Philosophy) also known as "the hill of beans" theory, best summed up by Humphrey Bogart in the following exchange in the final scene of "Casablanca":

Ingrid Bergman: And I said I will never leave you.

Bogart: And you never will. I've got a job to do, too. Where I'm going, you can't follow, what I've got to do, you can't be any part of. Ilsa, I'm no good at being noble, but it doesn't take much to see that the problems of three little people don't amount to a hill of beans in this crazy world. Someday you'll understand. Not now. Here's looking at you, kid.

Geek: A person who has no sense of humor; i.e., anyone who doesn't like this book. Also, anyone who bites the heads off live chickens and snakes for money.

Guys: Sex.

Hairdressers: People who spend a great deal of time inhaling and sticking their fingers in toxic chemicals but, unlike asbestos workers, coal miners, and those who dispensed Agent Orange in Vietnam, are not yet known for any peculiar warts, coughs, or lesions. But these things take years.

Hors d'oeuvres (or-derv'): French for "Would you like some sex before dinner?"

IHOW (eye'-how): International House of Women. A Greenwich Village brownstone that is headquarters for Titters, Central. (See Titters.) Also known as House of Wayward Women, Confused Women, Funny Women, Sexually Peaking Women, Wild and Worried Women, and Wage-Earning Multi-Occupational Women, but mainly it's just a bunch of crazy gals.

Irony: Bigger than sarcasm, but not as big as satire.

Kneecap: A handwoven, wool-blend cap favored by those in wheelchairs during cool weather.

Literate: What you become when you buy this book.

Method Training: School of acting where Paul Newman, Marlon Brando, and James Dean all learned how to cry, and play movie death scenes in a cruciform position.

Mouseburger: A wallflower, stick in the mud, spinster, old maid, prune face, or person with cooties.

Parody: Kind of like satire, but not really. See Satire.

Philosophy: An involved, confusing, and bewildering theory developed to explain anything that's involved, confusing, and bewildering. This leads to disorientation, chaos, and bedlam—at least that's our philosophy.

Pinky Shake: Often confused with the "hippy hippy shake," this expression of friendship involves the interlocking of your pinky finger and the pinky finger of a friend. Wanna shake on it?

Plagiarism: To steal the writings or ideas of another and get caught. Also known as "pulling an Alex Haley."

Pressure Points: Wherever it feels good when you sit in front of the jets in a hot tub, those are your pressure points. Don't ever let a Japanese person touch them.

Proletarian: A breakfast roll served with or without fruit but always with coffee. Especially popular in France, where they consume it with *café au lait,* which is a festive drink that celebrates the arrival of morning. Interestingly, the Spanish have a similar drink called *café óle!,* which they drink with their native breakfast roll, the *peón.*

Putz: Jerk, dork, stupid mahoney, boob, or Gerald Ford.

Recherché: French term meaning "sought after," also the original name of Cher when she was working in France with Sonny under the names "Soleil et Recherché" (the French thought they were brilliant, especially their rendition of "Je t'ai, Babe," which the rock critic for *Le Monde* described as *"formidable"*).

Sarcasm: Wouldn't you like to know?

Satire: Kind of like parody, but not really. See Parody.

Sex: See Guys.

Sextant: A navigational instrument used for measuring the altitude of celestial bodies; in the sixteenth century, a common sailor's term for the euphemism "rocket," as in, "Hey, baby, I've got a rocket in my pocket."

Sinatra, Frank: A little guy with a big voice. Now in the autumn of his years, this skinny kid from Hoboken sky-rocketed to the top of the heap, fell off, and climbed back up again, just like that little old ant. So from three ladies with the laughing face who wanna wake up in the city that never sleeps, we just wanna say, it was a very good year (for those who think young), so set 'em up, Joe, there's no one in the joint except you and me, and that's why Chicago is my kinda town. Yeah!

Style: Best defined by fashion dictator-for-life Idi Amin Dada Diana Vreeland, who said, "It gets you down the stairs."

Subway Chili: Put two medium-size cans of whole peeled tomatoes into your purse, grab a couple pounds of ground meat, cadge a few onions, swipe a bag of beans, and don't forget the hot sauce. Now, head quickly for the F train, hop the turnstile, and go home. Combine ingredients in a pan. Set iron on "synthetic" and bring mixture to a slow boil. Enjoy!

Titters: A humorous state of mind; developed by a fun-loving and eclectic cult group of women who like to get down, get funky and write.

Tone: The thing you hear when you pick up the phone. If you don't hear it, then your phone is dead, and you should phone the phone company, if you can find a phone with a tone, or figure out which phone company to phone.

Yurt: A tent; the Afghani equivalent of "the *Playboy* pad."

Acknowledgments

Design and Art Direction by Judith Jacklin

Original artwork and photography by:
Edie Baskin, John Daveikis, Lynn
Goldsmith, Judith Jacklin, Jill Mariani,
Laila Nabulsi, Deanne Stillman, and Mary
Wilshire.

Editorial Associate: Laila Nabulsi

Editorial Assistants: Jean Jacklin and
Katherine Rezucha

Copy Editor: Red Wassenich

Production Assistants: Rhea Braunstein,
Lee Katz, Katie Kehrig, and Karen
Krenitsky

NOTHING WITHOUT LABOUR

SPECIAL THANKS to the following:
Edie Baskin, Sheila Beatts, Bob Blanton and Brand X, FPG
(Freelance Photography Guild), Floyd Byars, Esmé, Bruce Goldstein,
Phyllis Grann, Kenneth Kneitel, Candace Lake, Pierre Laroche, Terry
Lee, Ron Leif, Christopher Little, Howard Mandelbaum, Linda
Mitchell, Sam Mitnick, Mystique Modeling Agency, Julie Nisson,
Chris Schillig, Barry Secunda, Penny Stallings, Eleanor Stillman,
Thatcher Waller, Rex Weiner, and Fred Weiss.

MODELS:
Anne Beatts, Heidi Berg, Floyd Byars, Cisco, Rhonda Coullet,
Christina Engelhard, Michael Fracasso, Judith Jacklin, Laila
Nabulsi, Gilda Radner, Abdal Sharif, Ameer Sharif, Kauthar Sharif,
Deanne Stillman, and Whisper.

PHOTOGRAPHS AND ILLUSTRATIONS were
supplied by or are reproduced by permission of the following:
Edie Baskin, page 238; Bruce Coleman, Inc./Norman Mosallem, page
214; Rhonda Coullet, page 245; John Daveikis, page 6; Eastfoto, page
228; FPG/Photoworld, pages 10, 18, 98, 110, 122, 125, 130, 139, 169;
FPG/Brook Elgie, page 160; FPG/Leonard Lee Rue II, page 140;
FPG/W. Luthy, page 160; Lynn Goldsmith, cover and author photo;
Lou Grubb, cover retouching; Judith Jacklin, miscellaneous and
sundry; Laila Nabulsi, page 200; Jill Mariani, pages 170, 214, 221,
223, 225, 242; Regents of the University of California, page 19
(© 1964); UPI/Bettmann Archive, pages 34, 134, 186, and back cover;
Deanne Stillman, pages 166, 174, 178, 183; and Mary Wilshire, pages
30, 58, 68, 69, 72, 80, 150, 151, 154.

Lyrics to "What a Wonderful World"
by Sam Cooke, Lou Adler, and Herb Alpert
© 1959 by ABKCO Music, Inc. All
Rights reserved. Reprinted by
permission.

Lyrics to "Mr. Ed" copyright © 1960,
1962 by Livingston & Evans, Inc.,
publisher and owner of all rights
throughout the world.

NOTHING WITHOUT LABOUR

ABOUT THE AUTHORS

Photo by Lynn Goldsmith.

The TITTERS Three: Anne Beatts, Judy Jacklin, and Deanne Stillman.

ANNE BEATTS
Anne Beatts was an editor of the *National Lampoon,* a writer for the original "Saturday Night Live," and the creator and producer of the TV series "Square Pegs." She co-edited *TITTERS: The First Collection of Humor by Women* (Macmillan, 1976) and *Saturday Night Live* (Avon, 1977). She is the only writer in New York or Los Angeles not currently at work on a screenplay.

JUDITH JACKLIN
Judith Jacklin worked for the art department and the "Radio Hour" at the *National Lampoon.* She designed and art directed *TITTERS, Animal House* (21st Century Communications, 1978), and *Blues Brothers: Private* (Perigee, 1980), for which she won the 1981 Art Directors Club Distinctive Merit Award. She also co-wrote *Blues Brothers: Private,* and a lot of really good letters.

DEANNE STILLMAN
Deanne Stillman was the co-editor of *TITTERS,* the co-author of *Woodstock Census: The Nationwide Survey of the Sixties Generation* (Viking Press, 1979), and the author of *Getting Back at Dad* (Wideview, 1981). Her work has appeared in many magazines, and she was also a staff writer on "Square Pegs." She still harbors a crush on former Cleveland Indians outfielder Tito Francona.

GUEST EDITOR: EMILY PRAGER
Emily Prager has been a contributing editor of the *National Lampoon* and *VIVA,* and at present writes a satire column for *Penthouse.* She performed in and co-wrote the film *Mr. Mike's Mondo Video.* She is the author of *A Visit from the Footbinder* (Simon & Schuster, 1982). She speaks twenty-four languages, holds a black belt in karate, and recently studied to be a midwife. Other than that, she's a perfectly ordinary woman.